John, 1–3 John

Preaching the Word

Smyth & Helwys Publishing, Inc.
6316 Peake Road
Macon, Georgia 31210-3960
1-800-747-3016
©2019 by Prince Raney Rivers and Abby Thornton Hailey
All rights reserved.

Library of Congress Cataloging-in-Publication Data

Rivers, Prince Raney, author.
John, 1-3 John / by Prince Raney Rivers and Abby Thornton Hailey.
p. cm.
Macon : Smyth & Helwys, 2019
Preaching the word
Includes bibliographical references and index.
LCCN 2018044463
ISBN 9781641730914
1. Bible. John--Sermons.
2. Bible. Epistles of John--Sermons.
I. Title.
BS2615.54 .R58 2018
226.5/06--dc23

2018044463

Disclaimer of Liability: With respect to statements of opinion or fact available in this work of nonfiction, Smyth & Helwys Publishing Inc. nor any of its employees, makes any warranty, express or implied, or assumes any legal liability or responsibility for the accuracy or completeness of any information disclosed, or represents that its use would not infringe privately-owned rights.

John
Prince Raney Rivers

1–3 John
Abby Thornton Hailey

Dedication

*This book is dedicated to
my father, Dr. Prince Rivers (1936–2010),
and my mother, Ann R. Davis (1939–).*

Prince

*This book is dedicated to
the good people of Broadneck Baptist Church
in Annapolis, Maryland,
who teach me every day
what it means not just to preach the word,
but to live by it.*

Abby

Contents

Part 1: John

Acknowledgements	3
Preface	5
1. Who Is Jesus?	7
2. It's Not about Us	15
3. Finding What You've Always Wanted	23
4. The Miracle at Cana	31
5. Spring Cleaning	39
6. The Necessity of New Birth	47
7. Trust God	55
8. The Gift of God	63
9. Contagious Christianity	71
10. Believe It Before You See It	79
11. Why Jesus Broke the Rules	87
12. The God Who Satisfies	95
13. Homily for Christian Leaders	103
14. Doing the Will of God	107
15. The Path to Freedom	115
16. Can You See?	123
17. Inside the Heart of God	131
18. Resurrecting Faith	139
19. Giving God the Best	145
20. Searching for Something More	153
21. Training Day	161
22. A New Way to Love	169
23. Living above Our Fears	177
24. Staying Connected	185
25. Courageous Faith	193
26. When Jesus Prayed	201
27. What Will We Do about Jesus?	209
28. What Happened at the Cross?	217
29. It Is a New Day!	225
30. Four Words We All Need to Hear	233

31. When Jesus Shows Up	243
32. Where Do We Go from Here?	251

Part 2: 1 John

Acknowledgements	263
Preface	265
1. What You've Seen and Heard	267
2. What's New . . . and Old	273
3. Buying into the Lie	279
4. Remember Who You Are	285
5. What Is Love?	291
6. Discerning the Spirit	297
7. Who God Is . . . and Why It Matters	303
8. Bearing Witness	309
9. What We Know	315

Part 3: 2 John

1. Making Connections	323

Part 4: 3 John

1. Welcome and Authority	331

Part 1

John

by Prince Raney Rivers

Acknowledgements

As with any writing project, there are many people to thank who contributed to the final product. First, let me express my deepest gratitude to the wonderful people at Smyth & Helwys for the invitation to be a part of this series. Keith Gammons and Katie Cummings have been more than generous in their support and patience. Katie's extraordinary editorial work has undoubtedly enhanced this collection of sermons. I am grateful for the invaluable comments from Chanda Stegall, Margie Scott, Ann Davis, Francine Madrey, Charlotte Purvis, and Sharon Bell, all of whom made this manuscript better. Chanda Stegall is one of the most capable executive assistants anywhere. I am indebted to her for her wisdom and patience. I am also indebted to the members of United Metropolitan Missionary Baptist Church in Winston Salem, North Carolina. Serving this congregation for eleven years was one of my life's unexpected blessings. I also want to thank past and present staff members, including my extraordinary assistant, Jessica Smith, and a former Minister of Discipleship, Reverend Tasha Gibson, whose deep love for God is evident in all she does. Finally, I could not have completed this project without the faith and steadfast hope of my loving wife, Monica. She has been a kind critic and helpful contributor to my preaching for over twenty years.

I also wish to offer a word of deep appreciation for the congregation I am now blessed to serve, Union Baptist Church of Durham, NC. Our journey together has just begun, but you have already shown yourselves to be followers of Christ; as it is written, "By this everyone will know you are my disciples, if you have love for one another" (John 13:35). You make it a joy for me to do what Jesus asked of Peter, "…Feed my sheep" (John 21:17). I am looking forward to whatever God will do with our partnership as pastor and people. Thank you for your support and, most of all, your deep hunger for the Word of God. I love you.

—**Prince Raney Rivers**

Preface

Even the most attentive parishioner may find it difficult to connect the preacher's attempts at continuity in the pulpit week in and week out. The lectionary helps, but even that trustworthy guide does not eliminate the challenge of engaging and inspiring the congregation while being faithful to the shape of the biblical story. This is why I was so pleased when I was invited to be a part of the Preaching the Word commentary project. I had never preached through a book as long or as substantive as the Gospel of John. The challenge seemed both delightful and daunting.

I announced my homiletical plans to the good people of United Metropolitan Missionary Baptist Church, where I served at the time, unsure of how the members would respond to the idea of taking this journey through the entire gospel of John. While they were accustomed to sermon series, the average length of a typical series was four weeks. To their credit, they encouraged this series every step of the way. Preaching through the gospel of John resulted in thirty-two sermons and could have easily been thirty-five or forty.

Once the series began, the Spirit transformed it into a partnership between the pastor and the people. Each Sunday I asked two or three people to read the Scriptures in a dramatic (but not melodramatic!) fashion. Biblical parts were assigned as if readers were delivering lines in a play. This approach to reading the passages went so well that I soon began to wonder if people were showing up for the Scripture readings instead of the sermon. In either case, the mood in those holy moments was saturated with the presence of God.

It was an honor to be asked to preach from John because it's different than the synoptic Gospels. John offers a unique perspective on the life of Jesus. Because this publication is one volume in a commentary series, I have sought to accomplish two tasks in each sermon. First, I attempted to give the hearers and readers a sense of the context of the text. I tried not to be too academic. In some places I admit I could have provided fewer exegetical details without compromising the sermon. Second, I tried to communicate the bold proposition of John's gospel: believe and live. It is my sincere hope that as you enter this great story, you will find or rediscover the promise of faith and abundant life in Jesus of Nazareth, the Son of God.

Who Is Jesus?[1]

John 1:1-5, 10-14

Today we are beginning what I hope will be more than just a sermon series. My prayer is that this trip through the Gospel of John will be a spiritual pilgrimage.

A pilgrimage is a journey, but not just an ordinary journey. A pilgrimage is not for sightseeing. A pilgrimage is not like a vacation. A pilgrimage is an inward journey. You may go somewhere physically, but you do not have to. Pilgrimage is not so much about the destination as it is about what happens to us on the way—what happens to our faith, what happens to our heart, mind, and soul.

Keep two words in mind throughout this series: *believe* and *life*. The reason the Gospel of John was written is plainly stated in John 20:31: "... these are written so that you may come to *believe* that Jesus is the Messiah, the Son of God, and that through believing you may have *life* in his name" (emphasis mine). This is why we are on this pilgrimage—to believe so that we may have life.

What we believe about Jesus determines what we think about God, about Christianity, about ourselves, about what truly matters, and ultimately about the way we choose to live. The Gospel of John goes to great lengths to tell us who Jesus is.

Matthew, Mark, and Luke have many similarities in the way they talk about Jesus. They cover the same period of time and share some of the same stories. They use some of the same language. John is different.

John's distinctiveness may be why it's one of the most treasured books in the New Testament. We read moving passages from the Gospel of John at Easter. We reference comforting quotes from John at funerals. Every child who has had to memorize Scripture has probably learned at least one verse from the Gospel of John because it contains the shortest verse in the Bible, "Jesus wept" (11:35, NIV).

John is different. John does not have as many miracles as the other Gospels. John has almost none of the parables found in other Gospels. John has many of the stories and sayings that have captured the imaginations and strengthened the faith of many, many generations of believers. Only John has stories like the raising of Lazarus from the dead and the late-night encounter between Jesus and a Pharisee named Nicodemus, when Jesus explains what it means to be born from above.

John expands our understanding of who Jesus is. This is true from the first chapter and first verse of the Gospel: "In the beginning was the Word . . . ."

At the opening of Matthew, Mark, and Luke, we are told something about the early days of Jesus's life. Mark begins as John the Baptist baptizes Jesus in the Jordan River. Afterward, the devil tempts Jesus in the wilderness, and then Jesus calls his first disciples.

Luke fills in a few more details. Luke tells us the most about the birth of Jesus. He describes the visitation of the angels. He shares the experiences of Mary and the shepherds. He even tells a personal story about the time Jesus ran off from Mary and Joseph when he was just twelve years old. They found him in Jerusalem in the temple, debating the elders.

Matthew adds a few particulars that Mark and Luke do not mention. In Matthew, we hear how Joseph was involved in the birth of Jesus and how the magi followed a star in the eastern sky until they came to a manger in Bethlehem where Mary had given birth. Matthew even provides a genealogy of Jesus that traces the family tree all the way back to Abraham, tying Jesus inseparably to his Jewish past. Matthew's point was that the same God at work in Abraham's life was now with us in Jesus of Nazareth.

And since today is the Sunday before Christmas, we might expect to hear about the manger or angels or wise men. But John does not begin by telling us about a baby wrapped in swaddling clothes. The Gospel of John starts a long, long time before Jesus was baptized in the Jordan River. John commences well before the time when Jesus was a little boy. John rewinds the story past the manger, past the shepherds and wise men, past the angels, and even past Mary and Joseph. John goes so far back that he leaps over lives of Solomon, David, Ruth, Jacob, Isaac, and Abraham.

For John to tell us who Jesus is, he has to go all the way back before creation: "In the beginning was the Word, and the Word was with God, and the Word was God" (vv. 1-2). He was with God in the beginning.

When John said "in the beginning," he was not talking about the day Jesus was born. That was not the beginning. The beginning was the time before time began. The beginning was the time before what is came into being. The beginning was the time before creation was created. The beginning was not the manger. The beginning was when nothing had yet been created and all that existed was God. This is where we begin.

The Gospel of John does not start out this way to *explain* Jesus. Who can explain the infinite to the finite? Rather, John is making a statement of faith about Jesus. That is all we can really do. And as far as the Gospel of John is concerned, that is enough. We cannot explain every mystery, but we can say what we believe: "In the beginning was the Word."

If the phrase "in the beginning" sounds familiar to you, you may be thinking about the words from Genesis 1, which is probably what John wants us to do. John 1:1 is likely drawing on the language of Genesis 1:1 to make a profound point. Just as Genesis was about creation, the Word is about new creation, which is the Gospel's first claim about Jesus. Jesus is the Word that was in the beginning, the Word that was with God and the Word that was God.

There are two ways we should understand what John means by "Word." First, in Genesis, everything came into being when God spoke. The world came into being as a result of God speaking things into existence. Psalm 33:6 says, "By the word of the LORD were the heavens made; their starry host by the breath of his mouth" (NIV). God did not have to put the world together piece by piece, like so many of the toys and games that will be unwrapped later this week. God did not have to read blueprints, prepare a budget, or do a feasibility study to see if the creation of the world was a viable project. God did not have to hire contractors and get building permits to make oceans or create continents. God only had to speak and it was so.

God *said*, "'Let there be light,' and there was light" (Gen 1:3). God *said*, "Let the earth put forth vegetation: plants yielding seed, and fruit trees of every kind on earth that bear fruit with the seed in it" (Gen 1:11). And it was so. God only had to say a word, and that which was not came into being. The Word of God is the wisdom of God and the creative power of God.

The second way to understand the "Word" comes from the translation of the Greek term *logos*. *Logos* is divine reason. *Logos* is the mind of God (cf. 1 John 1:1). *Logos* is the divine principle that governs the order of the universe. According to the Greek way of thinking, the *logos* is how everything that is came to be.

So John combines these two ideas when he says, "In the beginning was the Word" in order to tell us something. He wants us to know that the Word has no beginning and no end. When creation was being created, the Word was there. When God made a covenant with Abraham, the Word was there. Before any star was born, before the moon began to shine, the Word was right there with God and the Word was God. No one could see the Word, but the Word was always there because the Word is the *source* of everything that is. This will be an important theme throughout the Gospel of John.

John not only says the Word was with God and the Word was God but also that the Word brought all things into being. Verse 3 says, "All things came into being through him, and without him not one thing came into being." The passage from Genesis 1 said that in beginning God created the heavens and the earth. Connect that with John 1, and it tells us that when God created the heavens and the earth, all things were created through the Word.

We live in an era when we have such enormous capabilities in science and technology to make and reshape reality the way we want it. We need to be reminded that the source of all things is God. Everything that exists, including you and me, came into existence not purely by our own effort or will but by the creative power of God. If God were to stop creating this instant, everything that is would instantly disappear. All matter would disintegrate. God is the sustaining power that holds the universe and all things in the universe together—every planet, every family, and every being.

The good news is that as the Gospel of John unfolds, it will become clear that God intends to make all things new. Since God is the source, God has the power to create something out of nothing. God can take a life that has fallen down one too many times, speak a word of restoration, and raise it back up again. God can find those who have drifted far away from God and speak a word of reconciliation that brings them back home again. God can take what looks like little and speak a word of abundance and it will become all we need. The Word that was with God in the beginning is the source of a new creation.

Today we can celebrate the Word who was at the beginning and is the source of all things and is no longer hidden behind the scenes. The Word has come to center stage. By the time we get to verse 14, John says that the Word came out where all can see his glory. And everyone who saw the Word was surprised by what they saw.

The Word became known in the most unexpected way. The Word of God did not come as a bolt of lightning. The Word did not appear as a spirit or in a dream. "The Word became flesh and lived among us" (v. 14). This is what happened in the manger on Christmas morning. Jesus of Nazareth was the Word that was with God, the Word who was the source of everything that is, and the Word that became flesh. This is John's statement about who Jesus is.

Christians have come up with a name for the Word becoming flesh. We call this moment the *incarnation.* Incarnation means "in the flesh." Incarnation tells us that we can affirm two realities about Jesus. First, Jesus was fully God. The *Word* became flesh. Jesus was not similar to God. Jesus did not just have a really close relationship with God. Scripture tells us that the Word *was* God, which is to say the Word was the very same substance as God.

The second thing we believe about Jesus is that he was fully human. The Word became *flesh.* We sometimes downplay this affirmation about Jesus, but this is the part that makes Christmas worth celebrating. God became one of us.

The way Paul put it, Jesus, "though he was in the form of God, did not regard equality with God as something to be exploited, but emptied himself, taking the form of a slave, being born in human likeness" (Phil 2:6-7).

The Word became flesh. Sometimes we hear the word "flesh" and think about sin or evil. But that is not what John means. To say the Word became flesh is to say that the invisible God became a human being. Jesus did not just seem human. He was fully divine and fully human. We cannot explain how this happened, but by faith we believe it. Scripture affirms that Jesus's humanity was just like yours and mine. "We do not have a high priest who is unable to sympathize with our weaknesses, but we have one who in every respect has been tempted as we are, yet without sin" (Heb 4:15). Jesus was fully human. He got hungry. He felt fatigue. He suffered. He wept. He knew the ache of loneliness. He experienced the bitterness of betrayal. He knew the joy of friendship. He knew the delight of laughter and the power of love.

This is who Jesus is.

He is the Word, the divine reason who existed before anything was created, who took on flesh and was born of a woman. This is why *every* life matters. And this is why we do not separate the physical from the spiritual or the sacred from the secular. The Word became flesh. If God became flesh, how can we divide our lives into spiritual stuff and secular stuff? Everything belongs to God. God fills all things, is in all things, and is through all things.

It would be enough to say that the Word became flesh, but John goes on to say that the Word "lived among us" (v. 14). The Word did not become flesh and then slip off to hide in a cave. Jesus did not ascend to a remote mountain where only certain people could see him by appointment. When the Word became flesh, he chose to live smack dab in the middle of our mess. Jesus was even born in a manger. He dined at people's homes. He hung out with sinners. He attended weddings. He visited the forgotten. He touched the untouchable. He helped the hopeless. The Word made his dwelling among us.

The good news in this is that there is no place we can go where God is not already there. There is no place we can end up where God cannot reach us. There is no depth to which God will not descend to bring us back up again.

The Word has made his dwelling among us. Jesus came to live among us not just to let us see what God is like, although that would be enough. He did not come just to give us a safe exit from this world. Jesus came in the flesh to show us how to live in a new way "in the world."

He came to teach us how to live a life of spiritual freedom and trust in God, a life filled with faith, amazing grace, and liberating truth. When people have lost their way, they do not need a lecture. They need a living example, so "the Word became flesh and lived among us" (v. 14).

Some say that the translation "lived among us" is not quite vivid enough. A better translation might be the Word "pitched a tent" or "camped out" among us because Jesus was on a temporary assignment. That's good news—the Word became flesh and pitched his tent among us!

The Word becoming flesh is the foundation of our faith. It concerns our everyday lives. John says that in the Word was life, and that "life was the light of all people" (v. 4).

In other words, if we are looking for life, and I hope we are, we will find true life in the Word that became flesh, which is Jesus. One of the problems Jesus had is that when he came to offer people life, they told him that they already had life. They did not want what he had to offer. As it says in verse 11, "He came to what was his own, and his own people did not accept him."

People did not understand he was offering them life that was different from the life they had. They had the kind of life that one can attain through achievements and accomplishments and possessions. They had the kind of life that comes along with status and prestige, titles and independence. But this is not the kind of life Jesus came to give. He came to give the life that is the gift of God.

He came to offer life that is fruitful and vibrant, hopeful and purposeful. His gift is a life lived in God, with God, and for God. Jesus has this life, he is this life, and he came to give it away. His life is a "light" that can guide us through darkness.

We need this life. What we call life is often so far from real life. What we call life is often nothing more than "keeping up with the Joneses." It will become evident when we read in John that human beings have a way of exchanging real life (life God wants to give) for something that looks like real life (resembles it but does not compare). We will, as Paul Lawrence Dunbar poetically penned, "wear the mask."

> We wear the mask that grins and lies,
> It hides our cheeks and shades our eyes—

But now that the Word is among us, the masks are no longer necessary.

We can come out of darkness into the marvelous light. There is always a darkness that wants to drive Jesus away. There is always a darkness tempting us to choose to live in fear rather than in love. There is always a numbing darkness that accepts injustice and embraces inequality.

The good news is that darkness is never strong enough to overcome the light. Jesus came to give us life, and not just more of the life we already have. He came to give us something better. He came to give us something more. John says that to all who receive Jesus, to all who embrace him, to all who welcome him, to all who want to be with him, to those who believe in his name, he gives the right to become children of God.

That's who Jesus is. He is the One who can give us a new name. He is the One who can give us a new purpose. He is the One who can give us new hope. When the light in him is the light in us, he scatters the darkness. When the light in him is the light in us, he uncovers the truth. When the light in him is the light in us, he leads us in paths of righteousness.

Hear this good news! The Word became flesh. He has made his dwelling among us. He is God with us. No one believed it would happen, but *we* have seen the glory of God. No one thought you could see the glory of God and live, but we have seen his glory.

He walked the streets of Jerusalem.

He blessed little children.

He is the only begotten son.
He came from the Father.
He is full of grace and truth.
And his name is Jesus.

Note

1. This sermon was preached on the fourth Sunday of Advent.

It's Not about Us[1]

John 1:6-9, 15-34

Permit me to share a parent-child story that speaks to who we are as Christian leaders. During the Christmas holidays, I took a bike ride with my children, Cory and Julienne. Julienne's bike still has the training wheels on it. Pink ribbons hang from the white handlebars. The bike has a white, plastic basket on the front for carrying small items. When I put a bottle in the basket that I did not want to carry, she protested loudly.

Cory and I reassured her that the bottle in her basket was not a big deal. But she said, "If this is in my basket, people won't see my light on my bike." Her comment led to a heated debate with her brother, who said, "Actually, it's not a light. It's a reflector." Being the stubborn four-year-old that she was, Julienne insisted that it was a light.

My daughter helped me understand something about Christian leadership. We get confused about the difference between lights and reflectors, too. A light gives off its own brightness. A reflector gives off the light that comes from another source, not its own light.

As Christian leaders, we are not called to be lights as much as we are supposed to be reflectors. The light that shines through our lives should be a reflection of the Son of God. John the Baptist testified that he was not a light. He was a reflector. His mission was not about John. His mission was to be a witness to the light of the world.

John the Baptist stands out as one of the most unique personalities in all of the New Testament. Before Jesus presented himself to the world as the Christ, he revealed himself to John the Baptist. John plays such a pivotal role that none of the Gospel writers say much about Jesus without first mentioning John, the son of Elizabeth and Zacharias, often referred to today as John the Baptizer.

John's birth was predicted by an angelic promise, no less than that of the patriarch Isaac or the great warrior Samson. When our children are born, we typically have hopes of what they might become. Very few parents have expectations that their children will grow up to make ready a people for the Lord or possess the spirit and power of Elijah. John was special.

We can commend John for many reasons, but perhaps Jesus said all that needs to be said about John: "Truly I tell you, among those born of women no one has arisen greater than John the Baptist" (Matt 11:11a). This is high praise coming from the lips of a man who was crucified for the sin of the world. John never reigned as king over the nation of Israel. John did not command armies to victory in dangerous battles. John was a man who wore camel hair, preached repentance, ate locusts and wild honey, and baptized throngs of people in the Jordan River. Yet Jesus said there is no one greater born of women than John the Baptizer.

Therefore, we can only conclude that Jesus has his own way of measuring greatness. Jesus does not measure greatness by counting the followers we have on social media. Jesus does not measure greatness by the titles we hold, the labels we wear, or the incomes we earn. One day, if we live long enough, someone is going to occupy our office and take our title.

Jesus measures greatness by the standards of the kingdom of God.

Jesus had so much respect for John because John believed that his service and his ministry were not about him: "There was a man who sent from God, whose name was John. He came as a witness to testify to the light, so that all might believe through him. He himself was not the light, but he came to testify to the light. The true light, which enlightens everyone, was coming into the world" (vv. 6-9).

If Christian leadership is not about us, what are our ministry and our leadership about? According to John, we are here to point people to Jesus. This is why John did everything he did. Before he was born, God set John apart for a special assignment. The nature of John's assignment is captured in three words that appear in this passage: witness, testify, and testimony.

John came "as a witness to testify . . . he came only as a witness to the light . . . now this was John's testimony" (vv. 7, 8, 19, NIV). We recognize these three words from the field of law. Lawyers put witnesses on the stand to testify in court. A witness is someone who has seen something. In the Gospel of John, being a witness also carries the meaning of putting one's life on the line. To give testimony is to affirm publicly what you have heard or seen. This is what John came to do. He came to be a witness. He was willing to put his life on the line to testify that Jesus was who he said he was. He spent his entire ministry pointing people to Jesus.

A famous painting by Matthias Grünewald depicts John the Baptist standing next to Jesus's tortured, lifeless body on the cross.[2] Jesus's mother Mary stands opposite John the Baptist at the foot of the cross, grief stricken. The beloved disciple, also known as the apostle John, holds Mary, consoling her upon the death of her son. John the Baptist, standing at Jesus's left, has what looks like the open Scriptures in his left hand. With his right hand, he uses his index finger to point. He points straight at the figure on the cross. Mary is weeping. The disciple is comforting Mary. But John the Baptist stands with an outstretched arm pointing to Jesus.

This was the artist's way of highlighting the mission of John the Baptist. John's singular mission was to say, "This is not about me. I am here to point you to Jesus." John's sole purpose was to point and say to anyone willing to listen, "This is who Jesus is." As the Scripture says, "He himself was not the light, but he came to testify to the light" (v. 8).

This is why his life speaks to Christian leaders today. Our assignment, first and foremost, is to serve so well that our work points to Jesus. Pointing sounds so simple, even trivial and insignificant, because naked ambition seems to be one of the virtues of modern civilization. The housing crisis that led to the Great Recession of 2007–2009 was largely brought about by old-fashioned selfishness and greed. In contrast, John was so content to humble himself that Jesus said no one born of women was greater than John.

John could have built his own movement, a cult of personality, but he only wanted to be a witness. He only wanted to point to Jesus. It is tempting to point to great people or successful programs or our long-stranding traditions, but our calling as leaders is to point to Jesus. He is the Word of God. "Through him all things were made; without him nothing was made that has been made" (1:3, NIV). In him there is life. In him there is forgiveness. In him there is hope.

At the top of every job description for every position in the church—from parking lot attendant to senior pastor—should be the responsibility of pointing people to Jesus. The way we usher should point people to Jesus. The way we give should point people to Jesus. Our level of commitment and follow-through should point someone to Jesus. John's humility perplexed the priests and mystified the Levites. An official delegation came out to the Jordan River to see John. They only had one question in mind. They did not come to confess their sins. They did not come to be baptized. They heard about the work that John was doing, so they came out to ask him if he was the Christ.

Had John the Baptist been a different kind of man, he might have easily said, "Why, certainly I am!" But John knew that if he was ever going to be of any use to God, it was just as important to know who he was *not* as it was to know who he was. John did not fail to confess, but confessed freely, "I am not the Messiah" (v. 20). We can find ourselves in a painful position when we try to be someone we are not. John knew who he was and he knew who he was not. "I am not the Messiah."

The priests and the Levites continued to press John. They figured that if he was not the Christ, he must be some other prominent figure predicted by prophets of the past. "They asked him, 'Then who are you? Are you Elijah?' He said, 'I am not.' 'Are you the Prophet?' He answered, 'No.' Finally they said, 'Who are you? Give us an answer to take back to those who sent us. What do you say about yourself?'" (vv. 21-22, NIV).

To do the work God has called us to do with humility, we need to know who we are. John knew who he was. He said, "I am the voice of one calling in the wilderness, 'Make straight the way for the Lord'" (v. 23, NIV). John knew his calling. He understood his identity. He was not Moses. He was not Elijah. He was not the Christ. He was a voice. Jesus was the Word. John only wanted to be a voice on behalf of the Word. If he could be a voice, then his living would not be in vain.

Jesus needs more voices today. He needs young voices and older voices. He needs women's voices and men's voices. He needs voices that can sing and voices that cannot carry a tune. Moses was not sure that God could use him to be a voice because he stuttered, but God used him. Esther was not sure her voice had enough authority to speak for God, but God used her. Who knows how you and I might point someone to Jesus simply by letting God use our voice?

John was a voice crying in the wilderness. He told those who came to see him, "I baptize with water. Among you stands one whom you do not know, the one who is coming after me; I am not worthy to untie the thong of his sandal" (vv. 26-27). Only a servant would stoop down and untie someone's sandals, and John said he was not even worthy to do that.

Few of us see the nursery volunteers on Sunday, but thank God someone is willing to stoop down to care for children and advance the mission of Jesus. Not many of us see the van and bus drivers on Sunday morning, but thank God someone is willing to get up a little early and drive people to church to advance the mission of Jesus. Only a few of us have the perspective to see who is working in the audio-video ministry each week, but thankfully God keeps raising up men and women who are like John, willing to go behind the scenes to serve the mission of Jesus.

John the Baptist was not only humble but also sensitive. When we come to verses 29-34, John helps us see that Christian leaders must be sensitive to the work of the Spirit. The day after the delegation came to John asking if he was the Christ, he saw Jesus coming toward him. When John saw Jesus, he said, "Here is the Lamb of God who takes away the sin of the world!" (v. 29). John knew Jesus was the Messiah because he was sensitive to the work of the Spirit.

John confesses that he could not have recognized Jesus as the Messiah without the illumination of the Holy Spirit. "I myself did not know him, but the one who sent me to baptize with water said to me, 'He on whom you see the Spirit descend and remain is the one who baptizes with the Holy Spirit.' And I myself have seen and have testified that this is the Son of God" (vv. 33-34).

John the Baptist could testify that Jesus was the Son of God because he was attentive to the work of the Spirit. There is no getting around the fact that as leaders who serve God, we cannot do anything well without the ongoing empowerment and guidance of the Spirit. This truth can be unsettling because the realm of the Spirit takes us beyond the typical way of seeing and decision-making. A mentor of mine told me that if I wanted to key in on what God was doing, I had to pay attention to clues because God always provides clues. We just have to train our eyes to see them.

Spreadsheets can give us good information, but they may not give us the last word on what the Spirit is doing. Clocks can help us tell time, but we cannot always make the Spirit conform to our schedule. The Spirit can mock our strategic plans and surprise us with answers so simple that we have to think like a child to understand them.

John baptized a lot of people at the Jordan River, but he had his eyes and ears tuned into the Spirit because only by the Spirit was he going to be able to recognize the fulfillment of his hopes. We can say the same about Christian leadership today. Some insights only come when we wait on the Spirit. Some opportunities only materialize when the Spirit moves. So as we lead we have to be sensitive to the ongoing, unfolding, unpredictable work of the Spirit.

John was a unique man. It is remarkable that he remained motivated and focused on his mission given all the years he waited on the Lamb of God to be revealed. And yet John 3 suggests that he did what he did because he had hope: "The friend of the bridegroom, who stands and hears him, rejoices greatly at the bridegroom's voice. For this reason my joy has been fulfilled" (3:29). Christian leaders need humility, sensitivity to the Spirit, and hope.

John had hope that his service had significance. He hoped that his voice was not falling on deaf ears. He had hope that his mission had purpose. He had hope that his labor was not in vain. He held on to this hope even when his own disciples did not understand.

Some of John's disciples came to him saying, "Rabbi, that one who was with you across the Jordan, to whom you testified, here he is baptizing, and all are going to him" (3:26). They were concerned that Jesus's movement was gaining momentum and John's was losing steam. They were concerned that Jesus would end up with more followers than John. But John was not concerned because he knew he was doing what God sent him to do. His hope was in the Lamb of God.

John said, "I am not the Christ, but I am sent ahead of him. . . . God sent me to be a witness and I have done that. God sent me to give my testimony and I have done that. God sent me to prepare the way for Jesus. I have done that. Now, he must become greater; I must become less" (paraphrase of 3:28-30). John lived with the hope that whoever believed in the Son had eternal life.

This hope is why John stayed at the Jordan baptizing: to point to the Son of God, to be a witness to the light, to testify to what he had seen because he knew that anyone who saw Jesus and believed in him would have eternal life. Every Christian leader needs this hope. We point and serve and trust because we know that in Christ there is eternal life. No more despair and gloom, but eternal life. No more shame and guilt, but eternal life. No more fear and bondage, but eternal life. Jesus has the gift of eternal life.

This is why we sing. This is why we serve. This is why we lead. This why we give. This is why we plan. This is why we care. This is why we show up. This is why we preach. This is why we pray. This is why we worship. This is why we praise. This is why we point to Jesus. What we do is not about us. Jesus is our hope. He is our redemption. He is our all in all.

Notes

1. This sermon was preached on the occasion of the installation of church officers.
2. Matthias Grünewald, *The Crucifixion,* altarpiece in Unterlinden Museum, Alsace, France (1512–1516).

3

Finding What You've Always Wanted

John 1:35–51

Every year at this time, magazine articles and new books promise to tell us how to find purpose, meaning, and true joy in life. If you want to find the perfect job, they tell you how. If you want to build your dream home, they tell you what you need to know. If you want to get in the best shape of your life, they will provide the perfect plan.

The trouble is that finding what we truly want is not as easy as it sounds. We often have to walk through our fears, move beyond the expectations of others, and overcome the opinions of our friends and family. Sometimes the things we think will bring us true satisfaction only bring us temporary happiness.

Howard Thurman often said to college students, "Don't worry about what the world needs. Ask yourself what makes you come alive, because what the world needs is people who are fully alive." If we were to ask the four people featured in this text, Andrew, Simon, Philip, and Nathanael, what they thought would make them fully alive, their answer might be similar to that of other Israelites living in first-century Palestine. They wanted to find Israel's Messiah.

Messiah was the name given to the person the Old Testament prophets declared would deliver Israel from its enemies. Messiah means "anointed one," which indicates that the Messiah would be chosen by God, set apart by God, and sent from God. Much to John the Baptist's delight, he lived to witness the day when the Messiah finally arrived.

This day was a monumental moment for John. His life's work had been to prepare people for the coming of the Messiah, and now the Messiah had finally come. This is what he always wanted. When you wait for something a long time and it finally happens, it can be hard to believe that the dream is becoming reality. John and his disciples were not dreaming. Jesus, Israel's Messiah, had come.

When John saw Jesus, he said, "Look, here is the Lamb of God!" (v. 36). Two of John's disciples immediately began to follow Jesus. John was not insulted by their change in loyalty. This is precisely why John had come. His sole purpose was to point people toward Jesus. John was content to decrease so that Jesus could increase. Mother Teresa once said, "If you are humble, nothing can touch you, neither praise nor disgrace, because you know who you are."

John knew who he was. He was not puffed up by the priests and Levites who thought he was the Christ, nor was he disappointed when his disciples followed Jesus. As far as he was concerned, everything was unfolding exactly as God intended. The Son of God was being revealed. John had waited his whole life for this. His disciples had waited for this. All their lives, they looked for someone to bring light into darkness. They longed for the affirmation that God was with them. When the Lamb of God arrived, John and his disciples realized that everything they had been waiting for had finally come.

We, too, spend a lot of our lives looking for something. We look for the perfect job only to discover that the perfect job means we have to work with imperfect people. We look for the perfect house only to realize that the longer we stay in the house, the more we want to change the way it looks. We constantly look for what we think we do not have. The good news of the Gospel of John is that the search for satisfaction is over. The Lamb of God has come. We now have what we've always wanted.

We have to go back to the Old Testament to understand the meaning of Lamb of God the way the disciples, including Andrew and Peter, understood it. When Israel was enslaved by Egypt, the book of Exodus tells us that God orchestrated their deliverance in the most surprising way. God instructed Moses to tell the Israelites to sacrifice a lamb and sprinkle its blood on the doorposts of their houses. The blood was a sign. At night an angel came from God and slew the firstborn sons of the Egyptians as a judgment against their oppression of the Israelites and their unwillingness to set Israel free. The angel passed over every home where the blood of the lamb was on the doorposts, and the Israelites in those houses were spared. Soon after this divine judgment, the Egyptians set Israel free.

Freedom meant they would not have to make bricks and build cities for Pharaoh. Freedom meant they would not have to live in the shadow of fear. Freedom meant liberation from the dehumanizing, denigrating life of bondage.

Each year afterward, the Israelites commemorated their freedom by sacrificing a Passover lamb in the temple. At the end of John's Gospel, Jesus is killed on the very day that the Passover lambs are sacrificed in the temple in preparation for the annual celebration of freedom from slavery in Egypt.

To say that Jesus is the Lamb of God is to say that he can make possible a new kind of freedom, a life of liberation, a new exodus, a way out of the bondage that keeps us living in prisons of fear and shame. We all have something from which we need to be set free. Here comes the Lamb of God who takes away the sin of the world!

Saying Jesus takes away the *sin* of the world (rather than the *sins* of the world) suggests that Jesus's death was not merely about our individual sins—the candy we stole as a kid or the lie someone told last week. Jesus's death atones for more than our individual transgressions. He came to take away the sin of the "whole world." In him, God was reconciling the world to himself. In him, God removed the stain and burden of sin that mars all of creation. Jesus came to defeat the enemy who is trying to steal, kill, and destroy the gift of abundant life. He came to take away the sin of the world.

Jesus came to break the power that separates the world from God. He came to pull the plug on the principalities that oppose God. He came to expose injustice, shine a light on darkness, and denounce every evil. He came to set us free. Jesus can free us from unforgiveness. He can free us from anger and bitterness. He can free us from fearful limitations. He can free us from anxieties that keep us up at night. He can free us from prisons of pain. He is the Lamb of God and he is the Messiah who came to liberate our lives. The question for us today is, have we found what we're looking for?

Andrew and the second disciple did not immediately walk up to Jesus. The text says they followed at a distance. Eventually Jesus turned around. Here is where we hear the first words directly from Jesus in the Gospel of John. So far, we have heard many wonderful words *about* Jesus. But now we hear for the first time from Jesus himself.

Surprisingly, Jesus does not say "bless you" or "grace and peace" or "you are forgiven." Jesus turns around and asks Andrew and the other disciple of John the Baptist, "What do you want?" (v. 38, NIV). Some translations say, "What are you looking for?"

On a literal level, Jesus asked a basic question of people who were following him. However, the question was also Jesus's way of looking beneath the surface into the heart and mind of Andrew and the other disciple. What do you want? What are you looking for?

Everyone is looking for something. Some people are searching for security. Some people are looking for true love. Some people are hunting for hope. Some people are in need of affirmation, respect, or understanding. Problems arise when we try to have our needs met by things or people who cannot meet them. A new car can take you to a destination, but it cannot give you purpose.

Jesus asked the disciples what they wanted to find out, what they were searching for. So often people come to Jesus expecting him to be something he is not. He is not an ATM. He is not a motivational speaker. He has not ever run for or held an elected office. He is not a nationalist. He does not carry the flag of any one country. If anyone is looking for that type of Messiah, they will be misinformed, disappointed, or confused.

Andrew and the other disciple did what my mother never liked her children to do when she asked us something. They answered Jesus's question with a question. Jesus asked, "What do you want?" The disciples said, "Rabbi . . . , where are you staying?" (v. 38). This is an interesting response that leads to the second truth about what the disciples found when they found the Messiah. When they found Jesus, they entered a relationship that leads to a new way of life.

Andrew and the other disciple wanted to know where Jesus was staying because they probably wanted to move the conversation to a deeper level. They did not want to simply talk with Jesus in the middle of the street. They wanted a closer connection. They wanted to spend time with him, to share their lives with him and to find out more about his life. They were not going to be satisfied with catching a glimpse of him every few weeks. If he was the Lamb of God, they wanted to go with him wherever he went. They wanted a relationship.

Faith is more than a list of rules. Certainly, there are behaviors that contradict and undermine faith, but Jesus did not begin with the rules. He started with an invitation to authentic relationship with him: "Come and see" (v. 39).

"Come and see" was an invitation to the disciples to have a deeper conversation. Jesus did not brush them off. He offered them the chance to get to know him. If we want people "out there" to come "in here," we have to invite them to come and to see. We cannot stand in judgment of them if their clothes do not meet our approval. We simply have to invite them to come and see. And we invite them because we know that when they encounter Jesus, they will find what they've been looking for.

"Come and see" is an invitation that leads to transformation. Maybe transformation does not happen all at once. But day by day we are transformed. This is what happened to Andrew's brother, Simon. After Andrew and the other disciple spent the day with Jesus, they enjoyed what they heard enough that they decided to tell others about Jesus. One sign that the Church is in authentic relationship with Jesus is the desire to share the good news with others. When Andrew encountered Jesus, Andrew knew that he had found what he'd been looking for. Afterward, the first thing he did was find his brother Simon and tell him, "We have found the Messiah" (v. 41). And he brought him to Jesus.

Sometimes the hardest place to share the good news is in our own home. The people who are least willing to hear what God can do may be the people we see every night at dinner. We can go to the prison and minister. We can share the consoling words of Christ at work. But our own spouse or son or daughter can be the first person to shut us down as soon as we bring up Jesus. Andrew took the chance.

Simon was receptive to what his brother told him. He wanted to know more so he came to meet Jesus personally. Jesus saw so much potential in Simon that he changed his name from Simon to Peter. Just as Jesus changed water into wine, once we find that Jesus is the one we've been looking for, we are no longer who we used to be. Once we find that Jesus is the one we've been looking for, we are no longer who we used to be. Paul said, "I have been crucified with Christ; and it is no longer I who live, but it is Christ who lives in me" (Gal 2:19-20).

According to the New Testament, we are now a chosen people, a royal priesthood, a holy nation, and a people belonging to God. We are now the beloved of God, more than conquerors, and fishers of men. We are now redeemed, blessed, and adopted sons and daughters through Christ Jesus. This is not who we were, but in Jesus this is who we are. And isn't this what we have been looking for? The chance to start over, the opportunity to begin anew, the affirmation that God accepts us?

Our name is no longer failure. Our name is no longer barren. Our name is no longer ashamed. Jesus changes our name as he did for Simon. To all who receive him, he gave the right to become children of God. We are the apple of God's eye. We are redeemed. Now we are heirs, even joint heirs with Christ Jesus.

Perhaps now is a good time to make an important theological point. So far we've been talking about what happens when we find Jesus. But the more we read, the more it seems that when we find Jesus we discover that he is actually the one who finds us. We would like to think that we found God completely on our own, but in reality God was on a search and rescue mission looking for us. "And the Word became flesh and lived among us" (1:14).

The disciples were looking for the Christ, but according to the text Jesus was looking for them, too. Jesus found Philip and said to him, "Follow me" (v. 43). Like Andrew and Peter, Philip followed Jesus.

Like Andrew, Philip went and found someone else to tell the good news, a man named Nathanael. Philip told Nathanael, "We have found the one Moses wrote about in the Law, and about whom the prophets also wrote—Jesus of Nazareth, the son of Joseph" (v. 45, NIV).

Nathanael thought Philip was being absurd. He did not believe that anything or anyone good could come out of Nazareth. Philip said to Nathanael the same thing Jesus said to Andrew: "Come and see" (v. 46). Nathanael had been looking for the Christ, but little did he know that Jesus was looking for him. Jesus knew things about Nathanael that no human being could have known.

This amazed Nathanael so much that he decided Jesus must have been looking for him before he started looking for Jesus, which could only mean one thing: Jesus was the Son of God, the King of Israel.

And it gets even better than that. Once Nathanael identified Jesus as the Son of God, Jesus told him, "You will see greater things than these" (v. 50). Nathanael had waited all his life, and now the day of the Messiah had come. He hoped all his life to see Israel's Messiah, and now the day had arrived when hope was standing in front of him. He had been looking and searching, and now the Son of God was with him and knew him by name.

Seeing the Messiah should have been enough, but Jesus said to Nathanael, "If you think this is something, you haven't seen anything yet. If you were amazed that I saw you under a fig tree before you saw me, I'm just getting started. If you were surprised that I knew your name, sit back and relax because you're going to see even more."

It is as if Jesus said, "You have some joy now, but you shall see greater things than these. Your cup is going to overflow. You have some hope now, but this is only the beginning. Stay a while with me. Put your trust in me. When I get through with you, you are going to be 'steadfast, unmovable, always abounding in the work of the Lord.' You have the beginning of faith now, but more is on the way. Eventually, you will be 'like a tree planted by the rivers of water whose leaves shall not wither; you shall bring forth fruit in season'" (1 Cor 15:58; Ps 1:3).

You will see power like you've never seen before.

You will experience joy like you've never known before.

You'll discover peace like you've never had before.

One day you may even see the "heavens opened and the angels of God ascending and descending," which shall be a sign that God is with you; God is for you; God is watching over you (v. 51).

Jesus is the Lamb of God who can lead us to true freedom. I don't know for certain what you are looking for today, but I do know that Jesus is looking for you. When he finds you, it may be hard to believe what he says. But follow him for a while and you will see that he is exactly the one you have been looking for.

4

The Miracle at Cana

John 2:1-11

John 2 is where the action begins. Chapter 1 was an introduction, but chapter 2 is when Jesus steps out boldly to let everybody know by his words and his deeds who he is and what he came to do. And this happens, of all places, at a wedding in Cana of Galilee.

Two days have passed since the incidents that took place in chapter 1. It is now the third day after Jesus called his first disciples. Jesus's first disciples had originally been disciples of John the Baptist. But once John's disciples met Jesus, they knew they were in the presence of one sent from God, the one for whom John the Baptist had been waiting. The disciples were Andrew and his brother Simon Peter, Philip, and Nathanael.

After Jesus met them he stayed with them for two days. On the third day, Jesus, his four new disciples, and Jesus's mother attended a wedding in Cana of Galilee.

In one way Jesus's presence at a wedding is not surprising, and in another way it is. It is not surprising because weddings in Jesus's time were huge. There was no such thing as a small, private ceremony like someone might have today. Weddings were big community rituals filled with days of celebration.

The owners of Alex's Café next to Hanes Park in the West End (a restaurant in Winston-Salem) are from the same part of the world where Jesus lived. They are Coptic (Egyptian) Christians, and sometimes the wife, who waits tables, asks me questions to learn about the similarities and differences between Coptic Christians and Baptists. One day we talked about weddings. She said that in her hometown, every wedding has 1,000–2,000 or more guests. I told her that was a big difference between her culture and mine, because no one I knew wanted to feed that many people.

Weddings in the Mediterranean world were big because the guest list went well beyond people you knew intimately. It included whole families and neighborhoods. The wedding was a celebration for the community that lasted several days. So, given this cultural practice of having a huge crowd at a wedding in a place as small as Cana, it isn't a surprise that Jesus, living nearby in Nazareth, was in the web of relationships invited to attend the wedding. Some have wondered if Mary was a relative of the bride or groom given her concern about the details of the party, but we don't know for sure.

At the same time, is it not a bit of a surprise to see Jesus at a wedding? After all, he is the Word that was with God in the beginning. He is the only begotten son of the Father, full of grace and truth. And he has time to attend a wedding? This wedding was not a dinner at the king's palace. This was not a private meeting with the governor of Rome. This gala was a wedding for a couple whose names are not even mentioned. But Jesus—Son of God, Lamb of God, and Word of God made flesh—was right there in the crowd with his disciples and his mother, Mary.

Maybe this is John's way of reminding us that Jesus is willing to be involved in the most intricate details of a person's life. There is no time he will not be there with us. He is present in the most ordinary moments of our existence. Jesus is God with us.

And since weddings are celebratory events, it also needs to be said that Jesus's presence at the banquet assures us that the life of faith is not meant to be a sterile, drab, dreary, and dry way of life. Jesus is not a killjoy. We do not have to wear a perpetual frown to be faithful. We do not have to shun celebrations to be followers of Christ. A wedding in Jesus's day was a party—a weeklong celebration with feasting, dancing, laughter, and joy. And Jesus was right there!

John 2:11 lets us know that what Jesus did at the wedding was the first of Jesus's miraculous signs. Jesus performs seven miraculous signs in the Gospel of John. Each miracle does more than just change an individual's situation. The miracles are signs. A sign is something that points to something else. When we are driving along the highway and see a sign for a gas station, we do not stop at the sign for the gas station to refuel. The sign tells us that the gas station is near.

The same is true for Jesus's miraculous signs. By the end of the wedding he is going to turn water into wine. Spring water will become chardonnay. But if all we see in this moment is wine, we have missed the meaning of the miracle. The wine is a sign that reveals what Jesus's ministry on earth is about, a sign that discloses what is possible when Jesus is leading our life, a sign that uncovers what can happen through the power of Jesus Christ for anyone who has faith in him.

The way Jesus performs the miracle at Cana suggests that God invites us to cooperate with God in order to see the power of God. Jesus could have performed this miracle by speaking a word, as he did when he calmed the winds and the waves. But that is not what happened. Jesus invited the people around him to cooperate with him in what he was doing. He is still doing so today. The question is whether we will we say yes.

We cannot say for sure how long the wedding had been going on, but at some point what should have been a jubilant gathering of family and friends almost turned into a disaster. Maybe more people showed up at the wedding than expected, or the host of the banquet was simply unprepared. Whatever the reason, when the wine was gone, Jesus's mother said to him, "They have no more wine" (v. 3, NIV). We don't see many interactions between Jesus and his mother. Mary only appears twice in the Gospel of John: once at this wedding and again at the foot of the cross.

Mary knew that running out of wine was not just an inconvenience. If you threw a party or a feast and ran out of wine, you had a major crisis on your hands. The rules of hospitality in Jesus's culture were among the most important features of society. Having an abundance of food and drink for your guests was a necessity, not a luxury. It would have been an insult to the guests and an embarrassment to the host to run out of wine.

Mary told Jesus, "They have no more wine." Jesus replied, "Dear woman, why do you involve me? My time has not yet come" (v. 4, translation mine). Both times Jesus talks to his mother in John, he refers to her as "woman." To us this sounds a bit rude, but the tone he used was most likely one of tenderness. He was not trying to offend her. Nevertheless, since Jesus is who he is, he has no obligation to respond to Mary simply because she wants him to do something.

Throughout the Gospel of John, Jesus is guided by one voice only—the voice of his Father. He moves when the Father tells him to move. He acts when the Father tells him to act. Jesus is not required to be at our beck and call. He refuses be made subject to our agenda. Even the relationship between Mary and Jesus had to change. Jesus was not only her son; he was also her Redeemer.

So Mary turned her attention to the servants and said to them, "Do whatever he tells you" (v. 5). She clearly knew who was in charge and had confidence that if anything could be done, Jesus would make it happen.

Verse 6 tells us that nearby stood six stone water jars, the kind used by the Jewish people for ceremonial washing, "each holding twenty or thirty gallons. Jesus said to [the servants], 'Fill the jars with water.' And they filled them up to the brim" (vv. 6-7). Jesus may do some of his best work with empty vessels. When we empty our pride, our fear, and our guilt, Jesus can do amazing things in and through our lives.

Jesus decided to do something about the problem, and he invited the servants to participate in the miracle. He sent them to get the empty jars and fill them with water. They needed to do their part before he could do the miracle.

Filling up six thirty-gallon jars with water was not as easy as turning on a faucet. Someone had to go get the water. This work would have taken considerable time, effort, and energy; but filling the jars was required preparation for the miracle.

Considering the work required to fill these thirty-gallon jars with water, we may have stumbled on a key in this text about what God calls us to do. When we want to see the wonders of God, we may have to work while we wait. Jesus can do miracles, but that does not mean we should not do something. Jesus did not speak water into the jars. Jesus did not wave his hands over the jars. He sent servants to fill thirty-gallon jars with water and bring them back to the banquet.

So many times we want God to change something but we don't want to give up anything. We want God to open doors, but we don't want to take the first step. We want to see an idea bear fruit, but we do not want to get dirty doing the hard work of preparation. For so many of his miracles, Jesus calls for human participation to work in cooperation with his divine power.

To one man Jesus said, "Stretch out your hand" (Matt 12:13). Then he healed the hand. To another person Jesus said, "Stand up, take your mat and walk" (John 5:8). And the man was made whole. To these servants Jesus said, "Fill the jars with water" (v. 7). Then he performed the miracle.

When we think about how we want our lives to be better, to be different, after we have prayed for God to do something, we should listen for what God wants us to do. Just like the servants in John 2, we should do whatever Jesus says and bring him whatever he asks for.

Put forth the effort, and he can provide the providence. Put in the hard work, and he can provide the breakthrough. The miracle at Cana called for the servants to cooperate with God in order to see the power of God. What work is God waiting for you to do? The command to fill the empty jars with water reminds us of God's call for us to be participants in God's transformation in the world.

Jesus told the servants to fill six stone water jars. Each jar held up to thirty gallons of water. The servants filled each jar to the brim. Quick calculations tell us that Jesus was working with as many as 180 gallons of water that he would turn into wine. That is a lot of wine. But what Jesus did was about so much more than wine.

In Scripture, abundant wine was evidence of the blessings of God. Wine was a symbol of joy, celebration, and festivity.[1] Therefore, the miracle reminds us that Jesus is not stingy or tightfisted when it comes to giving us grace. When Jesus gets ready to give grace, he holds nothing back. Even though the servants did not know what was about to happen, the size of the water jars—thirty gallons each—makes it clear that Jesus was about to do something monumental and extravagant.

Thankfully, God's extravagance is not limited to water and wine. Many of us know from personal experience that God gives extravagantly with everything. If you have ever seen the orange and yellow sun setting on the horizon at the ocean, you know that God showers the earth daily with bountiful beauty and grace.

God gives joy beyond measure. God gives new mercies each and every day. God's love is wider, higher, deeper, and longer than anything we have ever known. God forgives more than we deserve. God pours out incredible power when we are weak. God's peace surpasses all understanding. God's provision is not only enough but more than enough. God's grace is amazing.

We cannot use up, exhaust, or run out of what God gives. In chapter 10, Jesus is going to tell us that he came to give us life and life more abundant. God is a God of extravagant generosity. This is good news in a world where someone is always playing on our fear of scarcity and lack and insufficiency. Someone is always telling us that we need to have more if we want to be more. But in Christ, we have all we need. "In him was life, and the life was the light of all people" (1:4). When God gives grace, God gives it abundantly.

Jesus came to the wedding with all of his generosity and abundance, and changed it from disaster to delight. He can do this in our lives, too. He can do this in our world, whenever we are willing to cooperate with him and do as he tells us to do. Because the best part about this miracle is that it is not just a historical event. This is also a promise for today.

The promise is that God is making all things new. The prophet Isaiah said it best: "you will be called by a new name that the mouth of the LORD will bestow . . . . No longer will they call you Deserted, or name your land Desolate. But you will be called Hephzibah [my delight is in her] and your land Beulah [married] . . ." (Isa 62:2b, 4, NIV).

Jesus came to show the people that they could have so much more in life and from life if they would put their hope in him and bring him what he was asking for. The people expected to put water in jars and get water out of jars. The miracle at Cana is proof positive that transformation is at the heart of Jesus's ministry. Transformation is what the kingdom of God is about. Transformation is what Jesus came to do. The wine was the sign that Jesus came to bring a change.

He came to change hatred into love; sorrow into gladness; despair into hope; inactivity into courage; misery into joy; darkness into light; loneliness into community; blindness into sight; and, by the end of the gospel, death into life.

There is so much more that could be said about the miracle at Cana, but time and wisdom do not permit us to say it all. Perhaps the only other thing we need to say today about the miracle at Cana is that it is a sign that Jesus came to bring us inexpressible joy.

John is so keen on symbolism that it is not a stretch to say that wine running out is not merely a statement about what happened at the party; it is also a reality that we may experience in our everyday lives. Have we run out of wine?

Have we run dry of the joy we once had? Have we lost our grip on the peace we once possessed? Do we need more of the hope that gives us the motivation to live? Do we know where to locate the love that once held us together? Are we missing the faith to move forward? Can we summon the creative juices to inspire new ideas? Are we struggling to maintain the energy to enjoy the blessings of God? If so, it could be that the wine has run out.

Just as no one in the first century would have conceived of throwing a wedding banquet without sufficient wine, no life can be content today without the presence and goodness of God. We cannot have true joy apart from the love of God in our lives, so Jesus directed the servants to fill the jars to the brim with water. Once the jars were filled, he asked them to draw some out and take it to the master of the banquet.

And when the master of the banquet tasted what the servants drew out of the stone jars, he could not believe his taste buds. He knew the taste of the wine he had been drinking earlier. He knew that the custom was to save the inexpensive stuff until the end of the party when people did not know or care what they were drinking. But when he put the ladle to his mouth and tasted what Jesus had done—even though he did not know Jesus did it—he could not believe his senses.

He had never sipped wine so satisfying. He had never consumed wine so refreshing. And when God goes to work in our lives, when God goes to work through us in the world, there is still the promise that, just like the water in those earthen jars, we can be more than what we were, more than what we have been. Jesus still turns water into wine.

There are places of despair on this planet, some not so far away, that have nothing but water—the water of illiteracy, the water of despair; but once God can find some empty vessels to do what he tells them to do, he will turn water into wine.

There are relationships that are as dry as the desert, but when Jesus gets in the middle of it he will turn water into wine. There are people who need to know that "he that is in you is greater than he that is in the world" (1 John 4:4b). You may think you are only water, but once God gets hold of your life, he will turn water into wine.

And I don't know if you've ever had it happen to you or ever seen it happen to someone else, but you know when Jesus gets hold of someone's life. Life tastes different. We cannot explain it. We just know that something has changed. We cannot always comprehend it. We just know that we are no longer the same. Jesus took the water of our pain, the water of our failures, the water of our heartaches, the water of our disappointments and turned them into wine. And if there is wine, there will be joy.

Joy when the power of God prevails.
Joy when the grace of God forgives.
Joy when the love of God unites.
Joy when our life is transformed by the renewing of our mind.
Joy that the world did not give. Joy that the world cannot take away.
O taste and see that the Lord is good.

Note

1. "Wine," *Dictionary of Biblical Imagery*, ed. Leland Ryken, James Wilhoit, and Tremper Longman III (Downers Grove IL: InterVarsity Press, 1998) 954.

5

Spring Cleaning[1]

John 2:12-25

Spring cleaning is the age-old practice of getting one's house back in order after a long, cold winter. Bed linens are changed. Carpets are cleaned. Windows are washed. Winter clothes are put away. Closets are organized. Everyone from Martha Stewart to HGTV has advice on the best way to do spring cleaning.

We all have times when we need to do spring cleaning—not in our garages but in our minds and in our hearts. There are times when we need to pray as David prayed, "Create in me a clean heart, O God, and put a new and right spirit within me" (Ps 51:10). There are times when we have to sing the words of the Negro spiritual, "Fix me, Jesus. Fix me."

In this passage from the Gospel of John, Jesus is doing a little spring cleaning of his own. What Jesus does in the temple is not like anything we have seen him do so far. His actions are unsettling to some and challenging to others.

His aim is to put God's temple back in order. He came to bring people back to God. He came to lift people out of spiritual ruts and routines to save them from going through the rituals without any sensitivity to the voice of God.

This moment in his ministry is often referred to as the cleansing of the temple. This text is what John remembers happening that day.

After staying in Capernaum for a few days with his mother, his brothers, and his disciples, Jesus went up to Jerusalem. Even though the trip from Capernaum to Jerusalem involved traveling from north to south, John says, "Jesus went *up* to Jerusalem" (v. 13, emphasis mine). Due to the high elevation of that city, going to Jerusalem was always described as going "up" no matter where you started your journey. This is why some of the psalms have subheadings indicating they are psalms of ascent. Travelers sang the psalms while they went up or ascended to the hills on their way to worship and sacrifice at the temple in Jerusalem.

We know that it was springtime because John tells us that the annual Passover feast was about to begin. Passover was one of the high holy festivals of Judaism. Passover happened every spring to commemorate Israel's deliverance from Egypt through God's miraculous and mighty wonders. Each year Israelites from all over Palestine made the pilgrimage up to Jerusalem to celebrate Passover in obedience to Moses' command in Exodus 12.

Since the time of Moses, God's chosen people saw it as their duty to travel to Jerusalem each year for Passover. So Jesus made this journey to Jerusalem like so many of his Jewish ancestors before him. Only this year, Jesus was not merely a participant in Passover. He did not come to make a sacrifice in the temple. When Jesus arrived in Jerusalem for Passover this year, he showed up looking, acting, and sounding more like a prophet than an ordinary participant.

Prophets played a significant role in the life of Israel. They were inspired by the Spirit of God to speak to the people of God on behalf of God. Prophets did more than talk about the future. They also revealed God's nature, reminding hearers of God's holiness or God's sovereignty. Prophets communicated God's laws to people, as Moses did when he delivered the Ten Commandments to Israel. Prophets also called the people back to obedience, encouraged people to offer God sincere worship, and, at times, warned them of divine judgment.

Prophets were not always embraced warmly because their messages challenged the hearers more than the hearers wanted to be challenged. Micah once said to the people, "Woe to those who plan iniquity, to those who plot evil on their beds!" (Mic 2:1, NIV). The word of the Lord came to the prophet Zephaniah, "I will utterly sweep away everything from the face of the earth, says the LORD.... I will stretch out my hand against Judah, and against all the inhabitants of Jerusalem" (Zeph 1:2, 4). And what about the word of the Lord that came to Malachi? "But who can endure the day of [the Lord's] coming? Who can stand when he appears? For he will be like a refiner's fire or a launderer's soap" (Mal 3:2, NIV).

Sometimes prophets encouraged the people, but often their messages challenged the people in order to call them back to devotion to God. This is what Jesus came to do in the temple.

As far as Jesus was concerned, it was time to put God's house in order. It was past time clear out the clutter. Too many distractions were in the way.

So Jesus came to clear out and clean up. He came to make the temple what God always intended.

In many ways, the forty days leading up to Easter, or Lent, is the perfect time for (spiritual) spring cleaning. We can and should do this all year long, just like we should be generous all year and not only at Christmas. But as we emphasize giving at Christmas, Lent is the time set aside to ask God, "See if there is any offensive way in me, and lead me in the way everlasting" (Ps 139:24, NIV). This is when we check the habits that we really do not need and recover the habits we do need and no longer have. This is why Jesus came to Jerusalem. One of the things Jesus had on his mind when he came into the temple was worship. He came to call God's people to return to God-focused worship.

People were going about their business that day as if everything in God's house was fine. Money was exchanged. Sacrificial animals were bought and sold. People were going and coming. Everything was happening as it always did. This was big business. The priests and the merchants were making a lot of money.

When Jesus came in and looked around, he knew something was off track. He knew something was going in the wrong direction. He must have been heartbroken when he saw what had become of the most sacred and holy place in Jerusalem. He could see money changing hands, but he could not find anyone worshiping God.

But this was the temple! The temple was the center of religion, culture, and music for the Israelites. The temple was supposed to a place of prayer and worship and sacrifice. The temple was the one place on earth where the presence of God resided.

When Solomon dedicated the *first* temple in 2 Chronicles 7, he prayed until fire came down from heaven and consumed the burnt offering and the sacrifices, and the glory of the Lord filled the temple. Then the Lord appeared to him that night and said, "I have heard your prayer and have chosen *this place* for myself as a temple for sacrifices" (2 Chr 7:12, NIV, emphasis mine).

The temple was the place for meeting God, but what Jesus saw that day disturbed him. Somehow the temple had become a place where people honored themselves more than they honored God. So Jesus entered the temple and made his prophetic presence known. He came to the temple to call the people back to true worship.

Worship is not synonymous with going to church. Going to church is good, but it is not the same thing as worshiping God. Sometimes we go to church because it is what we have always done and we feel it is what we should do. Sometimes we come to church because someone made us come to church. But the motivation for worship is something more. The motivation for worship is what we know about who God is: "Great is the LORD, and greatly to be praised; his greatness is unsearchable" (Ps 145:3).

The reason for worship is gratitude for what the Lord has done: "The LORD is gracious and merciful, slow to anger and abounding in steadfast love" (Ps 145:8).

The inspiration for worship is God's love for us and our love for God: "Let me hear of your steadfast love in the morning, for in you I put my trust" (Ps 143:8). Jesus came into the temple to call the people back to worship.

"Making a whip of cords, [Jesus] drove all of them out of the temple, both the sheep and the cattle. He also poured out the coins of the money changers and overturned their tables" (John 2:15). Jesus's actions in the temple reveal that worship is a matter of utmost importance to God. Worship must not to be trivialized or turned into something so familiar (cozy and comfortable) that we forget we have come into the holy presence of the living God. Worship is a sacred and consecrated act of celebration, reverence, and humility before God. Genuine worship is still central to what God desires from us. God is not looking for on-again, off-again relationships. The great commandment is still the great commandment: love the Lord your God with all your heart, mind, soul, and strength. This is the essence of genuine worship.

So, when Jesus made a whip and used it to drive out everyone and everything from the temple, he was rendering judgment on the people for what had become of worship. This was a call to reset their priorities.

While the money being exchanged in the temple was necessary, the most vulnerable people were being exploited in the process. When worshipers came to the temple, they gave an offering in thanks to God for the blessings of God. Many pilgrims, because of the Roman occupation of Israel, only possessed coins with the Roman emperor's image. These coins could not be used in the temple because they bore the image of Caesar. Any non-Jewish money was considered unclean and could not be used in the temple. The Roman coins had to be exchanged for Jewish shekels.

In addition, some pilgrims came from great distances and could not bring animals for sacrifice so they had to buy animals once they arrived at the temple. But the problem was not that people exchanged money or bought animals.

The problem was in large part how people were treated when they exchanged coins and bought animals. The money changers charged astronomical rates to change the unclean Roman money into clean Jewish money. The sellers of animals fixed prices at high levels and sold inferior animals instead of healthy, unblemished animals. The sellers made a bunch of money, and many worshipers paid a price they could not afford. They had given up their love for God in favor of the love of money. How could they worship God and treat one another this way?

First John 4:20 says, "For those who do not love a brother or sister whom they have seen, cannot love God whom they have not seen."

Jesus did not and does not condone economic exploitation or a casual attitude about worship or the mistreatment of the poor, so he drove everyone and everything out of the temple in order to clean up God's house.

We would no doubt prefer a Jesus who approves of everything we approve of and likes everything we like, but that is not the Jesus who makes a whip out of cords. Jesus comes in with a passionate call to reset priorities.

People were more interested in revenues than redemption. People were more concerned about the collections than coming to meet God. People were more interested in what they had on than in what they gave to God. It was time to clean up God's house, renewing worship and resetting priorities.

We cannot help wondering what tables Jesus needs to turn over today. If Jesus came into our city, our state, our nation, and our world, what would he cast out? Would he cast out our payday lending and a minimum wage that is not a living wage?

If he entered our church, what would he clear out? Before we start pointing our fingers at the sins of others, let us remember that Lent is a time for *self-examination.* It is much easier to deal with the sins of others than with our own, but when Jesus turns over the tables, he confronts each of us with our own brokenness and sin so that we might return to God and offer God proper/better worship. He is calling us to take another look at ourselves to see what does not belong. He is calling us to reset our priorities.

It is good to give up cupcakes and Cokes for forty days—it really is—but let us do that in addition to examining ourselves. Lent is a time to consider where we need Jesus to do some spring cleaning.

Once the tables settled and all the animals had been run out, Jesus looked at those who sold doves and said, "Take these things out of here! Stop making my Father's house a marketplace!" (v. 16).

The most amazing part about what he says is the pronoun "my." Jesus does not say that this is "the" Father's house. He does not say that it is "our" Father's house. He says it is "my" Father's house. He does this because he wants everyone to recognize who he is. He is the divine Son on a mission to honor his Father above all else. Therefore, to be Jesus's disciple is to prioritize honoring God, even when it involves taking a risk. That's why Jesus cleared out the temple. He had come to do his Father's will.

Jesus was not the kind of person who made rash decisions or performed attention-grabbing stunts. He did not cleanse the temple to increase his visibility. He only wanted to fulfill his mission of honoring his Father. He acted courageously because he cared more about what the Father thought of him than what the crowds thought of him. Jesus came to do his Father's will even though it meant putting his popularity on the line.

He could have taken an easier path. After all, he had just turned water into wine. Had he continued with miracles like that one, the crowds would have made Jesus a king.

But Jesus had not come for his own reputation. Jesus was on a mission to honor the Father who sent him. He now invites us to join him in that same mission. We may have to clear out clutter, but let's honor God. We may have to get rid of confusion, but let's honor God. Give in a way that honors the Father; love in a way that honors the Father; serve in a way that honors the Father; care in a way that honors the Father.

Of course, honoring God is not always a big, spectacular event like this one. Sometimes honoring God is in the simple choices we make every day: being welcoming to someone who is new, caring for someone in need, and taking time to stop and listen when we have another appointment.

I told you that this image of Jesus was unsettling to some and challenging to others. Seeing Jesus act this way in the temple made people ask him to prove his authority to do what he did.

They wanted him to produce some evidence that he was qualified to speak for God and act on behalf of God in this way. If Jesus was going to say that the temple was his Father's house, they wanted proof that he had permission to speak this way about God. Because when he called the temple his Father's house, he was identifying himself as God's Son and as Israel's Messiah.

Jesus did not ever seem interested in giving people signs to make them believe. In John, the only answer Jesus gives to those who demand a sign is, "Destroy this temple, and in three days I will raise it up" (2:19). It sounded like Jesus was talking about destroying the temple that had been built out of massive stones. The people said to him, "This temple has been under construction for forty-six years, and you are going to raise it up in three days?" (v. 20).

They did not realize Jesus was not talking about the building. He was talking about his body. He was talking about his crucifixion and resurrection. "Destroy this temple, and in three days I will raise it up. That will be the only sign I give you."

In the meantime, Jesus wanted them to know that the time for animal sacrifice had ended. And the time to trust the Son of God had come. God was doing a new thing. There was no longer any need to come to the temple with sacrificial doves. There was no longer any need for the blood of goats and rams to be sprinkled on the altar.

The Son of God had come. The Word of God was with them.

The Lamb of God was in their presence. The King of kings was standing in front of them.

The people did not understand at the time, and the disciples did not fully understand until later.

Not until after they went with Jesus into the wilderness and watched him feed the multitudes.

Not until after they went to the pool of Bethsaida and watched him restore sight to a blind man.

Not until after they crisscrossed the Sea of Galilee and saw Jesus walking on the water.

Not until after they snuck into Bethany so Jesus could console Mary and Martha and raise Lazarus back to life.

Not until after they went with Jesus to the Mount of Olives where he prayed until he was ready to glorify his Father on the cross.

Faith did not come right away, but eventually it did come. After Jesus was crucified and raised from the dead, it all made sense. After Mary came running to them from the empty tomb saying, "I have seen the Lord," it slowly began to dawn on them (20:18).

After Jesus was raised from the dead, his disciples put it all together. That's when they believed the Scripture and the words Jesus had spoken. After the resurrection, they believed what Jesus had said about the temple of his body being destroyed and raised again in three days. That's when it all made sense.

But we do not have to wait until Easter to believe the words that Jesus has spoken. We have the benefit of knowing the whole story. We do not have to wait until he has been raised to reset our priorities. We do not have to keep walking in darkness for the next forty days.

Jesus knew we needed someone to turn us around. Someone to put things back in order. Someone to show us the way, light the path, and lead us in the way everlasting. Because we know the story, we do not have to wait until the resurrection.

We can trust him today. We can obey him now. We can listen to him now. We can find rest for our souls now. We can follow his voice now. We can worship him now. We can serve him now.

It is time for spring cleaning.

Note

1. This sermon was preached on Ash Wednesday.

The Necessity of New Birth

John 3:1-8

The birth of a child may be one of the most miraculous events we witness every day. Babies are born all the time, and since it usually happens without complications in our part of the world, we can easily lose sight of the mystery and the wonder of new life, at least until it happens to us or someone we know and love.

Throughout the world, there are many ways to celebrate a new mother and child, but one thing is the same no matter where you go. Regardless of nationality, ethnicity, or religion, every child begins their existence in the same way. No matter what language we speak or where we live, every human being on the planet starts as a single cell.

We survived the first several months of life inside our mothers' wombs. They carried us around in their bodies. They nourished us with their own food. When we emerged from the comfort and safety of the womb, we could not walk or talk. Look at us now! Today our bodies are highly organized, complex systems of cells, tissues, and organs capable of doing and thinking and feeling and believing. This is nothing short of miraculous.

When a child is born, relatives often gather around and talk about how much the newborn looks like the mother or father. People point out how much the siblings in the family look alike. They refer to the mother's eyes or the shape of the father's head. As the child grows, people talk about how much the child's features look like a grandparent or some other relative who is no longer living. Noses, feet, eyebrows, chins, cheeks, ears are all fair game when it comes to comparing a newborn baby to his or her ancestors. As we get older, sometimes we examine old pictures, and these similarities are so obvious we can see them ourselves.

Some adults resemble their childhood selves in surprising ways. You see the baby picture and look at them and there is no question that those big curious eyes leaping off the photograph belong to the same person who is all grown up. Their smile has the same slight twist to the right. The dimples are just as deep. Others of us look like completely different people, as if our childhood selves were abducted by aliens and replaced with the bodies we have today. In either case, in many ways, we are different people.

Over a lifetime, a person's body recreates itself over and over again. Cells are born and cells die. Tissues expand. Bones lengthen. Muscles grow. Physically speaking, we have changed so much that we have been reborn over and over and over again.

The purpose of this sermon is to probe the mystery of rebirth. Not the rebirth that occurs naturally in the human body because of growth, time, hormones, and aging, but the rebirth that is the transformative spiritual experience Jesus describes in John 3. New birth is the inward change that happens through the Spirit by God's grace when we believe in him.

New birth is one of the foundations of Christian life and faith. We see hints and references to new birth sprinkled all over the New Testament like bread crumbs dropped on a trail to lead us home.

- Romans 6:4 says, "Therefore we have been buried with him by baptism into death, so that, just as Christ was raised from the dead by the glory of the Father, we too might walk in newness of life."

- Titus 3:5 says, "[God] saved us, not because of any works of righteousness that we had done, but according to his mercy, through the water of rebirth and renewal by the Holy Spirit . . . ."

- 1 Peter 1:3 declares, "By his great mercy he has given us a new birth into a living hope through the resurrection of Jesus Christ from the dead . . . ."

Jesus knows that it is possible to be religious without being changed. So when he meets a man in the third chapter of John, he is probably hoping this man will see that there is more to the life of faith than trying harder and doing more. Being busy, successful, or nice are not enough. External change will not get the job done. This is what Jesus is trying to say to a man we know by the name of Nicodemus.

Nicodemus was an influential person in Jerusalem. The way Nicodemus is portrayed in John, he is not an easy person to figure out. He gets some things right and seems to get some things completely wrong.

For example, he came to Jesus out of his own curiosity and interest, which is commendable. Nicodemus praised Jesus for the miraculous signs he had already performed, but in the previous chapter Jesus did not speak highly of people who come to him only because of signs and wonders (2:23-25). Nicodemus sincerely wanted an audience with Jesus, but he did not seem to recognize fully who Jesus was. He referred to Jesus as "Rabbi" (3:2), which implied that he did not recognize Jesus as the Word of God who became flesh. He got some things right and some things quite wrong.

Nicodemus was a public figure. He was a member of the Sanhedrin, the Jewish ruling council, a prestigious and elite group in Jerusalem. But Nicodemus did not approach Jesus in the marketplace or at the temple. Perhaps to protect his reputation, Nicodemus came to Jesus at night.

Had he heard that Jesus changed water into wine? Was that why he wanted to speak with Jesus? Had Nicodemus seen Jesus turning over tables in the temple? Maybe this was why he wanted an audience with Jesus. Or could it be that he had been told John the Baptist was now directing people to follow someone else, and this made him want to know more about the man who was taking John's place? It is hard to say for sure, but Nicodemus was curious and cautious, so he came to Jesus under the cover of darkness.

Once Jesus and Nicodemus started talking, it did not take long for Jesus to realize that Nicodemus did not know as much as he thought he knew. Nicodemus said to Jesus, "Rabbi, we know that you are a teacher who has come from God; for no one can do these signs that you do apart from the presence of God" (v. 2). Jesus responded like the person being interviewed on television who never directly answers the question they are asked.

Nicodemus brought up Jesus's miraculous signs, and Jesus took the conversation in a completely different direction. Nicodemus told Jesus what he knew about him, and Jesus responded by telling Nicodemus what he needed to know about the kingdom of God. "I tell you the truth, Jesus said, no one can see the kingdom of God unless he is born again" (v. 3, translation mine).

Jesus does not say much about the kingdom of God in the Gospel of John. We know from Matthew, Mark, and Luke that the kingdom of God is not a place we can locate on a map. The kingdom of God is not governed by human monarchs. The kingdom of God is a way of life. The kingdom of God is Jesus's way of life. The kingdom of God is whenever and wherever the light of God shines in darkness. The kingdom of God is whenever and wherever God's grace overflows and we receive one blessing after another. The kingdom is when the people of God take care of one another. The kingdom of God is when forgiveness is offered, grace is given, and the love of God abounds. In the kingdom, the poor have enough and the stranger is welcomed. In the kingdom, power is used to build up, not tear down. Jesus came to reveal and lead us into this kingdom.

When Jesus showed some people the kingdom, they did not comprehend it. Others, when they understood what it cost to enter the kingdom, decided they did not want it. "He came to what was his own, and his own people did not accept him" (John 1:11).

Nicodemus's trouble was that he probably assumed he was already in the kingdom of God. After all, he was a Pharisee. He was a member of the Sanhedrin. Surely these credentials qualified him for the kingdom.

I have always imagined Nicodemus to be a stately, dignified man. He was intelligent, but Jesus's words confused him. What did Jesus mean by "no one can see the kingdom of God unless they are born again" (3:3, NIV)?

It meant that there is a way to experience genuine change—not necessarily quick change or immediate change, but definitely genuine change. We must be born again.

Jesus wanted Nicodemus to know that if anyone was going to see real, authentic, and deep spiritual change, new birth was necessary. Jesus uses a strong word in verse 7 when he says "must be." "Must" does not leave room for debate. The same word will come up again when he talks about the necessity of doing his Father's will. This was Jesus's way of saying that for genuine spiritual change to happen, new birth was nonnegotiable.

If we are going to have the same mind in us that was in Christ Jesus, we must be born again.

If we are going to live up to the calling we have received, we must be born again.

If we are going to work out our salvation, we must be born again.

If we are going to go beyond coming to church and step into being the church, we must be born again.

If we are going to become mature, if we will no longer be tossed back and forth by the waves, if we want to speak the truth in love, new birth is not optional. We must be born again.

The word translated "again" in the phrase "born again" is the Greek word *anothen*. *Anothen* has a double meaning. It means born "anew" and it means born from "above." We do not have a word in English that can communicate "anew" and "from above" at the same time, so most translations pick one or the other or use the word "again." But we should not think "either-or." We should think "both-and." To see the kingdom of God, to see genuine spiritual change, we must be born anew *and* born from above.

Anew because we are blessed but broken vessels that need to be put on the potter's wheel and made over again.

From above because only the power of God can do a new thing that lasts. New birth is necessary.

Nicodemus's status as a Pharisee was not enough. His membership on the Jewish ruling council was not sufficient. He needed an inward, spiritual transformation. The same is true for us.

Experiencing the kingdom of God, living a life of purpose, enjoying the power of the Spirit, the joy of forgiveness, the renewal of hope, the strength of God's power, the peace of God's presence, and the beauty of God's grace are the by-products of new birth.

If the change we desire goes beyond the superficial or cosmetic, we must be born anew and born from above. If we expect to conquer anger, get a handle on our emotions, and walk by faith more than we walk by sight, the first step is to be born anew and born from above.

Nicodemus thought this sounded like an impossible task.

He was used to being in control and making things happen. But he did not know how to make this thing called new birth happen. He was not even sure if it made any sense. "How can anyone be born after having grown old? Can one enter a second time into the mother's womb and be born?" (v. 4).

The good news about this seeming impossibility is that it is possible because it is not entirely up to our own effort, our own strength, or our own talent. Being born anew and from above is not something we do to ourselves; it is something God does in us and for us. New birth is a necessity, and it is also a gift of the grace of God.

To see a change, Nicodemus needed to stop trying to figure out how to make it happen and let the grace of God wash over him. He no longer needed to tell God how much better he was going to be. He only needed to ask God, invite God, let God, listen to God, obey God, and trust God to do a work in him.

New birth is a gift of the grace of God. New birth is not simply a doctrine or a spiritual buzzword that gives us access to certain religious circles. New birth is a gift. We cannot manufacture new birth using the latest technology. We cannot transmit it from one generation to the next. No one can lay hands on us and cause us to be reborn. New birth is the gracious gift of God through the Holy Spirit. This is why Jesus said, "Very truly, I tell you, no one can enter the kingdom of God without being born of water and Spirit. What is born of the flesh is flesh, and what is born of the Spirit is spirit" (vv. 5-6). In other words, God is the source of all life. God made life in the beginning. "All things came into being through him, and without him not one thing came into being" (John 1:3). And the same God who made all things in the beginning, the God of creation, is also the God of re-creation.

The newness we need emerges as we surrender to the love and grace of God. History and experience bear witness to God's willingness to give the gift of re-creation. Jacob began life as a trickster. He lied. He cheated. He stole. But after he had an all-night wrestling match with God, God gave him a new name and a new walk.

David stumbled and fell, but we can hear him praying, "Create in me a clean heart, O God, and put a new and right spirit within me" (Ps 51:10). God gave him a new beginning.

The apostle Paul once was a Pharisee who went by the name of Saul. Then he had an experience with the Lord. God changed his name and gave him a new purpose. He went from persecuting the church to preaching the gospel. He was so changed by the grace of God that he wrote, "But by the grace of God I am what I am, and his grace toward me has not been in vain. On the contrary, I worked harder than any of them—though it was not I, but the grace of God that is with me" (1 Cor 15:10).

And Paul is not alone. Some of us here today can say, "What a wonderful change in my life has been wrought since Jesus came into my heart. I have light in my soul for which long I sought; since Jesus came into my heart."[1]

Some of us are not as impatient as we used to be. We are not as self-absorbed as we once were. We are not as quick tempered as we used to be. We are more prayerful than we have been. Our compassion has increased. Day by day God has been making us new by grace through the Spirit. The Spirit is giving birth to spirit.

Sometimes new birth is viewed as a one-time event that happens in a person's life once they reach rock bottom and have nowhere else to turn. It

THE NECESSITY OF NEW BIRTH

is true that many people do meet God in some of the lowest points of their lives, and they have dramatic conversions. They can point to the day and time when they accepted God's grace and Jesus's Lordship over their lives. This kind of experience is real, but it is not the only way to experience new birth. New birth is a necessity. New birth is a gift of the grace of God. Jesus tells Nicodemus that new birth is also a mystery, yet we can always see the signs.

I was born on March 22 in Nashville, Tennessee, at Meharry-Hubbard Hospital at around 10:10 in the morning. I know this to be true. I have seen my birth certificate. My parents told me so. And yet I do not remember any of it. I do not remember the labor. I do not remember the weather. I do not remember the doctor. I do not even remember seeing my mother or what it felt like the first time she held me in her arms. But we all know my birth happened because I am standing in front of you right now. You can see the signs. There is no denying that my birth took place because here I am as a living, breathing human being. You can see the signs.

The same is possible with the new birth. It is a blessing to be able to recall the moment that it happened, if that is your story. But for a lot of people, Jesus's words in John 3:8 will ring true: "The wind blows where it chooses, and you hear the sound of it, but you do not know where it comes from or where it goes. So it is with everyone who is born of the Spirit." Jesus is making the point that when the wind blows, we do not see the wind. We only see the trees moving, which is a sign that the wind is blowing. This is how it can be when God gives the gift of new birth. It is a mystery when and how it happens to us, but we know it happened and is still happening because we see the signs.

New birth may happen a little here and a little there, but more and more each day we see the signs. We may not be able to say exactly when the contractions began or how long the labor is going to be, but we do know that God has been at work in our lives.

We may not recall when we began earnestly asking God to direct us, but we see the signs.

We cannot say for sure when we felt the desire to be more loving, but we see the signs. We may not be able to pinpoint what time it was when we came to accept that God loves us unconditionally, but we have seen the signs.

We still have room to grow. We have miles to go on the journey. We still have a need for God's grace, but the wind and the breath of God, the Spirit of God, is blowing on our lives. We can see the signs.

The Spirit is working. The Spirit is moving. The Spirit is molding. The Spirit is shaping and forming and purging and pruning. Each and every day, God is giving the gift of new birth through the Spirit. New birth is a necessity. New birth is a gift of the grace of God. New birth is a mystery made possible by the Holy Spirit.

Nicodemus wondered, "How can this be? How can a man like me be changed? How can my mind be renewed? How can a hard heart become tender? How can these things be, Jesus?" Well, when the Spirit goes to work, there is no limit to what God can do.

We have more power to love when the wind of the Spirit blows. We have more peace in the storm when the wind of the Spirit blows. The mind is renewed daily when the wind of the Spirit blows. We can put off the old self and put on the new self when the wind of the Spirit blows.

No longer do we have to be the same. When the Spirit moves, we become a new creation. Jesus said we *must* be born again. I wonder if the good news is not so much that we must but that we can be—that we get to be, that Jesus makes it possible for us to be—born again. Thanks be to God!

Note

1. Rufus McDaniel, Since Jesus Came into My Heart," 1914, retrieved from https://hymnary.org/text/what_a_wonderful_change_in_my_life_has.

Trust God

John 3:9–36

John 3:16 holds special meaning for me, but not for the reason you might think. One summer day, before I started seminary, I drove from Philadelphia to North Carolina. I was in my mid-twenties. The car I drove that day was not extravagant. It was a white, two-door Toyota Tercel, as I recall. Driving down the highway, somewhere on I-95 in the state of Maryland, I attracted the attention of a state trooper. The blue flashing lights came on behind me. I pulled the car into the emergency lane. My heart pounded with a mixture of nervousness and indignation. I produced my license and registration with a polite, courteous disposition.

The term "racial profiling" had not yet made it into the headlines in the mid-1990s, but I remember that the trooper felt comfortable enough to tell me that he stopped me because I "fit the description." I did not think to ask him at the time, "Description of what?" Being unaware of my rights, I gave him permission to search my vehicle with the assistance of his German shepherd partner. At some point during the search, he asked me where I was headed. I told him I was on my way to preach in North Carolina. Observing my youthful appearance, the trooper was understandably skeptical. He said, "You're a preacher? What's John 3:16?"

Without hesitation I said, "For God so loved the world that He gave His only begotten Son, that whosoever believes in Him should not perish but have everlasting life" (NKJV). He looked at me and said, "That was easy." Then he let me go on my way without a citation.

I am grateful for what did not happen that day, but the state trooper was misinformed when he said John 3:16 was easy. This verse is widely known—it is imprinted on license plates, written on posters at football games, plastered on street signs, spray-painted on bridges, emblazoned on billboards, engraved on key rings, and printed on silk-screened T-shirts. John 3:16 is everywhere, but I'm not so sure we want to call it easy.

Once we actually consider everything Jesus says right before and right after verse 16, we might want to say it is outrageously unbelievable, magnificently generous, astonishingly merciful, extravagantly gracious, seriously challenging, or breathtakingly beautiful. But I do not think we will want to call it easy. This is why the title of this sermon is "Trust God."

It is sometimes hard to know who to trust. Things and people may appear to be one way and turn out to be something completely different. If you keep up with the goings on in Washington, you may remember seeing articles or even video from Senate hearings to confirm presidential nominees for certain positions, like that of US Attorney General. The senators want to know if they can trust the person to do the job they've been nominated to do.

Stephen M. R. Covey, the son of the late Stephen Covey, has written a book called *The Speed of Trust*. Covey states,

> There is one thing common to every individual, team, relationship, family, organization, economy and nation throughout the world—one thing that if removed will destroy the most powerful government, the most successful business, most thriving economy and most influential leadership, the greatest friendship, strongest character and the deepest love . . . . That one thing is trust.

When we left off last week, Nicodemus seemed unable or unready to trust Jesus and believe what he said was true. Jesus admittedly said things that were hard to understand: "You must be born again. No one can enter the kingdom of God unless he is born of water and the Spirit. The wind blows wherever it pleases. You hear its sound, but you cannot tell where it comes from or where it is going" (John 3:3-8, paraphrase).

Nicodemus needed regeneration. He needed to be born anew and from above. He needed something that only the Spirit could make possible. Nicodemus was among the most highly educated and influential people in Jerusalem, but Jesus's words did not make sense to him. So Nicodemus asked Jesus, "How can anyone be born after having grown old?" (v. 4).

We cannot be too hard on Nicodemus. He is not alone in his struggle to trust God. A lot of people have wondered if God's promises can be trusted. God told Sarah that she was going to have a son in her old age and she laughed out loud. God asked her, "Is anything too hard for the LORD?" (Gen 18:14, NIV). In other words, "Don't you trust me?" God told Gideon he was called to save his people from the Midianites. Gideon wondered how he could do this since he was so young and from an insignificant family in the smallest clan in Israel. Gideon struggled to trust what God was saying to him.

Even today, the question remains. We doubt that the promises of God are sufficient for our needs, our hopes, and our situations. We wonder if it is too late or too hard to experience the joy of the Lord. We wonder if we have made too many mistakes to receive a blessing from God. We doubt whether we know enough Scripture, if we are spiritual enough or good enough or important enough to be included in the promises, the presence, and the peace of God. The Bible says it is so, but can we or do we really trust that it is so?

Part of what Jesus wants to say to Nicodemus is that it is not too late. It is not too hard. Depend on me. Trust me. What we need is available if only we would trust God: "For God so loved the world that he gave his one and only Son, that whoever believes in him shall not perish but have eternal life" (v. 16, NIV). The invitation to believe is what the Gospel of John is all about. John 20:31 says, "But these are written so that you may come to believe…and that though believing you may have life in his name." God wants to give us a fuller, richer, and more abundant life, and this life is the by-product of believing in Jesus.

"Believe" is the key word that holds everything together in John, and it is the root of Nicodemus's problem. He did not believe what God was doing in and through Jesus. So what does it mean to believe?

The word "believe" is used in more than one way in Scripture. A belief can be a strong conviction about the truth of something. Scripture usually refers to this type of belief as faith. Belief can also be a commitment or a willingness to trust someone. This is the kind of belief we are talking about today. To believe in Jesus, as far as the Gospel of John is concerned, is to put our trust in him and then act on that trust. To believe is to trust that what Jesus says is true and live according to that truth. To believe is to be confident that Jesus is who he says he is and then to order our relationships and values as if he is who he says he is. To believe God is to trust God.

Therefore, we can substitute the word "trust" almost every time we see the word "believe." "Yet to all who received him, to those who *trusted* in his name, he gave the right to become children of God" (John 1:12, translation and emphasis mine). This is what Jesus is saying to Nicodemus: Everything I am telling you about being born again comes down to one question. Will you trust me, or are you going to do it on your own?

Trusting God tests us because our human nature prefers to be in charge. Our humanity does not like to surrender its will, wait on God, be humble, or entrust itself to another. The human nature prefers to make its own way and live by its own rules, which is the opposite of trust in God.

When we trust only in our own strength and resolve, we cannot receive the transforming power of God's grace and the renewing radiance of God's love. When we are busy concocting new plans to win God's approval or the praise of other people, we will not enjoy the freedom of falling down in humility before God. This is what Jesus is saying when he makes Nicodemus the offer of a lifetime. But sooner or later, Nicodemus, just like us, had to make a choice about who he trusted.

Jesus knew that there would be many who wondered why they should trust him. So he spelled out in a speech to Nicodemus the reasons why. The reasons he gave then are just as valid now. In the first place, Jesus can be trusted because he was sent from God to work for our good.

Jesus came to heal us and to save us. Jesus came to make us whole and to rescue us from ourselves. So many things wound us over the course of a lifetime. We may be ridiculed and rejected, abused and offended, degraded and disrespected. Jesus came to heal us and to save us. He came from God to work for our good.

Every letter, every syllable, and every word of the gospel, including the message of new birth, begins with what God has done for us. God made the first move. Jesus said, "No one has ascended into heaven except the one who descended from heaven, the Son of Man" (v. 13). God always takes the initiative. In Jesus, God came from heaven to be with us. He is God with us. And if he is God with us, God has not forsaken us. If God has not forsaken us, God wants to be involved with us. If God wants to be involved with us, then God has come to help us.

Jesus was born of a woman, but he came from heaven. He was a human being, and he was fully divine. Jesus was subject to all the challenges and problems of life on this earth, but the earth was not his home. He came from the right hand of the Father. He came from eternity into time. He was with God in the beginning. Jesus was God coming to heal us and to save us. We only have to consider what he says about Moses and the snake in the desert.

The reference to Moses lifting up the snake in the desert goes back to Numbers 21:8. At that time, Moses was leading the Israelites out of Egypt through the wilderness. The people grew impatient with Moses, and they grumbled against God. They complained that Moses had brought them into the wilderness to die. They did not have enough bread or water. They did not like the taste of manna. They acted like they wanted to go back to slavery in Egypt.

The Lord responded to Israel's ingratitude by sending venomous snakes into the camp to bite the people. Realizing the error of their ways, the people came to Moses and humbled themselves. They confessed their sin against the Lord and against Moses. They asked Moses to intercede for them and pray for the Lord to take away the snakes.

And the Lord said to Moses, "Make a [bronze] snake and put it up on a pole; anyone who is bitten can look at it and live" (Num 21:8, NIV). Scripture then says, "when anyone was bitten by a snake and looked at the bronze snake [which had been lifted up on the pole], they lived" (21:9, NIV). Looking at the serpent on the pole healed the sick and they lived. This is the origin of the serpent used in the symbol for medical doctors today.

Fast forward to the end of Jesus's life. He, too, was lifted up on a pole. John never talks about Jesus being murdered or killed. He only talks about the crucifixion as God lifting Jesus up or glorifying him. So, Jesus looked ahead to his own crucifixion and resurrection and said, "The Son of Man must be lifted up," too (v. 14, NIV). Just as the bronze serpent was lifted up to heal those who were sick, the Son of Man will be lifted up. Just as those who looked at the serpent were healed, Jesus says everyone who believes in him, trusts in him, and commits to him shall have eternal life. He was sent from God to heal us in all the places we are broken, to heal us and make us whole again. Jesus came to heal us from invisible scars, from wounded souls and toxic relationships, spiritual dryness, wandering minds, and poisonous pride. He is working for our good; therefore, we can put our trust in him.

The text also makes it clear that Jesus is the fullest expression of God's love. We have to wonder why God would come down from heaven to be with us. After all, why would God identify so closely with humanity given our tendency to play hide and seek with God?

Why would God reach out so persistently to people in light of the fact that we govern the world as if God does not exist? We pollute the water and waste natural resources. Why would God choose to be intimately involved in our lives when we are prone to ignore the truth and quick to complain?

God gave an answer to this question once before. In Deuteronomy 7:7, the Lord said to the Israelites that he did not set his affection on them and save them because they were more numerous than the other peoples; but it was because the Lord loved them and kept the oath he swore to Abraham.

This same love is why the Son of God came to heal us and is working for our good. Jesus is the fullest expression of God's love. "For God so loved the world that he *gave* . . ." (v. 16, emphasis mine).

This one phrase would have been enough for a whole sermon. "God so loved the world." This is the reason God came to be with us in the person of Jesus Christ. This is why we can trust God. God loves the world. This is why God set out a way to redeem us. God loves the world. This is why God continues to be with us. God *loves* the world.

God does not love only clergy and missionaries. God's love is not limited to Baptists or Presbyterians. God's love is not confined to Christians or to North Americans. When Jesus says God loves the world, the term he uses for world means that God's affection extends beyond the borders of Israel. God's love is not limited to the children of Abraham and God's covenant people. God loves every single solitary person, place, and thing in all of creation.

God loves citizens and refugees. God loves Americans and Iraqis. God loves the rich and the poor. God loves our enemies and friends. God loves people who live in gated communities who can afford psychiatrists, and God loves the homeless who walk the streets with untreated mental illnesses. God loves nature and human beings. God loves criminals and law-abiding citizens. God loves lions, dogs, and eagles. God loves the world.

Nicodemus probably imagined a more exclusive God, a God who tolerated everyone but only truly loved Nicodemus and his people. A God who always stood on his side, with his nation, and for his causes. But Jesus turned that idea upside down. Jesus came as proof positive that God loves the whole wide world.

God's love story reaches its climax in Jesus Christ. There is no greater love than the love that became flesh and made his dwelling among us. Jesus did not come to punish us or to penalize us. According to his own words, he did not come to condemn us or to imprison us. "God did not send the Son into the world to condemn the world, but in order that the world might be saved world through him" (v. 17).

Because of God's great love, salvation is God's agenda. Jesus came to save us from self-destruction, save us from a life without hope, save us from the fear of death, save us from staring at the ceiling at night wondering if life has any purpose, save us from drifting, and save us from loving the wrong things too much and the right things too little.

Jesus came to lift us out of hopelessness and give us eternal life. Too often, we limit God's work to what happens after death. We make eternal life a synonym for heaven, but that is not what Jesus meant. Eternal life is a way of describing the new life that comes after the new birth; eternal life is a life lived in relationship with God (John 17:3); it is the spiritual quality of life we live in the presence of God each day.

God loves us so much that Jesus came to do something for us right now as well as in the future. Eternal life is a promise that includes today. Eternal life is peace with God today so that we are no longer fearful of an angry divine judge. Eternal life is being in the presence of God today so we can pray in faith. Jesus is the fullest expression of God's love, but this is not all Jesus tells Nicodemus about the reasons to trust him.

Jesus also says we can trust him to lead the way into a better and more abundant life: "But whoever lives by the truth comes into the light, so that it may be seen plainly that what they have done has been done in the sight of God" (v. 21, NIV).

I do not know if you have ever followed someone in a car only to discover that, while you were following them, they were leading you in the wrong direction. You thought they knew the way, but they did not. You thought they could take you where you wanted to go, but in actuality they could not get you there. You hoped their path was reliable, but in the end it was not.

In life there are always choices to be made. We need to decide which way we will go, what priorities we will set, and what relationships we will pursue. People will give us advice that we can use from time to time. But sometimes we need to know that we are following someone who knows the way. We need to have confidence that we are behind someone who is not lost. We need to know there is someone who can get us where we need to go.

Jesus said, "whoever lives by the truth comes into the light" (v. 21, NIV). He knows the way we need to go. He is the way. He knows the path we should take. He is the path. He knows how to lead us. He is the truth. If we trust him, he will lead us into the light.

The Christian life is not complete when it is viewed primarily as a set of dogmas or facts. We cannot find our way simply by means of what we know. We find our way and reach our destination by who we trust. The faithful have always found what they were looking for by trusting God, waiting on God, believing God. This is good news!

We may not know the historical background of the Twenty-Third Psalm, but we can still trust that the Lord is our shepherd; we can still trust that goodness and mercy will follow us all the days of our life. We can trust that if we hope in God, we will not be put to shame. We can trust that in times of uncertainty, God will be our refuge, strength, and a very present help in trouble. We can believe that with God all things are possible. We can have confidence that forgiven means forgiven.

When we trust Jesus, it is like walking in the light. When we do not trust Jesus, we are like Nicodemus, looking for Jesus in the dead of night. We often sing a song that says, "I will trust in the Lord. I will trust in the Lord. I will trust in the Lord until I die." For God so loved the world that he gave us Jesus. So, let those who know Jesus go out and show the world God's love. Amen.

8

The Gift of God

John 4:1-26

Sometimes we know when we have to do something. No one has to tell us. We just know. Life is not always about what we want to do or love to do or like to do or even feel like doing. A maturing life is also about doing what must be done.

If we want to be in a different place financially in the future, there are some steps we must take now. If we hope that our children will become faithful adults, there are no magic formulas, but there are habits we must practice. Some moments in life challenge us to do what we have to do.

We have to go back to school. We have to make the phone call. We have to put in the application. We have to have the surgery. We have to start the conversation. The time for procrastination eventually runs out.

Of course, avoiding procrastination is not the only reason to take action. We may also feel compelled to act when we are aware of a divine call upon our lives. The Spirit will not let us rest until we speak up and let our voice be heard. Sometimes we have been pushed, pulled, or drawn into action by a divine calling.

Divine calling is why Martin Luther King Jr. had to follow his dream and Marian Anderson had to sing. A divine calling is why Adam Clayton Powell had to run for political office and Sojourner Truth had to stand up and speak up. A divine calling compels us to take action.

At the beginning of John 4, we are told that Jesus left Judea and went back once more to Galilee. He was on a divine assignment. He lived on purpose and with purpose. His desire was to fulfill the mission the Father gave him. He had to go to Galilee. The question is why he had to go through *Samaria* to get there.

Jesus could have traveled from Judea to Galilee without going through Samaria. Israelites had deliberately mapped out routes that did not pass through Samaria. No self-respecting Jewish person ever wanted to go through Samaria. A feud had existed between Jews and Samaritans for hundreds of years. The discord was so intense that the two groups tried whenever possible to avoid contact with each other.

The conflict between Jews and Samaritans originated during the Old Testament, in the period after the exile, when the Israelites came back to Judea to find that the northern region had been settled by a group of non-Israelites. Over time, the non-Jewish immigrants intermarried with the Jews who were not taken into exile. The descendants of these mixed marriages became known as Samaritans. When the Israelites came back from exile, they despised the Samaritans because of their pagan worship and mixed ancestry. The Samaritans despised the Israelites because their return from exile meant competition for land and resources.

So, while it is true that going through Samaria was definitely the most direct route between Galilee and Judea, there were other ways for Jesus to get to Galilee. Therefore, the only reason he had to go through Samaria was because he wanted to do his Father's will. Specifically, Jesus had to go through Samaria because this was the time and place set for him to reveal the gift of God.

When he and the disciples came into Samaria, they stopped in a town called Sychar, a small village near the plot of ground the Old Testament patriarch, Jacob, had given to his son, Joseph. When Jesus came to this place, he sent the disciples to buy food and he sat down next to a well to rest. He was tired from the journey.

As Jesus sat near the well, a Samaritan woman came to draw water. It was around the sixth hour, or noon. The sun was high and hot. The air was dry. It was a good time for a drink of cool, refreshing water. Jesus said to the Samaritan woman, "Will you give me a drink?" (v. 7, NIV).

The Samaritan woman could not understand why Jesus was speaking to her. She was a Samaritan and he was a Jew. She was aware of the hostility between Jews and Samaritans, and she knew her place. She probably felt that this man who was speaking to her should have known his place, too. So, she asked Jesus how he could ask her for a drink since Jews did not associate with Samaritans. Jesus was going against the norms not only because he was a Jew speaking to a Samaritan but also because he was a man talking publicly to a woman who was not his wife. This kind of thing was unheard of and unaccepted. Cross-gender public conversations were so uncommon that verse 27 says when the disciples returned they were surprised to find Jesus talking to a woman, even though no one asked him why he was doing it.

Jesus refused to lower himself by labeling and finger pointing. He was not concerned about the woman's Samaritan heritage. He was not interested in the barriers set up by human prejudice. He came to bring good news. Jesus said to her, "If you knew the gift of God, and who it is that is saying to you, 'Give me a drink,' you would have asked him, and he would have given you living water" (4:10).

If she knew the gift of God? What did Jesus mean? We are frantically trying to pile up achievements, accomplishments, accolades, titles, raises, promotions, praise, and applause. Rarely do any of these things come to us as gifts. They all have to be earned, bought, or won. They require effort, connections, and good credit.

We have to jump through hoops, pass tests, win approval, earn tenure, pay dues, log overtime, impress supervisors, satisfy shareholders, meet deadlines, exceed expectations, nail presentations, and increase productivity. There is something to be said for achieving our goals, and yet it is a blessing to know that what truly satisfies comes from God as a gift. "For God so loved the world that he gave [as a gift] his only Son . . ." (3:16).

According to Jesus, the gift of God is living water that truly satisfies.

Living water has two meanings. Living water is what first-century people called running water, like the water in a stream. This is how the woman initially understood Jesus's words. She thought Jesus was offering her a source of running water of a quality that was superior to the well she normally used. This was what she thought Jesus meant by living water. Jesus had something else in mind, but she did not yet realize who he was.

As far as the Samaritan woman was concerned, the man talking to her was just another Jewish man. She had no reason to think there was anything special about him. She was not in Cana at the wedding when he turned water into wine. She did not hear John the Baptist declare Jesus to be the Lamb of God. Had she known who he was, had she known that sitting right in front of her was the Son of God, had she known that she was face to face with the gift of God, she could have asked him, and he would have given her living water.

The woman hears Jesus's offer of living water, but she has heard it all before. To her this sounds like one more empty promise. First of all, she has come to the well prepared to work, and Jesus has not. She has the proper equipment for drawing and carrying water. Jesus has nothing. How is he going to give her something to drink, especially living water? The well is deep, so she gives Jesus a history lesson.

"Are you greater than our ancestor Jacob, who gave us the well, and with his sons and his flocks drank from it?" (v. 12). She thinks he is talking about fresh spring water. This is almost like Nicodemus asking if a man can go back into his mother's womb to be born a second time.

Jacob was the grandson of Abraham and a patriarch of the Israelites and the Samaritans. This woman knows that the patriarch Jacob was a magnificent man. He is celebrated in Scripture. She does not know who this is sitting on the well daring her to ask him for living water.

The Samaritan woman asks if Jesus thinks he is greater than Jacob, because only someone who is greater than Jacob can supply better water than the water in Jacob's well. It just so happens that Jesus is greater. He is the Word that was with God in the beginning. He is greater. Through him all things were made; without him nothing was made that has been made. He is greater.

He is greater than every cause. He is greater than every king and ruler. He is greater than every nation and tribe. And, because he is greater, the water he gives us is better.

The living water he offers is the Spirit of God, the life-giving presence of God. This is the water that truly satisfies. This is the gift of God. It is a gift that brings true fulfillment and joy and forgiveness and peace and power. It is water to quench our spiritual thirsts, meet our deepest needs, fulfill all of God's promises, and live up to our highest hopes.

When we go through seasons of spiritual dryness, we need Living Water. When the spiritual well is running low, we need Living Water. When we are weighed down by long periods of physical or emotional pain, we need Living Water. When emotional demands come at us from all directions, we need Living Water.

Thankfully, this is the gift of God. Thankfully, we can now have the peace that surpasses all understanding. It is the gift of God. Thankfully, we can have the joy of the Lord as our strength. It is the gift of God. Thankfully, God pours out his Spirit into our hearts to give us a hope that will not disappoint us. This is God's gift.

If the Samaritan woman had known the gift of God and who was asking her for a drink, she could have asked him and he would have given her living water. The same goes for us today. All we have to do is ask.

Asking is embedded into the logic of faith. Asking is not begging. Asking is not earning. Asking is believing. Asking is being open and ready to receive. Asking is trusting that when we reach out, God will be there to receive us.

Maybe someone told us not to ask God for anything. We should only be thankful. Jesus said it is okay to ask. When there are hurts that need healing, ask God. When there is faith that needs growing, ask God. When there is a need that has not been met, ask God. When there is a way we cannot figure out, ask God. "Ask, and it will be given you; search, and you will find; knock, and the door will be opened for you" (Matt 7:7). The foundation of faith is not bargaining or coercing or manipulating. We have a generous God who invites us to ask. When we ask, God will give us living water, the life-giving water of the Spirit of God. This is the gift of God.

A second and perhaps less obvious way of understanding the gift of God is that we have a Savior who really sees us.

It has already been mentioned that it was unusual for Jesus, a Jew, to have a conversation with this woman, a Samaritan. What's interesting is that to have a genuine conversation with someone, you have to pay attention to them. You have to notice them. You have to really see them.

It was a gift for Jesus to see this woman because for whatever reason she was trying to avoid seeing and being seen by anyone.

Her attempt to go unnoticed is suggested by the fact that she came to the well to draw water at noon. Anyone with good sense came to draw water early in the morning before it got too hot. This woman came to the well when no one else was around. She did not want to be seen. She was living in social isolation.

Far too many sermons about the Samaritan woman have been based on the belief that she must have lived an immoral life, which would explain why she came to the well at noon.

Some have even called this woman a prostitute. But we cannot actually come to that conclusion based on what the Bible says. The Bible says she came to draw water at noon. Noon is light. Light in the Gospel of John represents faith and belief. So it is unlikely that John wants us to see her as immoral. The Bible also says she has had five husbands and the man she is with now is not her husband. Prostitutes do not have husbands. This woman has been married five times. Jesus never forgives her of sin, and she never confesses immorality.

While it may be the case that the Samaritan woman was not respectable to the people in her village, that does not necessarily mean she was immoral. Jesus says she has had five husbands and the man she now has is not her husband. The reason for her situation may be what is known as the Levirate marriage laws.

The custom in Israel was that when a husband died, his male next of kin married the widow. A brother, uncle, or cousin married the wife of his deceased male relative. There were no social security benefits or pension plans back then. A widow would have been destitute without a male head of household. This arrangement was intended to help her, but the next of kin had to willingly accept this familial obligation.

It could be that this woman was caught in a pattern where the male relatives did not want her, so she was being passed off from one relative to the next and the last one had not married her. It could be that she had been widowed five times and not married by the next of kin. Either scenario would have resulted in her being a social outcast, but not immoral or a prostitute. But the fact that Jesus talked to her meant that while others rejected her, he took notice of her. He was concerned about her. He wanted to be near her. He saw her.

When Jesus told her how much he knew about her, she knew that he saw her. All of her. He saw the stuff she did not want anyone to see. And because his gaze was gracious and not condemning, she began to see him, too. She said, "Sir, I can see that you are a prophet" (4:19, NIV).

Jesus sees who she is. She begins to see who he is. Her faith is starting to unfold. Now that Jesus notices her, she does not have to pretend to have it all together. She does not have to act like everything is okay. Jesus sees her completely, and he still wants to bless her.

I am of the opinion that what a lot of people truly want and really need is to know that they are seen. Children want to know that their parents see them. Parents want to know that their teenagers see them. When young people feel invisible, they may act out in order to be seen. To be seen lets us know we are not insignificant. Our lives count. Someone hears what we are saying, cares about how we feel, and is interested in what we are going through.

It is a gift when someone takes the time to see us. Today we can rejoice that Jesus sees us. We are not anonymous or nameless anymore. We are not shielded by shadows any longer. Whether we are unemployed or underemployed, Jesus sees us. If we are divorced, Jesus sees us. Wounded—Jesus sees us. Single on Valentine's Day—Jesus sees us.

He sees our joys and our pains. He sees our successes and our failures. He sees our hungers and our joys. He sees our going out and coming in. He sees us when we are near and when we are far off. He sees our waiting and our worries. He sees where we are and where we have been. He sees what we show and what we try to hide. The Lord sees us. David said in Psalm 139:1-3:

> O LORD, you have searched me and known me.
> You know when I sit down and when I rise up;
> you discern my thoughts from far away.
> You search out my path and my lying down,
> and are acquainted with all my ways.

God sees us.

Jesus said in Matthew 6, "Do not worry, saying, 'What shall we eat?' or 'What shall we drink?' or 'What shall we wear?' For the pagans run after all these things, and your heavenly Father knows that you need them" (vv. 31-32, NIV). God sees us.

God sees that the gift we need is not a temporary fix. We need something greater to satisfy our souls. God sees that the gift we need is power to rise above the storm. God sees that the gift we need is truth to set us free. God sees that the gift we need is the faith to trust him when we cannot understand him.

God sees that we need Living Water. Not the water in Jacob's well. Not a cheap imitation sold online. Not some gimmick hawked on late-night television. That is the kind of water that will only leave us thirsty again. We need the Living Water.

"Come to me, all you who are weary and burdened, and I will give you rest" (Matt 11:28, NIV). That's living water. "Take my yoke upon you and learn from me . . . . For my yoke is easy and my burden is light" (11:29-30, NIV). The wait is over. The promise is true. Believe in him and he'll give you what you've been searching for. Jesus is the gift of God. He has forgiveness in his cross. He has power in his word. He brings salvation through his love. He provides hope with his grace. All we have to do is ask. If we drink the water he gives, we will not thirst again. Are you thirsty?

9

Contagious Christianity

John 4:27-42

Have you noticed that certain people are gifted at spreading the word? They always have the most up-to-date information about what's going on. It's hard to say for certain how they get their information, but whenever you want to know something or want to verify what you have heard, you know who to call.

The technology we have today allows us to spread the word about almost anything faster than most of us ever thought possible. As a kid, I thought the fax machine was the most amazing piece of technology ever. A piece of paper went into the machine and then printed out on slick, glossy fax paper in another office across town or around the world. That was incredible. Technology has come a long way since the fax machine.

All anyone needs to spread the word today is 280 characters and a mobile phone, and a message can travel around the world before the sun goes down. Someone can post a picture on social media that is viewed by hundreds if not thousands of people and then shared with many, many more. Ordinary people can make international news.

When the word first began to spread about Jesus, ordinary people who believed in him told others about him. Jesus did not have a marketing campaign or a major advertising budget. He grew up in a small, insignificant village called Nazareth over two thousand years ago, and he certainly didn't have Facebook or Twitter. But his name is known throughout the world because after people experienced his extraordinary grace, they could not keep from telling someone else.

Getting the word out about what God is doing and has done in Jesus is evangelism. Evangelism is the lifeblood of the church. Evangelism is highlighted in our congregation's mission statement: We will enlist all people through fellowship and discipleship. Enlisting is evangelism.

It turns out that one of the greatest evangelists in the New Testament may be the unnamed woman Jesus met on his way through Samaria. After hearing her testimony, an entire village wanted to know more about Jesus.

Jesus came through Samaria on his way from Jerusalem up to Galilee. He stopped at Jacob's well to rest and sent the disciples into the village to buy food. As Jesus rested at the well, a woman approached on her way to draw water. Jesus asked her for a drink of water. John pointed out all the reasons the woman was surprised Jesus spoke to her. He was a Jew and she was a Samaritan. She was a woman and he was a man.

But Jesus informed his unsuspecting guest that if she knew who he was, she would have asked him for water, and he would have given her living water, water to satisfy her thirsty soul and bring her eternal life. His offer piqued her curiosity. She wanted to know more. The conversation continued, but the subject quickly changed from water to relationships and then to worship.

The woman did not understand everything Jesus said to her, but she was sure about one thing. She said to Jesus, "I know that Messiah is coming.... When he comes, he will proclaim everything to us" (4:25). Like every other Jew and Samaritan, she was waiting on God's Anointed. So Jesus dropped a bombshell. He stepped out of the shadows of anonymity and made himself known. "This Messiah you are waiting for, I who speak to you am he" (v. 26, translation mine).

She had not realized it, but the man standing in front of her was the Messiah. He was the seed of David. He was Daniel's Ancient of Days. He was Isaiah's Suffering Servant. He was the Messiah. No one knew for sure when the Messiah might come, but her eyes had been opened. Could it really be that Jesus was the Messiah?

This is the good news at the heart of evangelism: Jesus is who he says he is. Good news is not a program of the church. Good news is not the harmony of the choir or the inspiration of the preacher. Good news is a person. Good news is Jesus who is the hope of the world and who is with us here and now.

The Samaritan woman immediately dropped her water jar, went back to town, and told everyone she saw, "Come, see a man who told me everything I ever did. Could this be the Messiah?" (v. 29, NIV). The Samaritan woman went back to her village, spreading the word about Christ. She may not have known it at the time, but she was doing the work of evangelism. She has become an example of what happens when we spend time with

Jesus. Our awareness of who he is grows and matures. Did you notice that about her?

At the beginning of the chapter, she only saw him as a Jewish man. Then she came to see him as a prophet. Later, Jesus told her he was the Christ. That is when she went home to spread the word. After we have tasted living water and we have worshiped God, it is our privilege to share the good news: Jesus is the Christ, the Son of God.

But let's be honest. The word "evangelism" sometimes conjures up images that make many people—God-loving, God-trusting, faith-filled people—feel a little uncomfortable. It's not that we do not want to share good news. It may be that we have seen too many methods of evangelism that did not feel right, look right, or sound right to us. We have seen briefcase-carrying pedestrians going door to door questioning and challenging people on their religious views.

We have seen people use business sales techniques trying to pressure people to pray a prayer of salvation. In fact, C. S. Lovett wrote a book in 1959 titled *Soul-Winning Made Easy* to teach people how to use his soul-winning plan adapted from corporate sales strategies. It shaped generations of evangelism training. Other people think of evangelism as asking the person, "If you died tonight, where would you spend eternity?" This question may inspire more fear than faith. Others think preachers or professional ministers are the real evangelists.

Of course, God can use any of these methods if God chooses, but we also have the testimony of the Samaritan woman, who offers us a new vision for sharing the good news.

What she did was simple, sincere, and amazingly fruitful. By the time she finished, a whole village wanted to know more about Jesus. This is what she did: She did not sit around at the well and wait for the village to come to Jesus. She went back to her village to proclaim the good news to the people. This is instructive for the church in every age. We cannot expect people to find God and join the church as already mature Christians. Like the Samaritan woman, we may have go where the people are and take the good news to them.

I met a man last week who told me he had been raised by atheist parents. He grew up in a home where there was never any positive exposure to God, so it never occurred to him to visit a church. Some people will never hear the good news unless we go to them like the Samaritan woman who went back to her village.

Lots of people may never come to our Christmas programs. We have to go to them. People may not automatically come to our revivals. We have to go to them. There are people who will not visit our Bible studies or come to Vacation Bible School. But with creative and imaginative ministry, we can take the good news to them. What if we had a Bible study outside the walls of the church? You can probably think of a few good ways of taking the good news outside these walls. Evangelism is the lifeblood of the church.

It is worth noting that the Samaritan woman took the good news and shared it with the people she knew best. She did not go to someone else's neighborhood. She went to her village. One key to doing evangelism with integrity is to build genuine relationships first. We must care before we share.

If we share before we care, we will make assumptions about people based on factors that do not tell the whole story. We may presume that when people live in low-income housing or come from a single-parent household or attend a low-performing school, they do not already belong to a church or do not know God. Similarly, we may presume that if people live in a nice house in a nice neighborhood, they already know the good news. But people need Jesus in wealthy neighborhoods just like they need him in tenement housing and everywhere in between. We simply need to care before we share.

Jesus did not announce that he was the Messiah until after he took time to have a compassionate conversation with the Samaritan woman. This sounds simple enough, but the impact is profound. People do not care how much we know until they know how much we care. Some people will never want to know how much Christ loves them until they see how much *we* love them.

This is why it is my prayer that any evangelism we do as a church in our neighborhood will not be restricted to the traditional models of witnessing where we hand out tracts and ask strangers if they are saved. My prayer is that our evangelism will involve taking time to talk to people, eat with people, and know people as human beings with no agenda other than relationship.

My hope is that our evangelism will *not* begin by asking people what their needs are. That may sound strange, but when we start the conversation by asking people what they need, we set up a relationship where they are always in the position of being needy and we are always in the position of providing what we think they do not have. But if people have been made in the image of God, they have more than needs. They also have abilities and gifts. They have strengths. And think of how powerful it would be to discover what people can do before we ask them what they cannot do.

Relationships matter when it comes to evangelism. If we do not take the time to build trust, why should anyone think that they can trust in our God? If we do not show compassion with no strings attached, why should anyone think that God's love is unconditional? Just as the Samaritan ran back to her own village to share the good news, we cannot always wait for people to come to Jesus. We must build relationships and take the good news about Jesus to the people.

It is also fascinating to see that the Samaritan woman's evangelism was so effective because of what she said when she returned to her village. "Come, see a man who told me everything I ever did. Could this be the Messiah?" (v. 29, NIV). She began her short speech with two simple but powerful words: "Come, see." She did not start with "You must" or "If you do not." She started with genuine offer. "Come, see."

"Come, see" is an invitation. "Come, see" is hospitality with open arms. "Come, see" is asking without wanting anything in return. This is how to do evangelism. This is how to share the good news. We extend an invitation. We do not manipulate. Evangelism is not imposing on others. Biblical evangelism is extending an invitation in word and deed. Come, see.

The people heard what the woman had to say about Jesus and they began to wonder along with her, "Could this man be the Christ?" We do not have to argue with people about creeds and dogma. Just invite them to come and see. We do not have to guilt anyone into worship. Just pray and extend an offer for them to come and see.

Come, see these people at this church who made me feel like I was a neighbor and not a stranger. Come, see a church where people got to know me by name before they tried to fix my problems. Come, see a ministry that offers healing for the mind, body, and soul. Come, see men striving to do better. Come, see women aiming to be wiser. Come, see God's love in the hands and feet of ordinary people. Could this be the power of God at work?

About this time in the text, the disciples returned from their village grocery run. They urged Jesus to eat, but Jesus refused. Instead he gave them a final lesson in evangelism. Jesus made it clear that the mindset for effective evangelism is to be convinced that the time is *now*.

Jesus did not stop to eat the food the disciples brought him. He said, "My food is to do the will of him who sent me and to complete his work" (v. 34). Then he told them a proverb: "Do you not say, 'Four months more, then comes the harvest'? But I tell you, open your eyes and look at the fields! They are ripe for harvest" (v. 35, translation mine). Jesus could see that the opportunity to share the good news was not in the distant future. The opportunity for someone to know him was in the present moment. This was the meaning of his parable.

He was not talking to the disciples about agriculture. The harvest he noticed was people. The point of the proverb was that he could not stop and eat the bread, dates, and cheeses the disciples brought him because there was something much more important he had to do. Perhaps he could already see the crowd of people coming to see him from Samaria led by the woman he'd met at the well. The fields were ripe for a harvest.

Jesus could not put his mission on hold to eat lunch. There are times when he did step away to rest, but not this time. Someone had just become curious about whether he was the Christ. Someone had just become sensitive to the presence and power of God. He wanted to be fully focused on the work of bringing one more person into relationship with God.

God calls us to be sensitive to the opportunities around us to share hope and peace and joy. God invites us to open our eyes and look at the fields. The fields are ripe for harvest. The time is now.

People need the hope of the gospel today and not tomorrow. Wandering hearts need peace today. There are people who need to be released from spiritual bondage today. People have burdens that need to be eased immediately, not next week. All we have to do is open our eyes to see the fields are ripe for harvest.

Maybe that is our challenge. Our eyes are closed to what God is doing around us. What might happen if we looked? If we looked, we would see the prisons filled with young women and men who are hungry for guidance and compassion. If we looked, we would see private clubs where people sometimes pretend to be happier than they really are. We would see college campuses where students truly want to know if their life matters. The fields are ripe for harvest.

We just have to keep in mind that the work of evangelism is not totally our work. Evangelism is God's work through us. Jesus said one sows and another reaps. But in the end, the harvest will come.

"Come, see." All we have to do is extend the invitation. All we have to do is tell the story. And what a story we have to tell. Jesus was born in Bethlehem and grew up in Nazareth. He was baptized in the Jordan and filled with the Holy Spirit. He was the Word. And the Word became flesh and made his dwelling among us. No one taught like him. No one performed miracles like him. No one ever loved like him.

He came to his own, but his own did not receive him. He was despised and rejected by humanity. But he kept on loving. People doubted his divinity. But he kept on loving. He was betrayed by Judas and tried by Pontius Pilate. But he kept on loving. He was crucified on Friday. But he kept on loving.

He died on Friday. He stayed dead on Saturday. But, because he loved us, he rose with all power early Sunday morning.

We've got a story to tell. A story that life is stronger than death. A story that God's love is stronger than the world's hate. A story of sins forgiven, blessings undeserved, and unspeakable joy. Go tell this good news.

10

Believe It Before You See It

John 4:43-54

Everything John has written about Jesus up to this point has focused on inspiring us to believe in Jesus. In the prologue, which is the beginning of chapter 1, John 1:12 tells us, "But to all who received him, who *believed* in his name, he gave power to become children of God." After Nathanael confessed Jesus to be the Son of God and the King of Israel, Jesus praised him saying, "You *believe* because I told you I saw you under the fig tree. You will see greater things than that" (1:50, NIV, emphasis mine).

After Jesus turned water into wine, the disciples put their faith in Jesus. In chapter 3, Jesus met a man named Nicodemus who did not understand faith. Although he was an official and a leader in Israel, Nicodemus struggled to believe that by faith through the power of the Spirit someone could be born anew and see the kingdom of God.

Sentence after sentence. Story after story. Chapter after chapter, Jesus has one main question in his mind in the Gospel of John: do you believe? Anyone who believes has life. To find life a person must believe. Surprisingly, Nicodemus, a high-ranking man who was an "insider" in Israel, struggled to believe, but when Jesus went into foreign territory in Samaria, he met an ordinary woman who was an "outsider." She believed and even led others to believe. Ironically, Jesus failed to find belief where he should have found it, and he found belief in the most unlikely places.

Belief, or faith, changes the way we see our life and the world around us. Faith alters our perception and gives us a new take on reality. Faith is the assurance that with God's help we will get wherever we are going even if we do not know when or how. Faith is confidence that God's foolishness is still wiser than the world's wisdom.

To have the abundant, full, satisfied life that Jesus came to give, we must have faith. To have faith is to trust. Trust is orienting our life, setting our mind, and turning our thoughts to depend on, wait for, and hope in God.

Jesus is once again issuing the call to trust him as he returns to Galilee, the region of his birth. As Jesus goes back home, verse 44 mentions parenthetically that he once used the proverb that prophets are not honored in their own country. We have comparable expressions in our contemporary culture, such as "familiarity breeds contempt" or, as another person puts it, "familiarity may not breed contempt, but it takes the edge off admiration."

Therefore, we might be confused when we read that as Jesus returned to Galilee the Galileans welcomed him. Countless commentators have remarked on these verses. A prophet has no honor in his own country, or the Galileans welcomed Jesus? Which is it? If a prophet is not honored in his own country, why does John say the Galileans welcomed Jesus?

Raymond Brown, widely respected for his scholarship on the Gospel of John, suggests that both statements are true in a manner of speaking. The Galileans welcomed Jesus, but it was not the kind of welcome Jesus deserved. Brown suggests that the welcome of the Galileans was similar to what happened in John 2:23 after Jesus impressed a crowd when he performed miracles at the Passover feast. Many people saw the miraculous signs and believed in his name, but Jesus would not entrust himself to them, for he knew all people.[1]

People believed in Jesus's name, but Jesus did not entrust himself to them because their belief was not for the right reasons. They believed because they liked the miracles, not because they had faith in the Messiah. The same dynamic could have been in play when Jesus went back home. Jesus came back to the place where he had turned water into wine, so quite naturally the people welcomed him. However, they did not honor him.

It is worth keeping in mind that a vast difference exists between welcoming Jesus and honoring Jesus. The crowds welcomed Jesus because he could perform wonderful works, but they did not honor him by altering their priorities. They welcomed him because he saved a wedding banquet by producing more wine, but they did not honor him by serving him as the King of kings. What about us? Do we just welcome Jesus or do we honor him?

Welcoming Jesus is treating others well when they treat us well. Honoring Jesus is blessing those who persecute us and praying for those who persecute us. Welcoming Jesus is wanting to receive more of his blessings.

Honoring him is asking him how we can be a blessing to someone else. The people of Galilee had no problem welcoming Jesus, but they did not genuinely honor him. Just as John wrote in chapter 1, "[Jesus] came to what was his own, and his own people did not accept him" (1:11).

Once he arrived in Galilee, Jesus made his way to the village of Cana. Without a doubt, the people of Cana must have remembered his miracle of water turning into wine. At the time, it must have been the most spectacular event people had ever seen. But this time Jesus will do even greater things than they saw him do before. God is like that, you know.

God is not limited by anything God has done in the past. The first miracle changed water, an inanimate substance, into wine, another inanimate substance. This time Jesus is going to change human lives. This time Jesus will take on the biggest, strongest enemy there is when he snatches someone out of the jaws of sickness.

But before he can proceed with the miracle, he has to overcome one spiritual challenge. Jesus never promised a path of discipleship without challenges. Lent is the season when we are called to embrace the challenge of discipleship. We do so as another way to move our faith forward by relying more on God's grace than we do on ourselves.

The challenge in Cana, and maybe for some of us, was to believe without visible evidence. Up to this point, people believed in Jesus because they saw something. They experienced a miracle. Then they believed.

When Jesus called Nathanael, Nathanael believed because Jesus knew his name before Nathanael told him. The first disciples put their faith in Jesus after he turned water into wine. The Samaritan woman believed because she was impressed with Jesus's prophetic insight: "Come, see a man who told me everything I ever did. Could this be the Messiah?" (4:29, NIV). She became a believer because of what he knew about her. Like Nathanael and the other disciples, she believed because she saw evidence of what Jesus could do.

As faith develops and matures, the challenge is to believe *before* we can see. We all desperately want to see, but the key is to have hope when we do not yet see the cavalry coming to save us. We all prefer to have proof, but faith is pressing forward in the face of rejection or setbacks. We are more confident when we have visual confirmation, but sometimes we must pray as if it is so, before it is so, until it becomes so. Faith is trusting Jesus enough to believe it before we can see it.

No one knows this better than the one John identifies as "a certain royal official" (v. 46, NIV). The man's name is not given, but his identity is interesting. He was a royal official. This suggests he was a high-ranking leader in the court of King Herod Antipas, the king who would later behead John the Baptist and eventually preside over Jesus's trial. Some interpreters think this royal official might have been a Gentile. We do know that he did not come to impress Jesus with his professional pedigree. He came to Jesus to present a deeply personal dilemma.

This man was not only a royal official, but he was also a caring and concerned father. He was a parent in pain. He had traveled a day's journey from the seaside village of Capernaum up hilly terrain to Cana because his son lay sick with a fever that threatened to take his life.

This man had access to power, but he could not do anything to make his son better. This man knew people in high places, but he knew no one who could cure his son's ailment. He worked for the king, but no royal decree was going to change the condition of his child. The royal official had so much working in his favor, and yet he was subject to the same frailties of life that we all are. Maybe that is why we can relate to him.

We are familiar with the fact that trouble does not ask our situation or station in life. Trouble shows up unannounced and uninvited. Trouble comes to the young and to the old. Trouble tests men and women. Trouble comes in all shapes and sizes. This man had finally come to the place in his life where he could not rely on his strength or his gifts. Someone he loved was hurting, and when that happens it can often hurt us just as much as it hurts that person. Only when the royal official was pushed to the limits of his wisdom and ability did he start looking for Jesus.

The man walked for half a day, up to Cana, and begged Jesus to come down to Capernaum to heal his son. He came all the way to Cana because he heard that Jesus was there, and by now Jesus had a reputation for doing signs and wonders. This is where Jesus taught the first lesson about believing before we see: genuine faith seeks the Savior and not the signs. The man asked Jesus to come heal his son, and Jesus responded to the man's plea in a surprising way. Jesus said, "Unless you people see miraculous signs and wonders you will never believe" (v. 48, translation mine).

Are we seeking signs or searching for the Savior? Jesus performed numerous signs and wonders, but the signs and wonders were never supposed to be the goal or the purpose of our faith. He changed water into wine, but not so that people would come to him whenever they ran out of wine. Jesus is not a divine bartender or a cosmic vending machine. He changed water into wine as proof of his authority over creation and to verify the claim that through him all things were made that have been made. This is why a maturing faith first seeks the Savior, not the signs and wonders.

But sometimes the way we pray contradicts this principle: "Lord, show me a sign and then I will do this or that. Do this miracle in my life or in my family and then I will believe in you." We all benefit from confirmation. But demanding signs is going too far.

Demanding signs has more to do with thinking that somehow God can be made to jump through the hoops that we set up for God. Demanding signs is the idea that God's purpose is to give us what we want when we want it. "God, if you do this, then I will do that." Demanding signs implies that the only way we can trust God is if there is some visible, observable evidence of God's activity that conforms to our expectations. This is a treacherous road to travel because we already know we cannot trust everything we see. Do you remember the picture of the dress that went viral on the Internet? Although the picture was in color, people could not agree on the color of the dress. It turns out that optical illusions are easy to create. You cannot trust everything you see.

People were more interested in what new thing Jesus might do for them than in who he was. Sign seekers are more interested in how much wine Jesus can make out of water than in how much he can change their lives.

Jesus will go on to perform more signs in John, but near the end of the Gospel, John makes this statement: "Jesus did many other signs in the presence of his disciples, which are not written in this book. But *these* are written so that you may come to believe that Jesus is the Messiah, the Son of God, and that through believing you may have life in his name" (20:30-31, emphasis mine).

So while we thank God for every sign of goodness and power, our deepest need is not for another miracle. What we need is a Savior. A sign cannot save us, but Jesus can. A sign cannot speak to us, but Jesus can. A sign cannot keep us company when we are lonely, guide us when we are wandering, comfort us when we are suffering, or protect when we are in trouble. A sign cannot dry our eyes, but Jesus, our Savior, can wipe our tears away.

What is a Savior? A Savior is someone who knows us better than we know ourselves. A Savior is someone who can forgive us of sins past, present, and future. A Savior is an intercessor who can pray on our behalf to the Father. A Savior is a liberator who can set us free from the powers and principalities of this world. A Savior is a reconciler who can restore our fellowship with God. Therefore, we put our trust in Jesus as the foundation of a maturing faith.

Jesus's refusal to come to Capernaum may have been discouraging at first, but the royal official and concerned father did not give up. He begged Jesus a second time to come down and heal his son. This father begged for Jesus's help because he knew the condition of his son.

What about us? Is there anything we need to bring to God today? Let me remind you that if Jesus is strong enough to handle a life that is on the brink of dying and a heart that is on the edge of breaking, he can handle whatever is going on in your life. Go ahead and ask him.

When we ask, we must remember that true faith requires us to rely on a sense other than eyesight. To put it positively, when we cannot see, we must build our faith on what we hear. Some things in life need visual verification. But to develop a faith that can handle the ups and downs of life, we have to shift the primary sense we use from seeing to hearing.

It is tempting to build our faith on what we see. If we see that things are going to work out, then we believe. If we see that the door is opening, then we believe. If we see that the problem is fixable, then we have faith. If we see that friends are coming to help us, then we do not fear. But the need today is to rely on what we hear more than what we see.

Our text confirms that the Galileans welcomed Jesus because they had *seen* all he had done in Jerusalem. But the royal official came from Capernaum to Cana because he had *heard* that Jesus was there. This troubled father got up early that morning and walked eighteen to twenty miles from Capernaum uphill to Cana in Galilee. He heard Jesus was in town. Based only on what he heard, he took more than half a day's journey to ask Jesus to come and heal his son.

The first time he asked Jesus to heal his son, Jesus said that faith based on signs is inadequate. The second time he asked Jesus to heal his son, Jesus said, "Go; your son will live" (v. 50). Jesus did not ask for the man's address. He did not even volunteer to go home with him. Nor did Jesus send any disciples on his behalf. Jesus sent the man home by himself. The man asked Jesus to come with him, and Jesus told him, "Go; your son will live."

And John says the man took Jesus at his word and departed. That's remarkable! He had no written guarantee. He had to go home relying only on what he heard. The man knew his son was critically ill when he left the house that morning. He heard what Jesus told him, and now he must go all the way back home walking by faith, relying only on what he has heard. "Go; your son will live."

The royal official could not see anything changing, but he believed because of what he heard. My spiritual imagination tells me he walked back talking to himself every step of the way. "My son will live. My son will live." He could not send a telegram or call home in advance, but he had a new sense of hope in his heart after hearing the words "your son will live."

The next day, before the man made it all the way home, his servants came to meet him and shared the news. "Your son is well. The fever broke. The boy is alive." They knew it because they saw it. But the official knew it because he heard it.

So, let this be an encouragement to us all. No matter what we are facing, we can believe it before we see it. Keep on walking and waiting. It has happened before. Abram could not see Canaan when God called him, but he left his father's house because he heard the word of the Lord. Moses had never organized a liberation campaign, but he went back to Egypt and demanded the emancipation of the Hebrews because one day he heard the word of the Lord.

We won't always see how the Lord is going to fulfill a promise, but we can believe God's word. We won't always see how the Lord is going to provide, but we can believe God's word. Do not be afraid. Take Jesus's word and go. We may not see it yet, but we can believe it now.

Note

1. Raymond Brown quoted in Frederick Dale Bruner, *The Gospel of John: A Commentary* (Grand Rapids MI: Eerdmans, 2012) 287.

11

Why Jesus Broke the Rules

John 5

Many of the breakthroughs in history have been made by people who broke rules. Conventional wisdom said "go left," but some individuals resisted traditional thinking and decided to turn right.

For thousands of years it was conventional wisdom that the earth was the center of our universe. Every captain who planned a sea voyage set sail convinced that the sun revolved around the earth. When everyday people imagined the earth, they perceived that they were standing on the bull's-eye of the universe. When priests taught creation, they used Scripture to validate their beliefs that the earth was at the focal point of the solar system.

In the year 1610, an Italian physicist and astronomer by the name of Galileo Galilei broke the rules. He published research that claimed the sun rather than the earth was at the center of the universe. Galileo broke the rules. This was the most radical news people ever heard. His views were so controversial that the Catholic Church forced him to renounce his position. But nothing changed Galileo's mind.

It turns out he was right, and his views ultimately changed the way people look at the world. It did not matter to Galileo that the priests quoted Scripture to prove their position. He believed the sun was at the center of the universe, so he broke the rules. The rest, as they say, is history.

I suspect that if we went around the sanctuary this morning, we would find that there are a few rule breakers in the congregation. You may have been born into a world of such low expectations that the rules said you would never achieve success. And because you broke the rules, God has made it possible for you to see and do things you never expected.

Hardly anyone in the Bible knew the rules better than Moses. We could say that Moses literally wrote the rules. After he led the Israelites out of Egypt, he went up to the top of Mount Sinai where God gave him the Ten Commandments. These ten laws were the foundation of Israel's relationship with God.

The first commandment said, "You shall have no other gods before me" (Exod 20:3). The second commandment said, "You shall not make for yourself an idol, whether in the form of anything that is in heaven above, or that is on the earth beneath, or that is in the water under the earth" (v. 4). The third commandment said, "You shall not misuse the name of the LORD your God" (v. 7, NIV). The fourth commandment is the one that connects with what happens to Jesus in John 5: "Remember the Sabbath day by keeping it holy" (v. 8, NIV).

Sabbath was the last day of the week for the Israelites. It began at sundown on Friday and lasted until sundown on Saturday. Sabbath was a day of rest. God created the world in six days and rested from creating on the seventh day. So God's people were called to rest on the Sabbath as a continual reminder that God's power and not human effort held and sustained the world. Our busyness and our plans do not keep the world spinning on its axis, the seasons changing, and the flowers blooming. Only God can do that.

The prophets who came after Moses commanded Israel to take the Sabbath seriously:

> Blessed is the one who does this—the person who holds it fast, who keeps the Sabbath without desecrating it, and keeps their hands from doing any evil. (Isa 56:2, NIV)

> But if you do not obey me to keep the Sabbath day holy by not carrying any load as you come through the gates of Jerusalem on the Sabbath day, then I will kindle an unquenchable fire in the gates of Jerusalem that will consume her fortresses. (Jer 17:27, NIV)

> Keep my Sabbaths holy, that they may be a sign between us. Then you will know that I am the LORD your God. (Ezek 20:20, NIV)

By the time Jesus came along, keeping the Sabbath was one of the most important religious rules. It was so important that the Pharisees and Scribes kept a record of what a person could lawfully do on the Sabbath.

John 5 is a turning point in the Gospel of John. When Jesus returns to Jerusalem, the first thing he does is agitate the religious leaders by healing on the Sabbath. Healing on the Sabbath was against the rules. Why would Jesus knowingly break a commandment?

When Jesus came to Jerusalem, he entered near the Sheep Gate, one of the entrances in the Jerusalem wall, where there was a pool known as Bethesda. This pool was a place of healing. It was a place where the infirmed were made well by the occasional stirring of the waters.

The pool was popular with people who lived in pain. Today this might include the poor, the hungry, the hopeless, and even the formerly incarcerated. John lumps people into three general categories but then singles out a particular person in the poolside crowd. He identifies one man marked by hopelessness and despair.

This man at the pool had been paralyzed for thirty-eight years. Jesus saw the man and asked him, "Do you want to get well?" (v. 6, NIV). This is a strange question to ask someone who has been paralyzed for thirty-eight years, but sometimes life can be stagnant for so long that we stop anticipating change. "Do you want to get well?" (v. 6, NIV).

Instead of answering Jesus directly, the man complained to Jesus that no one helped him into the pool when the water was stirred. Whenever he tried to get in, someone else jumped in ahead of him.

Jesus ignored the man's complaints and gave him a command. "Get up! Pick up your mat and walk" (v. 8, NIV). The man had been paralyzed for thirty-eight years, but Jesus told him to stand up. Miraculously, that is exactly what he did. He picked up his mat and walked.

This is Jesus's third miraculous sign in the Gospel of John. Certainly, there is much we could say about this sign. A man had been sick for almost four decades, and Jesus made him well. Someone had lived in desperation, and Jesus delivered him. That would be more than enough for a Sunday-morning sermon. We need this good news.

But there is more to this story than the miracle itself. John says the day on which this man was healed was the Sabbath. Moses had written about the Sabbath day in the fourth commandment. The Sabbath day was the day set aside to not work. The Sabbath in Jesus's time was guarded by legalistic rules and regulations.

Healing was considered work. To do any work on the Sabbath was against the law. To break the Sabbath was considered a transgression of the law. But Jesus defied conventional wisdom and healed on the Sabbath.

People celebrated when Jesus changed water into wine. No one became upset when Jesus's word healed the royal official's son. But when Jesus healed on the Sabbath, he crossed the line. He went too far.

Anyone following Jesus should be forewarned that there are times we must cross the line and break the right rules. We should honor laws that are in place for our common good, but there are unwritten rules that can keep a person from reaching his or her God-given potential. There are rules that tell us who to socialize with, what to do with our lives, and what our priorities should be. These are the rules that we need to challenge and break, but this is never easy. Just look at what happened to Jesus.

The Jewish leaders said to the man who had been healed, "It is the sabbath; it is not lawful for you to carry your mat" (v. 10). In the eyes of the Jewish leaders, this man had sinned by carrying his mat on the Sabbath day. The man defended himself, saying, "The one who made me well said to me, 'Take up your mat and walk'" (v. 11). In other words, the one who healed me is the one who broke the law. He's the one you ought to be looking for. I'm innocent.

From this point forward in the Gospel of John, Jesus will no longer be seen as only a miracle worker, prophet, or teacher. Because he broke the law by healing on the Sabbath, he will be considered by some to be public enemy number one. Verse 16 says, "That is why the Jews were out to get Jesus—because he did this kind of thing on the Sabbath" (MSG).

One reason Jesus healed on the Sabbath was to reveal his divine nature. He said to those who questioned him, "My Father is still working, and I also am working" (v. 17). The Sabbath was a day of rest, but rest did not mean God did no work on the seventh day. Babies were born on the Sabbath. People died on the Sabbath. Trees bloomed on the Sabbath. God evidently worked on the Sabbath.

If God were to stop working completely, everything and everyone would disintegrate. Creation would collapse on itself. God is always at work. God simply rested from the work of creating the world.

The problem Jesus faced is that when he told people why he healed on the Sabbath, he made a claim about himself that his opponents could not believe. Jesus did not say "the" Father is always at work, which would have put a safe, respectable distance between himself and God. He did not even say "our" Father is always at work, which would have emphasized God's relationship with everyone. Jesus said, "my" Father is always at work.

When his opponents heard Jesus use the personal pronoun "my" before "Father," they tried all the harder to kill Jesus because he was not only breaking the Sabbath but was even calling God his own Father, making himself equal with God. Equal with God meant he was calling himself divine. What God had the power to do, Jesus had the power to do. Jesus said, "What the Father does, the Son does. The Father loves the Son and includes him in everything he is doing" (v. 20, MSG).

This is why Jesus broke the Sabbath by healing. He wanted to reveal his identity as the divine Son of God.

God never stopped working graciously in the lives of human beings. God was always ready to show compassion to people in need. God always worked mercifully in the lives of suffering people. Therefore, since Jesus was God incarnate, he had authority to do the work of God, even on the Sabbath.

Jesus also broke the Sabbath to tell us something about God. Think about it. If Jesus will take the risk to heal on the Sabbath—knowing the cost of doing such a thing—that must mean that God will do anything to save us. There is no limit to God's compassion. The incident at the pool is a parable for how much God cares for us.

This pool had been around for years. People with pain had been coming to this pool for a long time. All kinds of brokenness surrounded it. Jesus could have waited until the next day to do this miracle. He could have waited until it was safe or convenient. But he did not.

He was on a mission to heal, save, and set free. He seems to have learned from his Father that there is no risk too great if it will save a life. God will stop at nothing to save us. Over the next several chapters in John, Jesus is going to face conflict and controversy, deserters and false admirers, critics and faultfinders, but he never turns back. He is determined to give us life and life abundant.

You may find this strange, but I am slowly making my way through a book about search dogs, German shepherds in particular. It's a good distraction to relax my mind before I go to bed.

The author is a professor at NC State who has a shepherd named Solo. The interesting thing about search dogs like Solo is that she does not go with rescue teams looking to find stranded hikers. She is called in when officers do not think the missing person is still alive. Solo is a cadaver dog.

The author makes the point that all dogs have a great sense of smell. But dogs like Solo that help grieving families get answers have more than a good nose. They also have an inner drive that sets them apart from other dogs and makes them stop at nothing to find what they are looking for.

When people want to hide a dead body, apparently they go to great lengths to make sure no one will find it. So, dogs like Solo have to be willing to go anywhere. They have to crawl through sewers. They cannot be timid about going into small spaces or be afraid of getting dirty.

Solo may have to walk through briar patches or thorny fields. But she does not whimper or turn back when a sharp point pierces her side and makes her bleed. Sometimes she has to cross rocky terrain to find what she is looking for. But she does not give up when she gets tired. She has a relentless inner drive to go wherever the scent leads her.

Thinking about Solo made me think of what Jesus did when he healed on the Sabbath. It is as if the Father sent the Son on a search and rescue mission to bind up the brokenhearted. And Jesus risked his life as proof that God stops at nothing to find us and save us.

He picked up the paralyzed man's scent as soon as he came into the city. He detected an aroma of hopelessness in the air. He noticed the fragrance of pain lingering in the atmosphere. Jesus followed the trail until it led him to the pool of Bethesda.

Jesus knew that healing on the Sabbath was going to bring out the worst in his enemies, but he could not wait to pour out his compassion.

Thirty-eight years was long enough. He knew that healing on the Sabbath was going to lead to persecution, but that was not his concern. "What the Father does, the Son does" (v. 17, MSG). Whatever it took and no matter what it cost, Jesus was willing to pay the price to heal the man.

And I think I know why.

Search dogs look for corpses and cannot do anything once they find a lifeless body, but Jesus looks for us because no matter what shape we are in when he finds us, he is the giver of life.

"Indeed, just as the Father raises the dead and gives them life, so also the Son gives life to whomever he wishes" (v. 21). Jesus gives life. That's why he broke the Sabbath. To give a person life.

"For just as the Father has life in himself, so he has granted the Son also to have life in himself" (v. 26).

Jesus will stop at nothing to save us.

Thank God Jesus broke the rules. The rules would have condemned this paralyzed man to one more day of suffering. Thank God Jesus emphasized love over legalism. Thank God Jesus pays attention to our pain.

He is the Son of God, Lord over the Sabbath, and he is worthy of honor. Whoever hears his words and believes the one who sent him has eternal life and has crossed over from death to life. How can we not give him honor when he came to give us eternal life? Amen.

12

The God Who Satisfies

John 6:1-15, 22-71

We were born hungry. Hunger is one of the first urges or cravings we learn to satisfy. (Someone may be thinking about how to do that even as I speak.) Actually, we do not have to learn to satisfy our hunger. The instinct to eat is in every healthy child that comes into the world.

Babies have an unmistakable cry with a certain pitch and volume that new parents soon learn to identify as the "you'd better feed me right now" cry. This cry may start off low and slow, but if the demand is not met in a reasonable amount of time, the cry intensifies until it reaches an almost unbearable decibel. This cry cannot be ignored. It becomes a shared language by which the parents know exactly what the child needs.

We are born hungry.

The marketing for Snickers has turned this fact into a popular advertising campaign. Individuals are depicted in commercials as upset, uptight, and frustrated because hunger has taken over their personalities. Of course, once they take a bite of a Snickers bar, they immediately transform back into their real selves. The tag line is something like, "You just aren't yourself when you're hungry."

The humor of the commercial quickly fades when we consider that in our present time, food has almost become a luxury for middle- and upper-income households rather than a human right for all. West of Highway 52 in Winston Salem, you will find at least ten grocery stores, two big-box discount stores, and a new grocery store under construction. You will find in these stores an array of organic fruits and a bountiful harvest of locally grown vegetables. But, east of Highway 52, you will find one, maybe two, full-service grocery stores. And anyone who cannot get to that one store in a car probably walks to a mom and pop corner store where healthy food is not likely to be found and the cost of unhealthy food is high. Or they may pay for transportation to take them to the one grocery store that is close by. Good-quality food has become a luxury for a few when good food should be accessible to everyone.

This may be partly why, throughout Scripture, God is moved to show compassion toward people who are hungry. God fed the prophet Elijah during a famine by sending ravens to bring him bread and meat in the morning and bread and meat in the evening. The psalmist praised God who rescued him from his enemies and who gives food to every living thing. In John 4, Jesus experienced hunger. Having walked miles and miles through Samaria, he stopped to rest and sent the disciples to buy him some food for the refreshment of his body. He can empathize with what it feels like to be hungry. Jesus knows what we need.

So when the crowds followed Jesus to the other side of the Sea of Galilee, John 6 reveals that he was unwilling to send them away without any food. Jesus turned to Philip, one of his disciples. Philip's hometown was nearby, so perhaps he was the spokesperson for the day. Jesus asked Philip, "Where are we to buy bread for these people to eat?" (v. 5). By "these people," Jesus was talking about the multitude that had come to hear him teach. We should be clear about the size of this crowd.

John says there were 5,000 men, but because this story shows up in Matthew, Mark, and Luke as well, we can read the other Gospels and notice more details. For example, 5,000 men is just the tip of the iceberg. Matthew says that the number 5,000 does not include the women and children. This crowd could have easily been 10,000 or 15,000, perhaps even larger.

Whatever the number, clearly the disciples had a problem. Where could twelve men who quit their jobs to follow a Galilean miracle worker buy bread for a crowd of 15,000 people? Even if they could find the place, they could not afford the price. Philip heard Jesus's question and did what we do in similar situations.

He immediately began calculating what it would take to solve the problem using only the resources he had at his disposal. He computed the cost of this outreach program in his head and quickly came to the conclusion that what he had was not enough. This cause was hopeless.

Philip said, "Six months' wages would not buy enough bread for each one to have a bite" (v. 7, translation mine). Clearly, Jesus did not understand complex, logistical challenges like feeding large crowds. Jesus was good to have around for the spiritual stuff, but he obviously did not know anything about economics and finance. Buying bread for a crowd this size was not feasible. The disciples did not have enough money. They were in a remote place. The hour was late.

Andrew seemed to agree with Philip, although initially he sounded like he was going in a different direction. Andrew said, "There is a boy here who has five barley loaves and two fish . . ." (v. 9). It sounds like he was about to say something radical, like, "We may not have much, but we are going to use our faith." That is not what happens. Andrew went on to say, "but how far will they go among so many?" (v. 9, NIV).

We are a lot like Andrew and Philip when we spend more time thinking about why something cannot happen than we do about what might be possible. Sometimes we have to remember that failure is not the worst possible outcome. It is far worse to look back on what we wish we would have tried but did not.

Thankfully, Jesus already had in mind what he was going to do. He instructed the disciples to have the people sit down. Luke tells us that Jesus had the people sit in groups of fifty. They sat on the green grass on a hillside beside the Sea of Galilee. It was spring, almost time for the Jewish Passover feast.

Jesus took the five loaves of bread and two small fish donated by a young boy in the crowd, and he gave thanks to the Father. Then he distributed the food to those who were seated, and everyone had as much as they wanted. It turns out they not only had enough, but because of the power of God, they had an abundance. They had so much food that the disciples gathered twelve baskets of leftovers after everyone had eaten and been satisfied.

This miracle seems far-fetched to the logical mind, but many of us have seen God do this again and again. God specializes in turning insufficiency into sufficiency. God knows exactly what we need. Our parents or grandparents may not have had much in the way of material wealth, but they somehow found a way to keep food on the table, clothes on children's backs, and even send some of us to college. Many laid-off workers have managed to keep their lives together because God is an expert in using what we have and turning it into more than what we need.

After people saw Jesus perform this sign, they began to think that if Jesus could do a miracle like this, he might be someone worth keeping around for a while. Think of what he could do for them. Think of what he could get for them. If they had a leader like Jesus, they could have everything they wanted. So they decided to make him a king.

Most people would be flattered to be asked to be a king, but Jesus never allowed people to make their agenda his agenda. He slipped away undetected. He did not want to be their king. At least, he did not want to be the kind of king they wanted him to be. They wanted a king who would give them bread for their stomachs and not ask for a change of heart. They wanted a king who would make life comfortable and convenient, not one who asked for commitment as a disciple. They wanted a king who kept them full, not one who expected them to use their faith.

The crowd followed Jesus because they wanted another miraculous meal. They are not so different from us today. We believe that the way to satisfy our deep hunger is with more power, material possessions, and fame. We talk about grace but live by the motto that God helps those who help themselves. We seek a God who will give us what we want and as much as we want.

The crowd in John 6 misunderstood the miraculous feeding with fives loaves and two fish. They looked for Jesus because they wanted more bread. From Jesus's point of view, they liked what he could do for them but were not willing to put their trust in him. Chasing after more bread meant they were merely working for food that spoils. They were working for food that was not going to last. They were working for food that tastes good today but is rotten and rancid tomorrow. They had set their sights much too low.

There is so much more to a relationship with God than simply getting more bread. The crowd did not need more bread. They needed someone in whom they could believe.

This is still the challenge we face in our own time. People have access to more than enough of the physical and material resources, but the lack of spiritual wisdom manifests itself in every arena—from the open, sometimes bigoted, hostility in political discourse to the unwillingness to pay a living wage for honest and decent work, from the defunding of public education to suicide bombers and the brutality of senseless government shutdowns and xenophobic debates about immigration, from our addictions to food and gambling to the fragmentation in our communities and the emptiness in our own hearts. All these are symptoms of a deep, unmet, spiritual hunger.

So, Jesus asked a question of those who came to him seeking more bread. He wanted to know if all they expected from God was bread. He asked if what they wanted from God was more and more food that spoils. Nothing is inherently wrong with physical bread. We need food to live. But our deepest hungers in life cannot be satisfied by food that spoils. We try, but it never works. It does not work because it is only temporary food. It is nothing more than food that spoils.

The timeshare we are so proud of—food that spoils. The dream house we think will make us happy—food that spoils. Our new shoes and new outfits—food that spoils. The new smartphone we must have every time a new model goes on sale—food that spoils. We can enjoy these things for what they are, but we have to remember exactly what they are—temporary.

Jesus came to invite us to work not for food that spoils, but for food that endures to eternal life, which he, the Son of Man, will give. Thankfully, what I need most is what Jesus is going to give. This is the grace of God. Jesus came to *give* us the food that endures.

When the crowd heard Jesus telling them to work for food that endures, they said, "What must we do to perform the works of God?" (v. 28).

They wanted this information from Jesus because they missed the meaning of the miraculous feeding of the multitude. There is no work one can do to obtain the food that endures to eternal life. There is no class to take. Food that endures is not a philosophical pursuit or an intellectual argument to master. It is about trusting God.

Jesus said the work of God is this: to *believe* in the one he has sent. We know from earlier chapters in John that belief is trust. To trust is to rely on someone. To trust is to be confident in someone. To trust is to know that the God who made you will never leave you. To trust is to know that you are not alone. The work God requires is to trust in, rely on, and have confidence in the One who came from God. As talented as we may be, we are not sufficient by ourselves. As connected as we may be, no one we know is capable of meeting all our needs. We need the food that endures. We need the true bread that came down from heaven.

Life demands too much of us to try to make it on the sugary, syrupy diet of pop culture and self-help spirituality. We need food that is more filling than the cotton-candy promises of prosperity preachers. We need a meal that is hardier than the fast food of prayerlessness. As my mother would tell us when we were children, we need to eat food that sticks to our ribs.

The demands of this life are often heaviest when we feel like we have the least to give. We have the heaviest load to carry when we have the longest road to travel. We have the most responsibility when we have the least amount of time. What we need for this journey is food that will not spoil. That is the only way we are going to make it.

If we intend to hold on to the great promise in Romans 8 that says we are more than conquerors, we need a diet that will not fail (8:37).

To live up to the image in Isaiah 40 that we will mount up with wings of eagles, run and not get weary, walk and not faint, we need food for the soul (40:31).

To be poised to persevere so that we can pray without ceasing, we need spiritual nourishment.

If we are going to put on the full armor of God and stand firm no matter what tries to bring us down, then every day we need to eat food that endures (Eph 6:10-20).

It happens to all of us; one day we come face to face with our own limitations. It may happen in our professional lives or in our relationships. But the day will come. Whenever it happens, we will feel a hunger that is unlike any other hunger we have ever known.

It is a hunger we cannot medicate. A hunger we cannot ignore. A hunger we cannot dress up. A hunger we cannot eat away or drink away. We will find ourselves craving food that endures.

What is food that endures? Food that endures does not rise or fall with the ebb and flow of the stock market. This food cannot be purchased at the mall or ordered from Amazon. This food is food that Jesus, the Son of Man, gives. Thanks be to God! We do not earn it. He gives! We do not produce it. He gives! We do not qualify for it by our good deeds. The Son of Man gives! Thanks be to God for this incredible gift.

God gives mercies that are new every morning. Mercy is food that endures.

God gives compassion that never fails. Compassion is food that endures.

God gives us purpose to live by. A divine calling is food that endures.

God forgives and enables us to forgive. Forgiveness is food that endures.

God gives peace in the storms of life. God's peace is food that endures.

God gives us his righteousness. His righteousness is a gift from God, and it is food that endures.

These are the gifts of a real and abundant life. Anything else is an edited, airbrushed, and cosmetically enhanced imitation of the real thing.

So the people said to Jesus, "Sir, give us this bread always" (v. 34). Give us the bread that gives life. Give us the bread that is true bread from heaven. We are tired of living a life without true joy. We are weary of coming to the end of each day asking why we do what we do. We have had enough of trying to keep up with the Joneses when the Joneses do not even know who we are. We want something better. Give us this bread.

This is when Jesus said to them, "I am the bread of life" (v. 35).

You do not need some*thing*. You need Someone. I am the bread of life. Anyone who comes to me will never go hungry. I am the bread of life.

Everyone who looks to the Son and believes in him shall have eternal life. I am the bread of life. Your forefathers ate manna in the desert yet they died. Eat this bread and you will not die. Put your hope in me and you will not be disappointed. Everything you need, I am.

Everything you hope for, I am. Everything that will make you whole and fill your life, I am.

I am the source of your strength. I am the center of your joy. I am the reason for your rejoicing. I am the bread of life. I am the promise in your pain. I am the bread of life. Anyone who comes to me will never go hungry. Anyone who believes in me will never be thirsty.

This is the good news that satisfies every hungry soul.

13

Homily for Christian Leaders[1]

John 6:16-21

It is possible for me to be in such a hurry to leave the house that I forget something I really need. I have my briefcase. I remember my keys. I drive out of the neighborhood. But by the time I'm a short distance from home, it occurs to me that I forgot something important, like my cell phone. At this point, I'm still close enough to turn around but far enough to be irritated.

So, I kick myself for being in such a rush and I turn the car around because there is no way I would keep going without my cell phone. My phone is often the primary way of communicating with others. Unless I am intentionally unplugging from technology, I do not want to leave home without it. When I do, I feel like something is missing.

There are periods when we can go for a long, long time and not notice that we are missing something we need. We may think something is in our purse or desk drawer, and not until we need it and look for it do we discover it isn't there. We think a tool is stored away in the garage, but when we want to use it, we cannot find it anywhere.

We encounter numerous people in Scripture who have a sense that something they need is missing. One young, wealthy ruler came to Jesus and asked, "What must I do to inherit eternal life?" (cf. Mark 10:17; Matt 19:16). He had so much, materially speaking. Still, he knew something was missing. A blind man approached Jesus, crying out for mercy. Jesus asked him what he wanted. The man said he wanted to see. He wanted to see like other people. He did not want to miss the sunsets or beautiful smiles. (Mark 10:46-52)

Spiritual leadership requires endurance and faith and compassion. Before we set out on this trip together, we need to make sure we have everything we need. In our text, the disciples find out exactly what that means.

It was late in the evening, and the disciples had spent all day with Jesus while he fed more than 5,000 people beside the Sea of Galilee. The disciples got into a boat and set off across the lake toward Capernaum. This was a journey they had taken many times before. Andrew and Peter were fishermen, as were James and John. They knew these waters like the backs of their hands.

The Sea of Galilee is a beautiful body of water. Technically, it is not a sea; it is a lake. The Sea of Galilee is actually situated almost 700 feet below sea level. Many stories in the Gospels center on the Sea of Galilee. Peter walked on the Sea of Galilee. The disciples netted a miraculous catch of fish in the Sea of Galilee. Jesus calmed a storm on the Sea of Galilee.

It is tempting to lump the story in John 6 with the other stories of Jesus and the disciples on the sea. But this story is different. John is not trying to teach us about Jesus's power over the storm (Mark), about what faith will do if we only step out of the boat (Matthew), or about the power of faith (Luke). Those are vital lessons we need to learn, but John is showing us something else.

The disciples set off in the boat to go to the other side of the sea. John is quick to point out one detail that is the key to this text. Jesus was not with them. For reasons John does not say, the disciples took this journey without Jesus being in the boat. This is not a passing thought or an insignificant detail. Jesus's absence from the boat had serious consequences.

Soon after they left in the boat, the sky darkened. Strong winds began to blow. The waters grew rough. The disciples were too far from shore to turn around and not close enough to their destination to have much hope for survival. And Jesus was not in the boat.

Strangely enough, it is possible to be on a journey that is directed by God but not be in the presence of God. The disciples were doing what they were supposed to do, but they were doing it on their own strength. Jesus was not in the boat. God can call us to serve and lead and work in the church, but we honor God most when we intentionally invite Jesus into the boat. We need to employ all of our intellect, experience, and know-how, and yet we cannot yield fruit for the kingdom unless Jesus is with us. As Jesus will say in John 15, no branch can bear fruit by itself; it must remain in the vine.

Specifically, we're talking about developing a life of prayer, sensitivity to the Scriptures, a Christlike attitude, and concern for the well-being of others.

The disciples had the know-how, but they did not have Jesus. Consequently, as the circumstances became more difficult—darkness, wind, and rough waves—they did not have any peace or power. Simply because we are on an assignment from God does not mean we will not face moments of adversity. Leadership is hard work. You will have meetings where everything goes smoothly. And you will have meetings where you will feel like the wheels have come off the bus. How we handle these moments will depend on whether Jesus is in the boat.

When Jesus, walking on the water, approached the disciples, they did not recognize him. The disciples were terrified at the sight of a strange figure stepping across the crests of the waves. So Jesus reassured them by saying, "It is I; do not be afraid" (v. 20). Once they recognized him, they were eager to take him into the boat. With Jesus on board, they reached the shore where they were heading.

Taking Jesus into the boat is an opportunity we have today and every day. He is willing to go with us. Will we take him into our boat? Do we want him in our boat? As leaders, my prayer is that we will see the meetings we hold and the committees on which we serve as opportunities for us to bring Jesus into the boat so we can safely land where God is taking us.

If our family is experiencing a storm, let's not push the panic button. Let's push the faith button. Take Jesus into the boat. If we need more volunteers to serve, let's not push the desperation button. Let's push the prayer button. Take Jesus into the boat. Let's not work against each other when we disagree. Let's work together because we know who is in our boat. There is no storm that can stop us when Jesus goes with us.

Let us pray: God who rules over the storms and the sea, be with us now. Open our hearts to your divine presence. May we see all of our work as an offering to you. Help us to surrender our will so that we might come to know and do your will. Be with us through all the winds and waves of life so that we can serve you with our whole heart and mind. Give us strength for the journey. In the name of the Father, Son, and Holy Spirit, Amen.

Note

1. The sermon was delivered at a churchwide conference for ministry leaders.

14

Doing the Will of God[1]

John 7

If you are like most people, you probably feel that although there are many things you could do and many things people want you to do, when you look past all the oughts and shoulds, there are really only a few things you *need* to do. And if you can ever get focused on those few things, you can experience more peace and joy in your life.

It is not always easy to identify what these few things are, but whenever a person catches a glimpse of what is most important, everything else fades into the background. When something incredibly good happens in our lives, that goodness can open our eyes and remind us of what really matters. Even when something tragic happens, in our suffering we are sometimes more sensitive to what we care about most.

Knowing what to do can spare us the trouble of making the wrong choice. Knowing what is best can save us from wasting precious time going in the wrong direction or taking action that will not bear any fruit. We can avoid relationships that are not going to last and habits that will not help us. We can better utilize our abilities and resources where they can do the most good for others.

Each of us will have a different answer concerning what we need to do. Some people need to forgive. Some people need to take care of a debt that is stealing their joy. Some people need to get busy before another opportunity passes them by. Not everyone needs to do the same thing. But there is one choice that is common to everyone who wants to see life become more of what it can be. We need to do the will of God.

To say that God has a will simply means that God is not neutral about our choices and decisions. God cares about the path we take. God is interested in our next move. God knows that our decisions can make a difference. Taking the time to consider what God wants is what we mean when we say we are "following the will of God."

The will of God is a big, mysterious idea, so let me share some background on the story in John 7 and, by considering the issues Jesus faced and the choices he made in the passage, try to communicate something about doing God's will in our everyday lives.

By now, it is obvious that Jesus is determined to do what the Father wants him to do. He has had chance after chance to save himself and avoid danger. He has had opportunities to take an easier path. But every time he had the chance to choose, he chose to do the will of God. Jesus knew that plots to take his life were percolating behind the scenes, yet he still went forward because he was determined to do the will of God.

He did not come to do his own work. He came to do the work of the One who sent him. When he went into the temple, as recorded in chapter 2, he saw transactions taking place that were not sanctioned by his Father. He could have looked the other way. Instead, Jesus turned over the tables in the temple and expelled the money changers and those who sold doves. He had to do the work of the One who sent him.

In John 4 when the disciples urged him to eat some food to refresh his body, Jesus told them, "I have food to eat that you do not know about.... My food is to do the will of him who sent me and to complete his work" (4:32, 34). In John 5, Jesus was condemned for healing a man on the Sabbath. Jesus responded to his critics by saying, "My Father is still working, and I am also working...the Son can do nothing on his own, but only what he sees the Father doing; for whatever the Father does, the Son does likewise" (5:17, 19).

Jesus had been sent. He was on assignment. Everything changes once a person sees his or her life as a divine assignment. Each day takes on new meaning and purpose and hope. God gives many and varied assignments. Raising children is an assignment from God. Our job might be our assignment from God. Our ministry in the local church might be our assignment from God. Contributing to the common good in the world is an assignment from God. Serving the underserved, reaching the unreached, and caring for the forgotten is an assignment from God.

This is how Jesus lived his life. This is why he was in Galilee. He was waiting on the Father to tell him what to do next. "But when the Jewish Festival of Tabernacles was near, Jesus's brothers said to him, 'Leave Galilee and go to Judea, so that your disciples may see the [miracles] you do'" (vv. 2-3, NIV).

Jesus's brothers dared Jesus to prove himself to the world. They taunted Jesus. "Don't stay behind the scenes in Galilee," they said. "Go to Jerusalem to the Feast of the Tabernacles and do miracles, signs, and wonders. Then everyone will know who you are. That's what you want, right?" It will become clear in a moment that what Jesus wanted was to do the will of the Father.

The Feast of Tabernacles, sometimes called the Festival of Booths, celebrated God's provision to Moses and the Israelites in the wilderness, a story that is told in the book of Exodus. The name of this festival refers to the fact that the celebration involved sleeping in tents for seven days to remember how God had provided for their ancestors for forty years in the wilderness.

The Feast of Tabernacles was a huge celebration. Throngs of people converged on the city of Jerusalem. To Jesus's brothers, this seemed to be the perfect time for Jesus to show his power to the crowds. He would have had a captive audience. If Jesus really wanted to impress people with his power, this was the ideal time to do miracles. "If you are the Christ, the Messiah, as you claim to be, you should go to the feast and let everybody see what you can do" (see v. 4).

We can assume that Jesus's brothers had a tone of sarcasm in their voices since John 7:5 says that even his own brothers did not believe in him. Jesus's claims of divinity sounded like the ramblings of an insane person. "I am the bread of life" (6:35). What did Jesus mean by that? Was he serious?

They had known Jesus as a boy growing up in Nazareth. If he was so special, he should prove it once and for all—go to Jerusalem and do something. But Jesus did not go.

This is often the hardest test in doing the will of God. The issue is not just knowing what to do but also when to do it and why. Jesus's brothers urged him to go to Jerusalem and do something amazing. They wanted him to perform signs to increase his popularity ratings, but Jesus would not show any signs at the feast. He was not interested in popularity. He only wanted to do what the Father told him to do when the Father told him to do it.

The brothers' advice to Jesus sounds a lot like what happened when the devil tempted Jesus to throw himself off a cliff in order for God to save him, which would lead everyone to believe in Jesus. He did not jump because doing the will of God involves the right motivation *and* the right timing.

Jesus told his unbelieving brothers, "The right time for me has not yet come; for you, any time is right" (v. 6, translation mine). John uses a Greek word for "time" that suggests more than time on a clock. When Jesus said the right time for him had not yet come, he was not saying, for example, that he could not go to the feast because it was only 9 a.m. and that he was not scheduled to go until noon. He was not talking about that kind of time.

The time he had in mind was time in the sense of the right season, the right moment. Whenever Jesus speaks of "his time" in the Gospel of John, he is referring to the time of his glorification, which is his death, resurrection, and ascension. People wanted to take his life and tried to take his life, but they could not lay hold of him before it was the right time. He slipped through crowds undetected because he would not be arrested until it was time. He did not linger in Galilee out of any fear for what he was going to face in Jerusalem; he simply did not want to go on his own timetable. He waited for the time the Father had set for him. Anyone who wants to do God's will has to pay attention to the times and the seasons in life.

When Jesus came riding into Jerusalem on the back of a donkey, the people cheered him while waving palm branches and lining the streets with palms. It was Jesus's way of announcing that God's time had come. It was time for blind eyes to be opened. Time for wounds to be healed. Time for Jesus's enemies to do what they were going to do. Time for God to do what only God could do.

One of the perennial challenges of the spiritual life is learning to wait on the timing of God. To you and me, a few days seem like sufficient time for God to hear and respond to our prayers. Certainly a week—seven days—is more than enough time for God to give us direction or move a barrier out of our way. Why does God take so long? Why does it take so much time for things to happen like we want them to happen, if they ever happen at all?

For one thing, God does not operate according to our carefully constructed calendars and neatly scheduled lives. We have to face the fact that there will be people and even our own thoughts that tempt us, daring us to act as if we are wise enough to set our own timetables.

But for anyone trying to do the will of the Father, there are times and seasons. There are times and seasons to move and times and seasons to be still. There are times and seasons to plant and times and seasons to harvest. There are times and seasons to build up and times and seasons to tear down and start all over again. There are times and seasons to work and times and seasons to enjoy the fruit of our labors.

Jesus told his brothers that any time was right for them because they were not concerned about the Father's will. They were preoccupied with what the world wanted. They were interested in what the world had to say.

But Jesus did not belong to the world. So he did not go up to the feast when his brothers told him to go. He stayed in Galilee.

Sometime later, after getting the okay from the Father, Jesus did go up to the feast. He did not go publicly, as his brothers wanted him to go. He went in secret. He concealed himself because it was not time for him to be arrested, convicted, and crucified. That time had not come. But it would.

Among the crowds that day, rumors circulated about Jesus. People had questions. Who is this person who feeds multitudes? Who is this person who claims to be the bread of life? Who is this person who says that the only way to have real life is through him? Some said, "He is a good man" (v. 12). These were the people who thought Jesus was a man of integrity. He was morally good. Others said, "He deceives the people" (v. 12, NIV). These were the ones who thought Jesus's claims of divinity were arrogant at best and outright lies at worst. One thing is certain, then as now: we have to decide what we believe about Jesus. Is he a good man? Is he more than a good man?

The Christian novelist and literary critic C. S. Lewis made this point when he wrote,

> A man who was merely a man and said the sort of things Jesus said would not be a great moral teacher. . . . You must make your choice. Either this man was, and is, the Son of God, or else a madman or something worse. You can shut him up for a fool, you can spit at him and kill him as a demon or you can fall at his feet and call him Lord and God . . . .[2]

The crowds debated Jesus's identity, but Jesus knew who he was. He was both Lord and God. Whenever we set out to do the will of God, we have to remember who we are. The debate going on at the Feast of Tabernacles was whether Jesus was a deceiver or a good man.

Jesus needed to remember who he was because everyone else wanted to tell him who he was and who he was not. His brothers dared him to go to the feast because they did not believe God had sent him. The crowds had opinions about him, but they only spoke in whispers because they feared the Jewish authorities. Some people asked how Jesus could be the Messiah, since they knew his mother and his brothers. Jewish leaders questioned Jesus's intellect because he had not graduated from their schools.

At a certain point during the feast, some of the people began to ask if Jesus was the same man the authorities were trying to kill. After all, he was teaching publicly and no one was stopping him. They wondered if the authorities had concluded that Jesus was the Christ. Other people wondered how Jesus could be who he said he was because he was not from the right part of town. To them, it was impossible that the Christ could come from Galilee. So the people were divided about Jesus.

Jesus, however, was not confused. He knew who he was. He was not perplexed about his identity. He was not puzzled by his uniqueness. He knew God had sent him. "My teaching is not my own. It comes from the one who sent me" (v. 16, NIV). Jesus knew who he was.

The times when we find ourselves at a crossroad are when we most need to remember who we are. Before we give in to fear, we have to remember who we are. Before we act on our feelings, we have to remember who we are. The moment we set out to do what God wants, something or someone is going to call our identity into question.

This is when we have to able to say, as Jesus said so many times, "I know who I am. I know to whom I belong. I know who called me. I know why I am here. I am made in the image of God. I am not what people have said about me. I am fearfully and wonderfully made. I am not an accident. I am a new creature. I am not forgotten. I am the apple of God's eye."

Let's not fool ourselves into thinking that when we choose to do something God wants us to do, the path will always be a smooth journey. Jesus will tell you that conflict is inevitable. He knew people wanted to take his life, and he went to the feast anyway. We sometimes only see Jesus as meek and mild, but he was bold and courageous, too. He knew the crowds misunderstood his ministry, but he went to the feast. He knew the leaders laughed at his credentials, but he taught at the temple. He could be bold and courageous because he never forgot who he was.

He was the Word of God. He was the Son of God. He was Israel's Messiah. He was the Savior who would take away the sin of the whole world. He was not about to turn around now. He made up his mind to do the Father's will.

And let's be glad that he did. Looking ahead in John, we see that things are not going to get any easier for Jesus. He is going to face more adversity and acrimony. He is going to deal with more troubles and traps. He is going to confront more criticism and complaints. All because he is determined to do his Father's will.

Some may say that it was easy for Jesus to do this because he was Jesus. It is true that Jesus was fully divine. But it is also the case that he was fully human. So he knows our hurts and our weaknesses. He is familiar with our faults and our frailties. And, thankfully, he makes a promise that he is available whenever we trust him and depend on him.

He makes a promise of power that can get us through the rough times.

He makes a promise that can take our prayer life to higher heights and deeper depths.

He makes a promise that can keep us moving forward when we feel like turning back.

He makes a promise that can renew our strength when our tank is on empty.

Doing what the Father wants is not always easy, but there is good news.

The good news, according to Jesus, is that for anyone who wants to do God's will, the power of God working within us is so much stronger than anything that is working against us. Whatever we need to do, we are not doing it on our own.

On the last and greatest day of the Feast of Tabernacles, Jesus stood and said in a loud voice, "Let anyone who is thirsty come to me, and let the one who believes in me drink. As the scripture has said, 'Out of the believer's heart shall flow rivers of living water'" (vv. 37-38).

The rivers, also translated "streams," of living water indicate the presence of the Holy Spirit. The streams of living water within are the indwelling of the Spirit of God. One songwriter said it this way:

> Something within me, Lord
> That holdeth the reins
> Something within me
> That banishes pain
> Something within me, Lord
> That I can't explain
> All I know I thank my God
> I've got something within me.[3]

A stream of living water. The presence of the Spirit. Wherever God wants me to go, the Spirit has the power to lead me. Whenever God wants me to move, the Spirit has enough power to direct me. Whatever God needs me to do, the Spirit has the power to reveal it to me. God is on our side.

When we are afraid, we can trust God. When we are in trouble, we can depend on God. Let us go from this place remembering who we are, ready and willing to do what God has called us to do. Amen.

Notes

1. This sermon was preached on Palm Sunday.
2. C. S. Lewis, *Mere Christianity* (New York: Harper One, 1952) 52.
3. Stephen Hill, "Something Within," *Freedom Band*, (New York: Spring House, 2001). Based on a hymn by Lucie Eddie Campbell, see www.hymnary.org/text/preachers_and_teachers_would_make_their.

15

The Path to Freedom[1]

John 8

The word "free" has multiple meanings. We use the word when obstacles or barriers are removed. Once the path is free of fallen trees, we can continue the journey. "Free" also implies that we received something without charge. This may be our favorite definition of freedom. "How much did you pay for those tickets?" "Nothing, they were free."

There is another way in which the word "free" is used. It has to do with the enjoyment of personal rights and liberty. "Freedom" in this sense is the opposite of slavery. The quest for freedom has sparked revolutions, protests, sit-ins, boycotts, and even *coup d'états*. One of the most famous sayings in this country about freedom is reported to have come from the mouth of the American revolutionary, Patrick Henry. Speaking at a political convention held at St. John's Church in Richmond, Virginia, in 1775, he said, "Give me liberty or give me death."

This freedom for which Henry was willing to die was written into the founding documents of the United States of America: "We hold these truths to be self-evident, that all men are created equal; that they are endowed by their Creator with certain unalienable Rights, that among these are Life, Liberty and the pursuit of Happiness."

Liberty, of course, is freedom by another name. And yet we have frequent, tragic reminders that freedom has not come to every citizen equally. People are subjected to bias that they are guilty until proven innocent, often with tragic, even fatal consequences.

Something in every human being wants to taste freedom. We were not made to be caged in and confined. Human beings can and do adjust to less than ideal circumstances, but oppression is not what we were made for. We were made to be free.

Luke 4 records Jesus's first sermon, in which Jesus quotes from a passage in Isaiah: "The Spirit of the Lord is upon me, because he has anointed me to proclaim good news to the poor. He has sent me to proclaim freedom for the prisoners" (4:18, NIV). Jesus came to set people free.

The trouble described in John 8 is that the people Jesus tried to liberate told him they were already free. Jesus said, "You will know the truth, and the truth will make you free" (v. 32).

If any group of people thought they knew the truth, it was the crowd that came to question Jesus while he was teaching at the temple. Jesus was teaching a crowd of people at the end of the Festival of Tabernacles when he was interrupted by a delegation of scribes and Pharisees.

These were the religious experts, Israel's trained teachers. They knew Jesus's perspective on the Law and thought his interpretation and application of it was lax. So the leaders wanted to put Jesus in a position where they could accuse him of breaking the Law. They set a trap so they could use Jesus's words against him.

The trap involved bringing Jesus to a woman whom they claimed was caught in the act of adultery. Somehow the man with whom she was caught conveniently got away before he could be detained for questioning, so they only brought the woman to Jesus.

The scribes and Pharisees had the woman stand before everyone. They wanted to shame her and trap Jesus. Her head hung low with guilt. She did not say a word. She had no right to speak on her behalf. Surely she must have trembled at the thought of what this angry, hostile mob might do to her.

The Pharisees quoted a section of the Law that said a woman in this situation should be stoned. Then they asked Jesus what he had to say (v. 5). If he agreed to stone her, he would be in violation of Roman laws that prevented the Jewish people from carrying out death sentences. If he did not agree to stone her, he would be in violation of Jewish Law, destroying his credibility in the eyes of the people.

At first, Jesus did not say anything. He simply bent down and wrote on the ground with his finger. Theories abound about what Jesus wrote on the ground that day. Some say when he used his finger to write on the ground, it might have been a gesture to highlight his divinity because God used God's finger to write the Commandments on stone tablets for Moses. Some say Jesus wrote down a list of the sins of this woman's accusers.

Whatever he wrote, the Pharisees continued questioning Jesus. "What are you going to do about this woman?" Jesus says a lot in this chapter, more than can we can possibly address in even two sermons. But it seems that there are several things he says about being truly free. The story about the woman accused by the Pharisees says that if we are ever going to be free, we must abandon a legalistic, judgmental attitude and embrace a spirit of forgiveness.

To the Pharisees, the problem was what this woman had done wrong. The problem was her behavior. However, Jesus saw things differently. He did not ignore or excuse adultery. The woman's actions were sinful, as were the missing man's, and Jesus said so (v. 11). But the issue for Jesus was bigger than the wrong behavior. He went after the motives, attitude, and intentions of the accusers. He highlighted their legalistic mindset. They had a critical spirit that made them just as guilty of sin. They were in bondage to the sin of a judgmental attitude. Jesus came to set them free.

Eventually, he straightened up and said, "Let anyone among you who is without sin be the first to throw a stone at her" (v. 7). He then bent down again and wrote on the ground. The crowd fell completely silent. By this time one of the accusers may have slowly relaxed his grip on the woman's arm and taken a step back. No one knew what to say. Who was going to throw the first stone? Who was without sin?

Jesus never argued that the woman had not done anything wrong. He simply knew that her accusers were just as guilty as she was. Saints are not always saintly, and the guilty are often the ones who simply happen, this time, to get caught. Jesus knew that the people who brought the woman to him were not overly concerned about what kind of behavior was right. They were controlled by a judgmental, hypercritical, holier-than-thou attitude. This was a problem because a legalistic attitude is one sure sign that we are not fully free. But when we embrace a forgiving spirit, the chains fall off.

Being judgmental may mean that we are insecure about some areas in our own lives; we are jealous or envious of others; or we think that we are somehow perfect in every possible way. News flash! "All have sinned and fall short of the glory of God" (Rom 3:23).

Judgmental attitudes are a way of hiding the fact that we may not feel like we measure up to someone else. Sometimes we try to make ourselves feel better by finding fault with others. So Jesus does not let this moment pass without teaching the teachers a lesson.

Jesus said, "Let anyone among you who is without sin be the first to throw a stone" (v. 7). Stones signified condemnation and hatred. Jesus was not saying that there are no standards. He certainly had standards. But it is one thing to hold each other accountable by the same standards and something else to act as though the rules apply to everyone else while we enforce them. So even though Jesus was without sin, he set the example of mercy by not throwing the first stone. He poured out grace because he was not interested in this woman's death. He came to give new life.

He came to set people free from the prison of a judgmental attitude. Jesus did not seize this moment for condemnation. This was a time for forgiveness. Forgiveness may be the only true remedy for a judgmental attitude. Forgiveness lets me be merciful with others because I know God has been merciful with me. Forgiveness lets me be patient with others because I know God has been patient with me.

When the Pharisees heard Jesus, they went away one at a time, the older ones first, until only Jesus was left with the still-standing woman. Jesus straightened up. "Where are your accusers," he asked. "Has no one condemned you?" (v. 10). And you can hear the relief and excitement in her voice when she said, "No one, sir" (v. 11). Jesus said, "Neither do I condemn you. Go your way, and from now on do not sin again" (v. 11). She was forgiven. She was free to live a new life.

When Jesus spoke again to the people he said, "I am the light of the world. Whoever follows me will never walk in darkness but will have the light of life" (v. 12). He not only frees us from a judgmental attitude through forgiveness but also frees us *for* authentic life as we obey him. Jesus is the light of the world. He is the one who guides us into new life if we will follow him. "Obedience" is a word we try to avoid, but Jesus makes it clear that freedom is found in keeping his word.

When Jesus called himself the light of the world, there was probably a collective gasp from everyone in the crowd. This is the second "I am" statement in the Gospel of John. His "I am" statements were significant because in the Old Testament, God alone was identified by the phrase "I am." Each time these two words came from Jesus's lips, he was claiming to be divine.

Declaring during the Feast of Tabernacles that he was the light of the world was not a coincidence. Worshipers attending the feast looked forward to a nightly ritual of the lighting of the golden lamps of the tabernacles. Candelabras were set up in the temple's court of the women. The lights burned brightly and musicians played festive tunes. The lamps were lit each night to remind people of God leading the Israelites through the wilderness by a pillar of fire (Exod 13:21-22). The light represented the presence and power of God. So when Jesus says he is the light of the world, he means he is the One who can lead us out of darkness so we can walk in the light.

But he can only lead us when we follow. We know the importance of light in our lives. Light determines how we well we can see. When we are in total darkness, our eyes can be wide open and we can still bump into things. Light shows us what we cannot see with our natural eyes. Light reveals. If your house is like mine, you have nightlights in strategic places so that people who get up in the middle of the night can find their way without tripping and falling in the dark.

By telling us we will not walk in darkness, Jesus is saying that if we follow him, we will not spend our lives tripping and falling over our failures and faults. We can live in the freedom of knowing we are following someone who is the light of the world.

As we obey him, his love becomes a radiant ray of compassion shining in a shadowy world of indifference. Just as plants grow toward the sunlight, the light of the world leads us to life.

When Jesus is our light, we are drawn to him in prayer, in fellowship, in worship, and in service. He is the source and the sustainer of our life. Obeying him is not necessarily easy. There are always other options, but none of them leads to life. So, why would we want to take any other path? Freedom comes through obedience. Freedom comes through forgiveness.

Finally, freedom happens when we start living what is true.

Bill Wilson, also known as Bill W., founded a life-changing movement in 1935. That movement is now a household name. I'm talking about Alcoholics Anonymous, or AA. AA has twelve steps to guide people into a life of sobriety.

One of those steps, number 4, is to "make a searching and fearless moral inventory" of ourselves. This is about learning to see the truth about oneself. Alcoholics live in a perpetual state of denial. They think they can handle their drinking. They think nobody knows how much they drink. They think their life is not that bad. They do not think they drink as often as they actually do. Until the alcoholic faces the truth, he or she cannot be free.

He has to affirm the truth that he cannot stop whenever he wants to. She has to recognize the truth that she uses alcohol to avoid facing reality. Alcoholics must "make a searching and fearless personal moral inventory" if they ever hope to be free. A person can go through life pretending to be someone they are not. But that is not freedom. A person can go through life mainly trying to please other people, but that is not freedom. Only the truth can make us free.

Our country is at a crossroads once again. As another family lays to rest its loved one who was killed by a mixture of fear and blatant disregard for human life, people still seem to be unable or unwilling to talk about the truth. The truth is that race still matters in so many ways that we wish it did not. No one is going to be free until we face the truth.

We cannot avoid the truth. We cannot sweep the truth under the rug. In the word of the poet William Cullen Bryant, "Truth, crushed to earth, shall rise again."[2]

Knowing the truth, according to Jesus, is holding to his teaching. Another way of saying this is that knowing the truth means we abide in Jesus's word. To abide is to make your home someplace. Making our home in Jesus's word means staying with his teaching. It is the act of living under Jesus's teaching in faithful obedience. To abide in Jesus's word is to make him the guiding wisdom for our daily life. Jesus does not give any specifics about how to do this. It is as if he wants to say, "Give your life to me and you will see that God is at work in and through me."

Anyone who recognizes that the Father is in Jesus, that Jesus is in the Father, and that he and the Father are one, discovers that the truth will set them free (v. 28).

In the crowd that day were descendants of Abraham who had never in their lifetime been slaves. However, Jesus knew that a person who has never been a slave from a legal point of view can still be in bondage from a spiritual, social, emotional, or intellectual point of view. We can be in bondage to the need to be known by other people. We can be in bondage to a fear of failure. We can be in bondage to trying to keep up the perfect image. So much can keep us in bondage, but the promise Jesus makes is that when the Son sets you free, you will be free indeed.

The Pharisees did not believe Jesus could deliver on this promise. They did not believe who he was. But Jesus said to them, "You are from below, I am from above; you are of this world, I am not of this world" (v. 23). "The one who sent me is with me; he has not left me alone, for I always do what is pleasing to him" (v. 29). "Your ancestor Abraham rejoiced [at the thought of seeing] my day; he saw it and was glad" (v. 56).

When Jesus mentioned Abraham, the Pharisees asked how he had seen Abraham, as Jesus was not even fifty years old. Jesus said, "Very truly, I tell you, before Abraham was, I am" (v. 58).

At last, there is someone who is strong enough and wise enough to set us free. The Son of God is here.

In times when it seems like we are powerless against the weaknesses in our soul, the Son of God can set us free. When we cannot find the way out of the shadows of sorrow, if we wait on him and abide him, the Son can set us free.

Follow him. He knows the way through the maze of life. Obey his word. He is the light of the world. Abide in him, for those whom the Son sets free are truly free indeed.

Free from the power of sin. Free from the punishment of sin. Free from guilt and shame. Free from insecurities and anxieties. Free from fears and lies we have believed about ourselves.

Finally, we can be free because God has shown mercy and forgiven us. We become free as we obey Jesus's word. Once we know this truth and live this truth, this is the truth that will make us free. Amen.

Notes

1. This sermon was preached April 12, 2015. On April 9, news media outlets aired dashcam video footage from an incident in South Carolina where Walter Scott, an African-American man, was shot while running away from a white police officer.

2. William Cullen Bryant, "Truth, Crushed to Earth, Shall Rise Again," 1837, retrieved from https://hymnary.org/text/truth_crushed_to_earth_shall_rise_again.

16

Can You See?

John 9

In the first four chapters of John's Gospel, Jesus's divinity is boldly declared. John 1:18 says, "No one has ever seen God, but the one and only Son, who is himself God and is in closest relationship with the Father, has made him known" (NIV). In chapters 5–10, Jesus's divinity is debated. Jesus told them he was the bread of life and the people said, "Is this not Jesus, the son of Joseph, whose father and mother we know? How can he now say, 'I came down from heaven'?" (6:42, NIV).

In John 9 we come near to the climax in this debate about Jesus's divinity. It is also near the end of the Feast of Tabernacles that started in chapter 5, at which Jesus performed the first healing miracle in the Gospel of John. John 9 records the sixth miraculous sign in the Gospel. It is one man's powerful testimony about what the grace of God can do in our lives.

When Jesus went to the Feast of Tabernacles in Jerusalem in John 5, he came to the pool near the Sheep Gate and saw a man who had been lying there lame for thirty-eight years. The man had been there so long that he had become socially invisible. Jesus came into town, saw him, and went to him right away.

Hurting people attracted the most attention from Jesus. Jesus did not look over, look beyond, or look past broken people. For John to say that Jesus saw this disabled man is to say that he took notice of him. Jesus paid attention to him.

In chapter 4, Jesus sat down at a well in Samaria. It is as if his mission was to sit there and wait for the woman who was trying to avoid being seen. Jesus paid attention to people others barely noticed.

The pattern continues in John 9, where we read some of the most comforting words in the New Testament: "As he walked along, he saw a man blind from birth" (v. 1). This man was a beggar who had been blind from birth.

The contrasts between blindness and sight and darkness and light are the central themes of this chapter. As with most themes in John, these phrases have a double meaning. On the one hand, Jesus came to fulfill the promise in Isaiah 35:5 that Israel's messiah would give physical sight to the blind. God has compassion on those who have physical needs. God is not indifferent to the needs that arise in our day-to-day lives.

On the other hand, not all blindness is physical. Some blindness can be a spiritual condition. Sometimes we can see, but spiritually speaking we are blind. Some people are physically blind, but they have 20/20 insight. We have heard the expression that love can make a person blind. We can feel so strongly about someone that even when everyone else can see that the person is no good for us, we are blind and cannot see it. Love is not the only force that blinds our eyes. A person can be blinded by pride, by greed, by fear, or even by loyalty. When someone is blind, it is hard to reason with them. We can give them advice until the cows come home. We can rationalize with them from sunup to sundown. But when we are blind, we simply cannot see.

So many of the people Jesus encountered during his ministry could see with their eyes, but they were spiritually blind. They could not perceive who he was. They did not understand his wisdom. They had ears, but they did not hear. They had eyes, but they did not see. They were so blind to who he was that at the end of chapter 8 that Jesus had to slip away from the crowds because they wanted to stone him to death for claiming to be God. They could not touch him because his time had not yet come. And this is when Jesus came into contact with the beggar who was blind from birth.

"From birth" means that this man had never seen daylight. "From birth" implies that he had never witnessed the bright orange glow of a summer sun setting behind the Mount of Olives. "From birth" means that this man had never seen the joy one can notice only in the delight of a smiling child. He had never seen his mother's face, either. "From birth" means that since the moment he entered this world, he lived in total darkness. He was blind, and his community did not accommodate his disability.

In John 5, Jesus healed a man who had been lame for thirty-eight years. The power to heal a man blind from birth goes beyond anything we have seen before. Healing someone who had been lame for thirty-eight years was impressive, but we can assume that person was born with the ability to walk and became lame. Now Jesus will heal someone whose eyes have never worked. This man was blind from birth.

Jesus's method of healing was unconventional to say the least. He spat on the ground and made medicinal mud using his saliva. He put the mud on the man's eyes and told him to go wash in the Pool of Siloam. When the man went and washed his mud-caked eyes in the Pool of Siloam, he immediately and miraculously began to see. Some miracles do not happen until after we do what the Lord tells us to do.

Surely the reference to Siloam was intended to make us think about Jesus since Siloam means "sent" and Jesus is the one God *sent* into the world. This means that the miraculous healing of this man born blind was not about any power in the mud or in a pool. The miracle happened through Jesus, the One sent from God. The miracle happened so we might see that it does not matter what the conditions are or what they have been. God is the God of creation and the God of re-creation, so even when God has to start with nothing, God can turn it into something. Jesus touched eyes that had never seen before. Light poured into the man's eyes, signals about the light reached his brain, his brain processed them correctly, and the man saw.

We can ask many questions about this man. At the beginning of the chapter, when the disciples saw the man for the first time, before he had been healed, they asked a question about him. They saw his condition. They saw his suffering. So they asked Jesus, "Rabbi, who sinned, this man or his parents, that he was born blind?" (v. 2). They clung to the false notion that wherever there is suffering in a person's life, there is a direct connection with sin. Their only question was whose sin is to blame.

Since the blindness was congenital, the disciples wanted to know if this man had committed sin in the womb or if his parents had committed sin before he was born. The disciples were looking for the traditional explanation of suffering and sin. They thought they could see.

There must have been something in this man's personal past to explain the unfortunate circumstances in his present life. They wanted to find some reason that he deserved his blindness. How quickly we forget. When the Pharisees brought the woman caught in the act of adultery to Jesus, she deserved death but Jesus gave her life. This blind man did not deserve to be blind. His disability was not because of his parents' sin or sin he somehow committed in the womb.

It sounds silly to hear the disciples ask if the man was blind because he sinned in the womb, but we are all at times drawn in by this idea. We can see bad circumstances as divine punishment handed down by an angry God. We want to attach a specific sin to every misfortune. It can be hard to see what God might be doing during the painful seasons of our life, but Jesus assures us that if we have eyes to see, we might notice God working for us rather than against us. Who sinned? This man or his parents?

Jesus quickly redirected the disciples' question. He was not concerned in the least with pinpointing a moral failure as the reason for this man's sin. And it is not because there is never a connection between sin and suffering. It is just that we cannot say every instance of suffering is directly caused by something that person has done wrong.

Were the children at Sandy Hook Elementary or their parents being punished? Were the four girls killed in 1963 in the bombing of Sixteenth Street Baptist Church being judged for their sins or their parents' sins? The book of Job teaches us that we cannot generalize our conclusions about the connection between sin and suffering. Job was upright and feared God. He prayed. He worshiped. But by the end of the second chapter, Job had lost his livestock, his children, most of his servants, his livelihood, the support of his wife, and his own health. His friends tried to get him to confess his wrongdoing, but Job made it clear that he had done nothing to deserve what happened to him.

Jesus did not answer the question of whether the man or his parents sinned. Instead, he changed the question into a statement about the purposes of God. Jesus said, "Neither this man nor his parents sinned . . . , but this happened so that the works of God might be displayed in him" (v. 3, NIV). This does not mean the man or his parents were sinless. This means that the cause of the man's blindness was less important than what God was going to do with his blindness.

No one may be able to tell why certain tragedies, disappointments, and difficulties have happened in our lives. But it is the case that God can work through whatever happens in our lives for God's glory. God can take an orphan and turn her into a loving parent. God can take a demotion and turn it into a dream career. God can take our hurt and turn it into a ministry to serve others who are hurting. We do not always know the cause, but if we have eyes to see, we will notice that, as Paul wrote, "in all things God works for the good of those who love him, who have been called according to his purpose" (Rom 8:28, NIV).

Jesus was trying to give the disciples spiritual vision. He was trying to get them to stop looking for someone to blame for the lack of light and start seeing how God might be at work through the darkness. Think of the difference this kind of spiritual vision would make in our lives. When we can see spiritually, our imagination expands from "why did this happen?" to "what work is God going to accomplish through this?"

Fast-forward in the story and notice that the healing changed the blind man so dramatically that when he came back from the Pool of Siloam, his neighbors were not sure he was the same person. What an affirmation it would be for God to work in my life to such a degree that someone had to wonder if I were the same person they once knew.

The man's neighbors saw him coming down the street. He was not walking the same way anymore. He did not have a stick to feel the road or an arm to steady him. This is how they were used to seeing this man. Now that he'd had an encounter with Jesus, however, something was different about him. He was standing up straighter than he used to. He had more confidence than he once did. Now he could see.

Not only did his neighbors question him but the Pharisees also asked questions. Their resentment toward Jesus has been building throughout the first eight chapters. People wanted to stone Jesus not long ago, so it did not help that Jesus healed this man on the Sabbath day, breaking at least two Sabbath rules. First, he healed on the Sabbath when it wasn't a matter of life and death. Second, he kneaded mud with saliva. Kneading was considered work and, therefore, unlawful activity on the Sabbath.

Keeping our attention on the man who had been blind, we see that his eyes were opened both physically and spiritually. When his neighbors questioned him, he affirmed that he was the same man who had once been forced to beg. Beyond that, he did not know much about his healing. He did not know where the person was who healed him. He only knew that the man's name was Jesus. That is as much as he could see.

When the Pharisees questioned him, some of them came to the conclusion that whoever healed the man was not from God because he did not keep the Sabbath. A few of them asked how anyone could do such miracles if he were not from God. They turned to the man and asked, "What do you say about him? It was your eyes he opened" (v. 17). In other words, "tell us about your experience."

Speaking about Jesus, the man said, "He is a prophet" (v. 17). He moved from the language of "the man they call Jesus" to "He is a prophet." Already he was growing in his spiritual vision.

The Pharisees were so bewildered by the miracle that some doubted the man had ever been blind. So they sent for the man's parents. They asked the parents if their son was born blind. The parents said that he was, but they did not—or would not—say how he came to see. Their son could speak for himself.

The Pharisees summoned the man a second time. Ironically, the more they challenged him, the clearer he began to see and the more he shared. The Pharisees ordered him to tell the truth although they could not see the truth. They were blind to the man's answers. They even threatened to throw him out of the synagogue if he didn't say Jesus was a sinner (see v. 22).

If we learn anything from this story, it might be that growing in spiritual vision increases the boldness of our faith. At the beginning, this man had been a beggar, one of the lowliest positions in Israel's culture. He had no pedigree. He had no wealth. But once he encountered Jesus, he had a testimony. He had boldness based on his experience of God's grace.

The man said to the Pharisees, "I don't know whether he is a sinner. One thing I do know, that though I was blind, now I see" (v. 25). What gave him the audacity to speak with such boldness in the face of so much hostility? What gave him the fearlessness to stand his ground when folks tried to intimidate him? This man was growing in his faith. He was getting clearer in his spiritual vision. He now felt that he had as much a right as anyone to live. His faith was getting stronger the more it was challenged.

This man was not emboldened because of something he discovered in a textbook about the doctrine of God's grace. This man was not encouraged because of an inspiring lecture or even a sermon on the goodness of God. This man believed because he had encountered firsthand the transformative grace of the living Lord. The Pharisees condemned him. They said he was unworthy to lecture them on what Jesus was able to do.

But nothing and no one can turn us around once we have experienced the power of God in our lives. People can tell us that something won't work and give us a litany or reasons why something cannot work. But that cannot deter the person who can say, because of their experience, "I was blind, but now I see," or "I was in darkness, but now I'm experiencing light."

Threaten me. I was blind, but now I see. Persecute me. Try to discredit me. I will not bow. I will not bend. Once my world was nothing but darkness, but now I see the light of day.

After a while, Jesus showed up again. He came back when he heard that the Pharisees threw the man out of the synagogue. Jesus found the man and asked, "Do you believe in the Son of Man" (v. 35). In other words, you are no longer blind, but can you see? I gave you your sight, but can you see? Your eyes are working now, but can you see?

Do you believe in the Son of Man?

The man said, "Tell me who he is so that I may believe in him" (v. 36, translation mine). Jesus said, "You have seen him, and the one speaking with you is he" (v. 37). The man said, "Lord, I believe" (v. 38). An experience of God's grace can change our testimony and enlarge our faith. We once were blind, but now we see.

We had a need, but now we see that the Lord provides.

We were confused, but now we see that the Lord is wise.

We had to confess our sins, but now we see that the Lord is merciful.

We see that the Lord loves us. We see that the Lord can heal a broken heart. We see that Jesus is living water. We see that he is the bread of life. The only question that remains is the one the formerly blind man asked the Pharisees: "Do you also want to become his disciples?" (v. 27).

17

Inside the Heart of God

John 10

God's love is unlike any other love. God's love is holy. God's love is righteous. God's love is everlasting. God's love is true.

Even knowing all this about God's love, it seems nearly impossible to fully comprehend how much God loves us. Yes, we sing about God's love and we teach God's love, but it strains the mind to imagine how long, wide, deep, and high the love of God really is. As is written in Ephesians 2, "But because of his great love for us, God, who is rich in mercy, made us alive with Christ even when we were dead in transgressions—it is by grace you have been saved" (vv. 4-5, NIV).

The hymn writer Charles Wesley was so captivated by God's love that he did his best to describe the heart of God through the words of one of the sweetest melodies of the church: "Love divine, all loves excelling, joy of heaven, to earth come down."[1]

We can find on nearly every page in the Bible some word or reference pointing to the extravagance of God's love. David wrote in Psalm 25:6, "Remember, LORD, your great mercy and love, for they are from of old" (NIV). And in Psalm 32 he said, "Many are the woes of the wicked, but the LORD's unfailing love surrounds the one who trusts in him" (v. 10).

Thankfully, God's love is not rooted in how God feels about us from day to day or moment to moment. God's love is constant. One day Charles Spurgeon, the great English preacher of the nineteenth century, was walking through the countryside with a friend. As they strolled along, Spurgeon noticed a weather vane on top of a roof. On the weather vane were the words "God is love." Spurgeon told his friend that the weather vane was an inappropriate place for these words. Weather vanes are changeable, but God's love is constant. Spurgeon's friend disagreed with him about the words. He said, "Charles, you misunderstand the meaning. That sign indicates the truth that regardless of which way the wind blows, God is love."

God's love does not change. God loves because God is love. People live every day haunted by the feeling that their lives do not matter, but our insecurity can be vanquished with the belief that God loves us. When we encounter icy stares of rejection instead of the signs of a warm embrace, our souls can find rest in the peace of knowing that God loves us. This radical and unrelenting love is exactly what was on Jesus's mind in John 10.

John 10 gives us a glimpse inside the heart of God. But before we dive all the way into chapter 10, it is important to recognize its connection with chapter 9.

Even though we have started a new chapter, the people Jesus talks to in chapter 10 about God's love are the same people he called blind in chapter 9. They are religious leaders in Jerusalem, the Pharisees.

The Pharisees were supposed to be spiritual leaders, and yet they knew so little concerning the love of God. They knew about the love of God intellectually, but wanting to stone a woman caught in adultery in John 8 and throwing the formerly blind man out of the synagogue in John 9 demonstrates how little they practiced the love of God. Some of the Pharisees were so intoxicated on status and prestige that they had lost their way. So Jesus found himself once again in a direct confrontation with the people who wanted to kill him.

There are many questions we could ask at this point. How had people who knew so much about God been able to treat the woman and the man in the previous chapters so callously and cruelly? How did people so well versed in the Law completely miss the commandment to love the Lord your God with all your heart, mind, soul, and strength and to love your neighbor as yourself? These questions are not intended to give us a license to stand back and point accusing fingers at the Pharisees, which is easy to do. Rather, we need to be mindful that we do not take the same path. The Pharisees started out with the best intentions. But what sense did all the rules make if no one ever knew the heart of God and no one was transformed by the love of God? Jesus knew this, so he told a short story about shepherds and sheep in order to lift up his own life as the supreme example of God's everlasting love.

> Very truly I tell you Pharisees, anyone who does not enter the sheep pen by the gate, but climbs in some other way, is a thief and a robber. The one who enters by the gate is the shepherd of the sheep. The gatekeeper opens the gate for him, and the sheep listen to his voice. He calls his own sheep by name and leads them out. When he has brought out all

his own, he goes on ahead of them, and his sheep follow him because they know his voice. But they will never follow a stranger; in fact, they will run away from him because they do not recognize a stranger's voice. (John 10:1-5, NIV)

The Pharisees did not fully understand Jesus's figure of speech, so Jesus graciously offered a full explanation. In verse 7, he says, "I am the gate for the sheep." He repeats himself in verse 9: "I am the gate." Some translations say "door" instead of "gate." Either way, this is the first of the two "I am" sayings in chapter 10. The second "I am" saying appears in verse 11: "I am the good shepherd." Taken together, these two sayings give us a look inside the heart of God.

Everyone in Jesus's audience would have understood exactly what was involved in being a shepherd, but I suspect I may need to do some explaining this morning since not many of us have experienced herding sheep.

The image of a shepherd was a common description of kings, rulers, and leaders. In modern business settings, few managers or executives would want to be compared to a shepherd. In Israelite society, the shepherds were the lowest of the low. They were regarded as half-wild, living and working, sleeping and eating, in the fields with the animals. But in the world of Scripture, there was no higher accolade for a leader than to be called a shepherd. Jesus was making a statement about the kind of leader he was and what he came to do in our lives.

For one thing, shepherds cared about their sheep. In ancient Palestine—even in the present day—shepherds did not treat their sheep as commodities. Shepherds looked after their sheep with tenderness and compassion. They typically did not raise sheep to be slaughtered for meat, except maybe for an occasional sacrifice. Shepherds raised sheep to be used for wool. They needed their sheep to be healthy, well fed, and safe.

Herding sheep was hard, dangerous work. So after a long day of grazing the sheep, the shepherd led the sheep into an enclosure where they would be safe during the night. Each village had an enclosure, and all the shepherds in that village brought their sheep into one enclosure for the night.

The enclosure was often a stone fence in the shape of a circle or a square, which was closed in on all sides except for a single opening where the sheep were led in at night and brought out in the morning. This opening was the gate or the door of the sheep pen.

At night, when the shepherds went to sleep, a hired hand, or a porter, might have been paid to keep watch at the gate. He literally stretched his body out in front of the opening so that the sheep would not wander out of the pen while the shepherds rested. In the morning, only the shepherd was given access to the gate and allowed to come into the sheepfold and take out the sheep. Keep in mind that the only legitimate way into the enclosure was through the gate. Anyone who tried to get in by coming over the wall was, as Jesus pointed out, a thief or a robber (v. 1).

Jesus said, "I am the gate" (v. 9). This tells us something about God's love. Since the gate provided access to a safe place of rest and a refuge for the sheep, and Jesus is the gate, then whoever comes to God through him will be saved. In this instance, salvation means safety in danger, preservation through trouble, and protection from thieves and bandits.

Gates regulate who or what comes in and who or what goes out. The gate of the sheep enclosure was often the only thing standing between the sheep and life-threatening danger.

Wolves might be hiding behind any rock. Thieves were on the prowl to steal a sheep away from its shepherd. But as long as the gate was secure, nothing could get into the sheepfold to harm the sheep. Therefore, since Jesus declared himself to be the gate (the door), we know that it is his mission to regulate who has access to the sheep. And because the hired hands only open the gate for the true shepherds of the sheep, we can count on Jesus to guard our lives the same way the gate provided safety for the sheep.

As the gate, Jesus lovingly and wisely inspects anyone or anything coming into or going out of our lives. As the gate, Jesus can get us into safety and get us out of danger.

This may be why some of our prayers are not answered the way we want them to be answered. Maybe we prayed about something, but Jesus did not open the gate and grant what we prayed for because he knows better than we do who and what works for good in our lives. Some things and some people he let into our lives, and some he did not.

Some jobs don't come through until he opens the gate. Some dreams have to wait until he opens the gate. Sometimes Jesus even has to be the gate to keep us from going out and looking for greener grass, thinking we can find a better God, a stronger hope, or a greater peace. He knows that we will only get lost and lose our way. As frustrating as it is, Jesus loves us too much to open the gate.

One problem in chapter 10 is that the Pharisees thought they were the gate. They thought their word was final about who was in and who was out. So when the formerly blind man lectured them for not knowing how God could open his eyes, they kicked him out of the synagogue.

Have you ever been told you could not come in or that you did not belong? Fortunately, the people who say these things do not decide the final verdict because they are not the gate.

Jesus came back and found the man he had healed. He let the man know that even though he had been kicked out of the synagogue, he still had a place in the family of God. Jesus not only keeps things and people out of our lives that will steal, kill, and destroy but also brings us in, keeps us in, and leads us into a more abundant life. Or, as *The Message* Bible paraphrase says in verse 10, a "better life than they ever dreamed of."

Have you ever thought about some of the signs that are on doors? "Employees only." "Authorized access only." "No trespassing." "Do not enter." The good news this morning is that while not everyone can enter certain gates and doors, when Jesus is the gate, all are welcome. "Come to me, all you that are weary and are carrying heavy burdens, and I will give you rest" (Matt 11:28). "Everything that the Father gives me will come to me, and anyone who comes to me I will never drive away" (John 6:37). The invitation is given. The call has been extended. The gate is open.

In verse 11, Jesus goes on to say even more about the heart of God. He declares, "I am the good shepherd" (v. 11). Jesus was probably thinking back to something the prophet Ezekiel said.

In Ezekiel 34, the word of the Lord came to Ezekiel, telling him to prophesy against the shepherds of Israel and say to them that they were guilty of only taking care of themselves. Of course, the shepherds the Lord had in mind were not the ones in the fields with actual sheep. The Lord was expressing dissatisfaction with the people who had been called to lead Israel as priests and kings. They were only taking care of themselves.

The prophet went on to say to those shepherds, "You eat the curds, clothe yourselves with the wool and slaughter the choice animals, but you do not take care of the flock . . . . You have not strengthened the weak or healed the sick or bound up the injured. You have not brought back the strays or searched for the lost. You have ruled them harshly and brutally" (Ezek 34:3-4, NIV).

This was what Jesus thought about the shepherds of Israel. He could not see anything in them that looked like the love and affection between a shepherd and his sheep. He could not see the heart of God. But that is exactly what we see in Jesus.

He never took advantage of sheep. He never tried to profit on the backs of sheep. He never cared more about himself than he did about the sheep. He was never at ease when the sheep were wounded or suffering. Today we see examples of leaders who say they are doing good, but they have no regard for the sheep. They make payday loans at interest rates so high that people became financially enslaved. They use their celebrity status as a license to make bombastic comments on social media, fueling fear and distrust in local communities.

Jesus, though, was a good shepherd.

One of the characteristics of a good shepherd is how well they know each sheep. This is why Jesus says the shepherd calls his own sheep by name and leads them out.

A fascinating fact about sheep herding in Jesus's day and even in Israel today is that when the shepherds wanted to collect their sheep, they did not use sheep dogs. They stood among the sheep that may have belonged to several shepherds and called their own sheep by name. The shepherd knew their names, and the sheep knew the shepherd's voice.

Jesus is the good shepherd who knows every sheep by name. Sometimes we fail to fully realize how uniquely we are made, but God knows us by our names and not by numbers.

Howard Thurman spoke to graduates at Spelman College in 1980 and encouraged them to listen in life for what he called the "sound of the genuine." He said, "Nobody like you has ever been born. And nobody like you will ever be born again. You are the only one."

This might be another way of saying that you and I have a name that only God knows, a name that makes us who we are. Our name sets us apart from another individual.

God took great care in naming people. Each name spoke to something significant about that individual, something that God recognized and noticed and valued as unique. Nobody like you has ever been born. This world puts pressure on us to fit in and conform such that when we are just a few degrees different than the norm, we can feel as though we do not belong, like no one knows our name.

But the good shepherd knows our name and calls us by name. Jesus knows every sheep—that's you and me—cares for every sheep, values every sheep. He knows our name. And that means more than the word by which people know us. Jesus knowing our names means he knows every detail of our lives.

The good shepherd knows our hurts. God knows our name. The good shepherd knows the prayers we pray. God knows our name. The good shepherd knows our gifts and our weaknesses. God knows our name. The good shepherd knows our fears and our disappointments. God knows our name.

The good shepherd knows our dreams and our doubts, our resources and our needs. God knows our name.

God not only knows our name but also calls us by name. And when the sheep hear the shepherd calling their name, they follow him where he leads. Sheep do not follow the voice of a stranger. Sheep do not follow the voice of fear, pride, ego, or popularity. Sheep listen for the voice of their good shepherd.

When we listen to the voice of Jesus the good shepherd and follow his voice, we inevitably find out how much he loves us. Because sooner or later a wolf is going to come, and a stranger will not protect the sheep. A hired hand is not going to defend the sheep. He will abandon the sheep and run away.

But the good shepherd will not leave the sheep. The good shepherd will never abandon the sheep. When the wolf comes, the good shepherd will lay down his life for the sheep. This is the essence of God's love.

Jesus was willing to give his life to give us life. Jesus was willing to lie down so that we could stand up. This is what he did on the cross. He laid down his life for the sheep. This is the depth of God's love.

For every sheep that is lost, he'll lay down his life to bring it back home. He is the good shepherd. For every sheep that is weary, he'll lay down his life to give it rest. He is the good shepherd. For every sheep that is wounded, he'll lay down his life to help it heal. This is the love of God.

He knows us by name. He is the gate of our life. He brings us life and life more abundant. He lays down his life in order to give us life. Then, after he lays it down, he picks it up again and he holds us in his hand.

No one can snatch us out of his hand. "My father, who has given [the sheep] to me, is greater than all; no one can snatch them out of my Father's hand. I and the Father are one" (vv. 29-30, NIV).

And so we can truly sing along with Charles Wesley:

Love divine, all loves excelling, joy of heaven to earth come down.
Fix in us Thy humble dwelling; all thy faithful mercies crown.
Jesus, thou art all compassion, pure, unbounded love thou art;
visit us with thy salvation; enter every trembling heart.[2]

Notes

1. Charles Wesley, "Love Divine, All Loves Excelling," 1747, retrieved from www.hymnary.org/text/love_divine_all_love_excelling_joy_of_he.
2. Ibid.

Resurrecting Faith

John 11

Up to this point in the Gospel of John, the disciples have already seen so much to inspire and motivate their faith in Jesus as the Son of God. This is significant because in one sense, faith should grow over time. Faith is never a thing we put on the shelf and say is complete. As the apostle Paul said to the Philippians, "Not that I have already obtained this or have already reached the goal, but I press on to make it my own, because Christ Jesus has made me his own" (3:12). Paul continued striving to reach just a little higher and go a little farther.

We do not see faith grow in the way that we can see trees grow or children grow. We cannot measure growth in faith on a chart or with a time lapse camera that takes pictures over time. Growing faith does not follow a neat, linear path. Nevertheless, faith does grow.

Growing faith opens up new possibilities. Growing faith enriches and enlarges our experience of life in the Spirit. In the Gospel of John, the word to describe faith is the word "believe." To believe is to surrender to, depend on, and trust in someone or something. In our culture, the basic approach to life is to first see and then trust. However, a growing faith challenges us to trust before we see.

The difficulty we face is that when we commit to trusting God, there is always something pulling us back to where we feel more comfortable, to that which is more familiar. Thankfully, the Lord never tires of leading and guiding us through experiences that help us trust God more and more.

One of the patterns we see in the Gospels is that faith, or belief, does not happen all at once. We need not feel ashamed if our faith in God did not blossom overnight, in one worship service, or after reading one particular passage of Scripture. We can see from the events of John 11 that often we pass through phases or stages that increase or deepen our belief and trust in the Lord.

The story in John 11 is unlike anything we have seen up to this point. The action begins when Jesus receives word that a friend named Lazarus is sick. Lazarus was from the village of Bethany. He was Mary and Martha's brother. We have not yet heard anything about Mary, Martha, and Lazarus in the Gospel of John, but these are three people Jesus knew quite well. Bethany was outside the city of Jerusalem. Jesus went to their home on his trips to and from Jerusalem to enjoy the gracious hospitality of his friends.

It is a wonderful thing when we know we are counted among the friends of Jesus. Jesus had plenty of admirers. He had countless observers. He had numerous spectators who came to watch him whenever a great miracle was performed. Even today, Jesus has many admirers, observers, and spectators. But why settle for admiration and observation when another dimension of relationship is available to us, one that goes beyond casual acquaintanceship? Why settle for what others tell us about Jesus when we can have the kind of closeness with him that allows us to hear his voice for ourselves?

Mary, Martha, and Lazarus had a sincere, intimate relationship with Jesus. They were counted among his friends. Because of this friendship, when Lazarus became ill, Mary and Martha did not hesitate to send word to Jesus that "the one you love is sick" (v. 3, NIV).

What a testimony to Lazarus's life that when Mary and Martha sent word to Jesus, they only needed to say that "the one you love is sick" (v. 3, NIV). They did not need to send a biographical sketch or even a name. They did not have to remind Jesus of who they were. It was enough to say that "the one you love is sick."

Lazarus's body temperature spiked, his energy bottomed out, and beads of cold sweat ran down the side of his face. Sickness can be devastating. Sickness can interrupt the normal routine of daily life. But strangely enough, Lazarus's sickness and ultimately his death proved to be a catalyst for Mary and Martha's faith.

The turning point in the growth of resilient and life-giving faith was that Mary and Martha were confronted with a crisis they could not handle on their own. To be sure, a crisis does not always make us grow in faith. We can choose not to grow. But often a crisis, a test, or a trial is the occasion when genuine faith begins to grow.

Lazarus's sickness and his death tested Mary, Martha, and the disciples because his sickness brought to the foreground the reality that being loved by God does not spare us from sadness, sorrow, or even death. Even the people Jesus loves encounter suffering. We should not excuse the unnecessary suffering that people experience as a result of abuse, exploitation, injustice, and prejudice. But the truth is that sometimes we can be right where God wants us to be and still experience the unforeseen and the unfortunate. We encounter roadblocks. Marriages have challenges. Children have troubles. Souls get weary. Friends are not always true. Families do not always stick together. Careers encounter setbacks.

Psychiatrist M. Scott Peck wrote a best-selling book decades ago titled *The Road Less Traveled.* The first words of that book are "Life is difficult." Peck did not write that life is difficult for some people. Having considered the clients he counseled over the years, he came to the conclusion that one thing common to us all is that life is difficult. Life is beautiful, and it is difficult. Life is a gift, and it is difficult. Life gives us much for which we can be thankful, and life is difficult.

Lazarus was Jesus's friend, but he was not exempt from the troubles of this world. Mary and Martha counted Jesus among their regular houseguests, but they were not spared from the vicarious pain we feel when someone we love is hurting. Jesus cared about them, but they were not immune to the hard parts of life. Fortunately, God can use crises to raise our faith.

The Scriptures go to great lengths to tell us this is so. Out of the mouth of Job we hear the words, "Though he slay me, yet will I trust him. Through all my appointed time, I'm going to wait until my change comes" (13:15, translation mine). The apostle James encouraged us, "whenever you face trials of any kind, consider it nothing but joy, because you know that the testing of your faith produces endurance" (Jas 1:2-3). God is able to bring something good out of the most challenging moments. We cannot be certain of how God will do this, but God does it. This is what energizes our faith when we face a crisis.

God can use a crisis to renew our minds, to revive our souls, and to rekindle our hope. God can use a crisis to encourage our perseverance, eliminate our fears, and build up our courage. God can use a crisis to purify our hearts, reorder our priorities, and make us stand still. God can use a crisis to work on us and to show us who he is.

Revealing himself seems to be the goal Jesus had in mind for Mary, Martha, and his disciples in John 11. After receiving the message that Lazarus was sick, Jesus stayed where he was two more days. Then he said to his disciples, "Let us go to Judea again" (v. 7). Jesus had been keeping a low profile for a few months because the Pharisees wanted to arrest him and kill him.

Thinking Jesus might not have remembered this significant, life-threatening detail, the disciples said, "Rabbi the Jews were just now trying to stone you, and are you going there again?" (v. 8). The disciples could only see a clear and present danger.

The disciples felt sure that Lazarus's sickness was going to lead to certain death for Jesus and probably for them. Going back to Judea was a risk they did not want to take. But Jesus knew it was a risk they needed to take. How about us? What is God calling us to do that can only be done if we walk by faith? The disciples wanted to follow Jesus, but following Jesus back to Judea did not make sense.

The beginning stage of faith was the crisis of Lazarus's sickness and the challenge of going back to Judea. John 11 goes on to suggest that if we do not give up at the moment of crisis, we will come to another stage of faith, which is choosing to believe that frustrations in life do not overrule the faithfulness of God.

When Jesus came to Bethany, he found that Lazarus was already dead. Lazarus had been in the tomb for four days, which meant the crisis was worse now than it was when Mary and Martha had sent word to Jesus. Four days was the definitive period for pronouncing someone dead. No one held on to hope of a miraculous recovery after the third day following a person's death. Many of the Jewish people believed that on the fourth day after a person died, the spirit left the body. Without the spirit, there was no hope for life to return. Lazarus was dead.

So when Jesus arrived at the home of his dear friends, Mary and Martha, as far as they were concerned, it was too late. Nothing else could be done. Martha summed up what everyone was thinking in her first words to Jesus.

Hearing Jesus was nearby, she went out to meet him. She said to him, "Lord, if you had been here, my brother would not have died" (v. 21). She knew that it had been four days since her brother died. Had Jesus arrived one day earlier, he might have been able to do something about Lazarus. Now there was only time for mourning.

We can hear in Martha's words that she did have enough faith to think Jesus could have kept Lazarus from dying. Nevertheless, she was disappointed in his delayed arrival. What had taken Jesus so long to get there? She sent word in plenty of time for him to do something about her brother's sickness. Jesus did not arrive when she called. Now there was nothing anyone could do because too much time had passed.

Jesus was not concerned about time. He only wanted Martha and Mary to know that if they recognized who he was, they would discover that delays do not have the last word. Sickness will not have the last word. Disappointment will not have the last word. Failure will not have the last word. God is faithful. This is the hope that raises our faith from day to day.

Martha affirmed her confidence in Jesus, saying, "But even now I know that God will give you whatever you ask" (v. 22). Two words let us know that although Martha was disappointed, her faith was still at work. She said, "even now."

"Even now" is the affirmation that the circumstances I am in are not enough to turn me around. "Even now" comes from the confidence that the frustrations in this life do not overrule the faithfulness of God. "Even now" expresses the assurance that nothing is too hard for God. "Even now" is the declaration that if God is for us, it matters not who is against us. "Even now" is the language of growing faith.

Jesus heard this expression of faith and said to Martha, "Your brother will rise again" (v. 23). Martha was a faithful Jewish woman who believed the teachings of the rabbis concerning life after death. She said to Jesus, "I know that he will rise again in the resurrection on the last day" (v. 24). She knew that she would see her brother again at a time that the prophets called "the last day." She knew that the righteous dead would be raised one day in the future. But that is not what Jesus had in mind. Jesus was not talking about the future. He was talking about Lazarus rising from the dead right now.

Jesus looked at this brokenhearted sister and said, "I am the resurrection and the life. Those who believe in me, even though they die, will live, and everyone who lives and believes in me will never die. Do you believe this?" (vv. 25-26).

Jesus invited Martha to realize that she did not have to wait until life after death to see her brother again. She did not have to wait until some distant future for something to change. Jesus is the resurrection and the life right now. Martha did not have to stuff her expectations into a bag labeled "someday." Jesus is the resurrection today. He is the giver of life today. Faith comes to its apex when it reminds us that wherever Jesus is, there is hope today.

Jesus did not say that he *will be* the resurrection. He said "*I am* the resurrection." This is the hope in every crisis: the Lord is able to raise dead things back to life *today*. This is the spring that catapults faith to the next level: whenever Jesus is at work, there is no limit to his power. This is a melody we sing when our hearts are heavy: I am the resurrection and the life. This is the ground of our faith.

Jesus saw Mary weeping and asked, "Where have you laid him?" (v. 34). The mourners led Jesus to the tomb. Jesus was so moved by the death of his friend that he stood there and wept. Jesus weeping is but one example of the vulnerability of God. God is moved by our misery.

Jesus stood at the entrance of the tomb and said, "Take away the stone" (v. 39). But by now there was no earthly reason to take away the stone. Lazarus had been dead four days. Martha reminded Jesus that the odor of decomposing flesh inside the tomb was going to be overwhelming. But Jesus said, "Did I not tell you that if you believed, you would see the glory of God?" (v. 40).

If you believe this, you will see that nothing is too hard for the Lord.

If you believe this, you will see that dead things can live again.

If you believe this, you will see that as long as Jesus is with us it is not too late to hope.

Jesus said to take him to the tomb. Take him to the problem that looks impossible to solve. Take him to the hurt that hasn't healed. Take him to the pain that lingers. He is the resurrection and life.

If you believe this, then there is a good chance your faith is growing. And if your faith is growing, you will discover that what you see now is not necessarily all there is to see.

They took Jesus to the tomb and rolled away the stone. Jesus prayed and then called in a loud voice, "Lazarus, come out!" (v. 43). And John says the dead man came out, his hands and feet still wrapped in linen. Jesus said, "Unbind him, and let him go" (v. 44).

And the man who was dead came out of the tomb alive. Lazarus was a walking, talking, living, breathing testimony to the power of faith and the power of God. And the good news is that even now, God is still raising what was dead back to life.

Do you believe this?

Yes, the wait has been long. Yes, the hurt has been slow to heal. Yes, the odds seem overwhelming. But Jesus is the resurrection and the life. Take him to the tomb. Let him speak life. That which was dead will rise again. Amen.

19

Giving God the Best

John 12:1-11

By now everyone living in the little village of Bethany must have heard what Jesus did for his friend Lazarus who had died.

Jesus walked up to a tomb containing the body of his friend Lazarus. He commanded that the stone covering the entrance be taken away. When the stone was removed, the stink and stench of death came rushing out of the cave like a flood, but Jesus did not flinch, faint, or back away. He lived up to what John told us about him in chapter 1: "in him was life, and [that] life was the light of all people" (v. 4).

Jesus looked up to heaven, thanked his Father, and said, "Lazarus, come out!" (11:43). Lazarus came out of the tomb still wrapped and bound by linen strips. People would not have believed it if they had not seen it. Lazarus was alive! It has been pointed out many times in the history of Christian preaching that if Jesus had not called Lazarus by his name, the whole graveyard would have been raised from the dead!

As you might expect, many people who saw what happened to Lazarus began believing in Jesus. Raising someone back to life was sufficient evidence for them to believe that Jesus was the Son of God. No one since the prophet Elijah had been so filled with the power of God that they could bring a dead person back to life.

This was a genuine resurrection, which is different from resuscitation. Medically speaking, resuscitation happens when someone loses consciousness but is not pronounced dead. Through CPR or some other life-saving measure, the person regains consciousness and full vitality. Resurrection is what happens after someone has died and there is no more life left.

This is why it was so amazing that Jesus could speak a word over a dead man's body and bring him back to life. It is just as Jesus told us in John 10:10: "I came that they may have life, and have it abundantly." It all comes down to one question. Will we trust him?

You would think that given Jesus's power over death everyone would have put their trust in him. But some people, according to John 11:46, went to Jesus's opponents and told them what Jesus had done. Once people reported to the Pharisees that Jesus had raised someone from the dead, the system of power and privilege immediately went to work to eliminate Jesus as a threat to the status quo.

This is not too surprising since Jesus's words and actions often caused division and even led to a falling away. For example, when Jesus said, "I am the bread of life. . . . Whoever eats of this bread will live forever; and the bread that I will give for the life of the world is my flesh," some of those who were with him turned back and did not follow him any longer (6:35, 51).

Jesus's words and actions separated the casually interested from the seriously committed. His words and actions tested loyalties and allegiances. This is why even after he raised Lazarus back to life, some of the people believed in him and some reported him.

When the chief priests and the Pharisees heard the report about Jesus, they called a meeting of the Sanhedrin. The Sanhedrin was the main court of the Jewish people at the time, functioning under Roman jurisdiction. The Sanhedrin consisted of around seventy members, chaired by the high priest. The members of the Sanhedrin were not necessarily devout, but they were influential and made important decisions concerning religious life. Seeing Jesus growing in popularity and power threatened their positions. They had to do something fast.

Jesus was doing miracles that inspired people to trust him more and be less afraid. And once someone is no longer afraid of death, once a person believes that death is no match for God's power, there really is not much you can hold over his or her head. So the Sanhedrin decided they had to get rid of Jesus.

Therefore, John says at the end of chapter 11, Jesus no longer moved about publicly among the people of Judea (v. 54). This is when the Gospel of John takes a turn. The first eleven chapters focused on Jesus's public ministry as he did miracles, signs, and wonders among the people. But now that the plot to kill him has intensified, he begins a more private phase of his ministry where he mainly focuses on his disciples and those closest to him.

This brings us to chapter 12. Given all the tension, unrest, and unease in the atmosphere in Jerusalem, we would think that anyone who knew Jesus would want to keep as far away from him as possible to preserve their own safety. Jesus was enemy number one. His face was on wanted posters in every corner of the city. Anyone who cared about his or her own life should not want to be anywhere close to Jesus.

So it's intriguing that in the twelfth chapter of John, just after we are told that the Sanhedrin was looking to arrest Jesus, we learn that Mary, Martha, and Lazarus are having a dinner party with him. The table has been set. The food has been prepared. The meal has been served. Everyone is having a good time.

This makes me wonder if one of the gifts of being in relationship with Jesus is that when the whole world is gripped by fear and anxiety, peace is still possible. It is possible to be in a storm and not be driven by the storm. It is possible to be calm when life is chaotic.

When was the last time we did something we should have been afraid to do, but faith gave us the courage to do it? Mary, Martha, and Lazarus knew Jesus was under surveillance, and yet they invited him into their home for dinner. This was an act of courageous commitment. This dinner party was to honor Jesus, and it was also to show him their gratitude.

All we have to do is consider what Mary does in the middle of the dinner party. The text tells us that Martha served while Lazarus reclined at the table with Jesus. In typical Near Eastern style, they did not sit in chairs for the meal, no matter how many Last Supper pictures portray the meal this way. People leaned on one arm next to the table with their feet going away from the table. They passed the food and ate with the hand that was free.

While the meal was served, Mary came into the presence of the men at the table, which was against cultural norms but seemed quite acceptable to Jesus. She came over to him with a pint of expensive perfume called nard. Mary poured this excessive, extravagant quantity of high-quality, pure perfume on Jesus's feet and began wiping his feet with her hair.

You can imagine the murmurs and whispers around the table. What is Mary doing? Why is she doing this? Why is Jesus allowing her to do this? Do they know what people might say? These are a few of the thoughts that were likely going through the minds of the guests at this dinner party when Mary poured expensive perfume on Jesus's feet and wiped his feet with her hair. If Mary was trying to keep a low profile given the death threats against Jesus, she went about it the wrong way. Mary wasn't concerned about what anyone thought. She did what she did as an expression of genuine gratitude. The nard was probably one of the most expensive items she owned. She gave Jesus the best she had to give because she was thankful.

Mary's gift was so extravagant that one of the disciples, Judas Iscariot, objected. "Why wasn't this perfume sold and the money given to the poor?

It was worth a year's wages" (v. 5, NIV). Not many of us can imagine taking something that's worth one year of our annual salary and putting it in the offering plate on Sunday morning (although no one will stop you!). But this is what Mary did to Jesus. She took expensive perfume, not the au de toilet. This was the pure, 100 percent, undiluted fragrance. Mary gave this lavish gift because she was thankful. And why shouldn't she be thankful?

Not long ago, she was at a funeral for her brother Lazarus. Not long ago, she was mourning helplessly in the face of death. Not long ago, she was crying, asking Jesus why he had not come to see her sooner. But now her brother was alive again. She could look into Lazarus's eyes once more. She could hear his laughter again. Jesus had raised him from the dead. For that reason, she felt obligated to say thank you by giving Jesus her best.

Perhaps we need to take a spiritual inventory of our lives. How well and how often do we tell the Lord thank you? When we think about what God has turned around, turned over, and turned back, our gratitude should be nearly impossible to restrain. If we are not careful, we will find ourselves giving God only what we think is required. Mary was not concerned about what was required because she was motivated by gratitude and love.

Giving out of love always goes beyond giving what is required. Just take a look at grandparents. Most grandparents have the mysterious capacity to look at a child and see all the joys and none of the responsibility. This allows them to give way beyond what is required and focus on love and gratitude for this new generation.

Mary could not help thinking about how blessed she was that she had her brother back alive. Her whole being overflowed with gratitude. She knew Jesus had done something for her that she could not do for herself. She knew he had made something happen that was beyond her power to make happen. And the realization that she had been a witness to and the beneficiary of God's power made her want to pour out this perfume and wipe his feet with her hair as a way to say thank you.

The psalmist asked the question, "What shall I return to the LORD for all his goodness to me? I will lift up the cup of salvation and call on the name of the LORD. I will fulfill my vows to the LORD in the presence of all his people" (Ps 116:12-14, NIV).

This is why I am so thankful to have something to give when it is time to give my tithe and offering. Sometimes we busy ourselves trying to figure out whether it is enough to tithe off the gross income or tithe off the net income because we do not want to make the mistake of giving God too much. We do not want to give more than is required. But we can be thankful today that God never calculates our blessings this way.

God has never asked God's self, should I bless my child with a gross blessing or with a net blessing? God has never asked how little God can give us. God just opens up God's hands and pours out blessing upon blessing upon blessing upon blessing so that we scarcely have room enough to receive the bounty. And these are not necessarily financial rewards. So many of the blessings we need money cannot buy!

We are alive—that's a blessing. We are still dreaming—that's a blessing. We have been knocked down, but we did not stay down—that's a blessing. Don't let anyone fool you. You can't beat God at giving no matter how hard you try. Mary gave her best because she was grateful for what the Lord had done.

Mary also gave her best because she knew she did not have much time left to serve Jesus. Mary could have easily decided to wait and say thank you to Jesus at some later time. She could have held back that expensive perfume until "someday," but she decided today was the day. It's tempting to say that we will get around to serving God or giving thanks "one day," but today is the day.

Judas objected to Mary's extravagance. John informs us that Judas did not object because he cared so much for the poor but because he was a thief. He kept the money for the disciples and he skimmed off the top for himself. Jesus silenced the critics by saying, "Leave her alone.... It was intended that she should save this perfume for the day of my burial. You will always have the poor among you, but you will not always have me" (vv. 7-8, NIV). Mary gave her best to God because she knew she did not have much time. It was imperative that she do whatever she was going to do now and not later.

This text has been twisted and taken out of context by people who suggest that there is no need to help the poor because they will always be with us. That is not the point Jesus was making. The emphasis was not on the persistence of poverty. The emphasis was on the brevity of the opportunity to do something for him. "You will not always have me" (v. 8). In verse 35, Jesus tells them, "You are going to have the light just a little while longer. Walk while you have the light, before darkness overtakes you."

Jesus was the light. He was saying that he was only going to be with the disciples a little while longer. He knew that his death would happen soon. Soon the Pharisees and the chief priests would arrest him. They would fabricate lies and falsely accuse him. He would be sentenced to death by crucifixion, and that sentence would be carried out on a hill called Golgotha. His hour was soon to come.

Mary was motivated to give this extravagant gift of love to Jesus because he was not going to be with her much longer. Time was running out. The fact that we do not have forever to serve God and to show gratitude to God should inspire us to be faithful with the time we do have.

The knowledge that time is short should encourage us not to hold back, hoard, and cling to everything we have as if we can take it with us when we die. And for many of us this isn't even about money. We give freely of our financial resources, but what about our time and our attention? Like Mary, each of us possesses something of great value that can honor God if we use it for God today and not tomorrow.

Some of us have a voice. We need to sing today. Some of us have wisdom. We need to share it today. Some of us have time. We need to spend it today. Some of us have money. We need to give it today.

Mary knew that one day it was going to be too late. One day the Father was going to call the Son back to his seat at the right hand of the Father. She was determined to do something now. This way, whenever the day of his crucifixion came, she would not have any regrets about what she did not do. She would not have any remorse about a missed opportunity to serve. She would be able to say that she did what she could with what she had while she had the opportunity.

John says a large crowd of people found out that Jesus was at Mary's house and came to see him. They came, John says, not only to see Jesus but also to see Lazarus. They came to lay their eyes on a man who was the only person they knew who made a round trip journey to and from death. Lazarus was the only man whose passport had been stamped for entry and exit to and from eternity. They wanted to hear the testimony of one who had slipped into the darkness of death and had been called back to the marvelous light.

But I think there is another reason they came to Mary's house. The crowd came to see Lazarus, and I think the crowd also came because they smelled the fragrance of Mary's perfume. When she poured the perfume on Jesus's feet, the fragrance filled the entire house. People in the front of the house could smell the nard in the back of the house. And I suspect that as high quality as the perfume was, the fragrance not only filled the house but also drifted out the windows. Once it drifted out, it floated down the street, and everybody whose nose caught the aroma wanted to know where it had come from. They were drawn to Mary's house, which inevitably drew them to Jesus.

And church, I submit to you that when we give our best to God, every deed, every word, and every gesture will leave a fragrance in the air. And that fragrance will spread far beyond us such that someone else will catch the scent of our service. And when they catch the scent of our service, what we have done for Jesus will affect untold lives in unknown places and in unknown ways.

When we give our best, what we do for Christ seeps out beyond the borders of our own awareness, and others experience the benefit of the good we offer to God. Who knows what will happen to the child we mentor? But someone will smell the fragrance. Who knows where they will go and the decisions they will make? Someone will smell the fragrance. When we raise an offering for Liberia, who knows how those gifts will contribute to the transformation of a child, a school, or even the entire nation. But someone will smell the fragrance. When you visit the sick, pray for the prisoner, care for the wounded, listen to the lonely, or sit with a hurting soul, you may never know how it will make a difference. But if you give your best, someone is going to smell the fragrance.

So give God the best that you have. Give God the best faith you have. Give God the best love you have. Give God the best surrender you have. Give God the best confession you. Because the Lord has given us the best. The best mercy. The best patience. The best grace. Now I know the answer to the question David asked: "What shall I return to the LORD for all his goodness toward me?" (Ps 116:12).

"All to Jesus, I surrender, all to him I freely give I will ever love and trust him, in his presence daily live."[1]

Note

1. Judson W. Van DeVenter, "I Surrender All," 1896, retrieved from https://hymnary.org/text/all_to_jesus_i_surrender.

20

Searching for Something More

John 12:12-50

In chapter 6 of the Gospel of John, Jesus satisfied a famished multitude by making a meal with only five loaves of bread and two fish. After everyone had eaten and people realized what Jesus had done, they began to say, "Surely this is the Prophet who is come into the world" (John 6:14, NIV). John says that Jesus knew the crowds intended to make him a king by force so he withdrew to a mountain by himself.

He clearly did not want to be their king. Yet in John 12, the day after Mary anoints Jesus with a pint of pure perfume, Jesus comes into Jerusalem where he is hailed as the ruler of Israel.

People took palm branches and went out to meet him shouting, "Hosanna! Blessed is the one who comes in the name of the Lord—the King of Israel!" (v. 13). Palm branches were familiar symbols of military victory.

But this time, Jesus did not withdraw right away and hide when the people hailed him as king. Had Jesus changed his mind? Did he now want to be made a king? We will see in a moment that the answer is no, or at least not really, but Jesus's grand entry into Jerusalem definitely attracted a great deal of attention.

A massive multitude gathered in Jerusalem for the annual Passover festival. Verse 17 indicates that among the people in the city was the crowd who had witnessed Jesus raising Lazarus from the dead. Other people who had not witnessed the miracle but had only heard about it learned that Jesus was coming, so they went to see the royal parade, waving palm branches and shouting, "Blessed is...the king of Israel!" (v. 13). They must have wondered if their king had finally come. If Jesus was their long-awaited king, then finally all their revolutionary hopes would be fulfilled.

Also in the crowd were Pharisees who now had all the evidence they needed to arrest Jesus. They saw him surrounded by throngs of people and said to one another, "See, this is getting us nowhere. Look how the whole world has gone after him!" (v. 19, NIV).

It was not quite the whole world going after Jesus, but John was clear that word about Jesus had definitely spread beyond the regions of Galilee and Judea. Also in the crowd were *Greeks* who came up to Jerusalem to worship at the Passover festival (v. 20). We do not know exactly where they came from, but we do know they were searching.

Life seems to be a perpetual search. We search for friends. We search for purpose. We search for contentment. We search for recognition. We search for fulfillment, for love, for peace, and ultimately for God. The search for God is, of course, the search beneath almost every other search. We were created to know God and be in relationship with God. And the aspect of God within us will not stop searching until we are found by the One who made us. We do not know where these Greeks started their search, but they came to Jerusalem asking, looking, and searching for the Messiah.

The Greeks made their way through the thousands of people who came to Jerusalem for the Passover festival and they found Philip, one of Jesus's disciples. Philip's name was of Greek origin and he was from Bethsaida, a city that was known to be friendlier to Gentiles than other Israelite towns. Perhaps they thought Philip was someone they could trust and someone who would accept them. Whatever their reason for choosing Philip, they made one remarkable request: "Sir, we wish to see Jesus" (v. 21).

What they meant by this request is not stated in the text, so allow me to suggest a few possibilities. Did they want to have a conversation with Jesus? Did they want to watch Jesus perform miracles and signs? Did they want to become followers of Jesus? Whatever their intentions, these pilgrims had come to Jerusalem with one aim in mind. They wanted to see Jesus.

Who can blame them for wanting see Jesus? If they heard even half of what we have heard so far about Jesus, it isn't terribly difficult to understand why they wanted to see him. They wanted to see the man who healed a person who'd been lame for thirty-eight years. They wanted to see the person who had gone into the temple, turned over the tables, and chased out the money changers and those who sold doves.

They wanted to see the hands that had multiplied loaves and fishes, to sit with the teacher who called himself the good shepherd. They wanted to see the prophet who had been anointed by Mary and to lay their eyes on the source of the power that had raised Lazarus from the dead after four days. They wanted to see Jesus.

This is the one conviction that every church, every preacher, and every servant of God has to keep in mind or else we will surely lose our way. Crowds may gather and heap praise for the work that we have done, but in the end let it be our prayer that when the crowds gather, they see more than *us* and more than *our* work. Let it be our deepest desire and highest hope that someone will see Jesus. People show up on Sunday morning tired, weary, and searching. So before any song is sung, let the prayer under our breath be "Lord, let them see Jesus." Before any sermon is preached, let the preacher whisper, "Lord, in this message let them see Jesus." In every community outreach, in every Sunday school class, in every worship service, and in every program, let us hope that the result is that someone sees Jesus.

John did not say the Greeks wanted to talk to Jesus. He said they wanted to *see* Jesus. His choice of words was probably not an accident. Seeing has played an important role in the Gospel of John. When John the Baptist gave his testimony, he said that he had seen, perhaps in a vision from God, that the man on whom the Spirit came down and rested would be God's chosen one. When John's disciples saw Jesus they asked him, "Rabbi . . . , where are you staying?" (1:38). Jesus replied, "Come and see" (v. 39). Later, Jesus encountered a man who was blind from birth. He had never seen in his lifetime. Jesus healed the man and then asked him if he believed in the Son of Man. The formerly blind man asked, "'And who is he, sir? Tell me, so that I may believe in him.' Jesus said to him, 'You have seen him, and the one speaking with you is he.' He said, 'Lord, I believe.' And he worshiped him" (9:36-38). Seeing is believing. Believing is seeing.

So one has to wonder what these Greeks had in mind when they told Philip they wanted to see Jesus. Did they want to merely watch Jesus and make observations so they could tell the people back home that they had seen the wonder-working peasant from Galilee? Or did they really want to see him? Did they really want to believe in him? Did they finally want to put their faith, hope, and trust in him? If so, why did they want to see Jesus now?

It could be that they heard the cries of the crowd as Jesus entered the city of Jerusalem. This text narrates the day we call Palm Sunday, which lets us know we are getting closer to the end of Jesus's earthly life. Palm Sunday was the first day of the last week of Jesus's ministry on earth. When he came into Jerusalem, the crowds hurried out to meet him.

They waved palm branches and shouted, "Hosanna!" (12:13). We treat this word like a term of praise or even another name for God, but it is actually a prayer petition. Hosanna means "Save now, I pray." Had the Greeks come searching because "Hosanna" was a prayer that they had prayed many times before? "Save now, I pray." Had the Greeks come to see Jesus because they were searching for someone who could save them? Why did they want to see Jesus?

Unfortunately, if they listened to the crowds, they may have gotten the wrong idea about how this salvation would take place. The crowds believed Jesus was a conquering king coming to save them by way of military victory. Their misunderstanding is evident when we see how Jesus responded to their shouts of "Blessed is the one who comes in the name of the Lord—the King of Israel!" (v. 13). Conquering kings rode horses, but Jesus took a page from the prophet Zechariah and climbed on the back of a young donkey. The Old Testament prophet had written, "Do not be afraid, daughter Zion; look, your king is coming, sitting on a donkey's colt" (see Zech 9:9).

John 12:16 says, "His disciples did not understand these things at first." They could not see who Jesus was because they expected him to be something he was not. He was not the defender of one nation. He was not the protector of one group of people. Jesus came as the Savior for the whole world. Jesus turned the wisdom of the world upside down.

People were looking for a powerful king, but he arrived as a humble servant. People expected an army to follow behind him. He brought nothing more than a few disciples who often did not grasp what he taught.

If we want to see Jesus—really see him for who he is—there are a few ways John 12 helps us in our journey. After the Greeks asked Philip to see Jesus, Philip went to tell another disciple, Andrew. Andrew and Philip went together and told Jesus.

As Jesus has done so many times before, he responds to a direct request in what seems like an indirect way. It is as if he wants Andrew and Philip to know that seeing him—really seeing him—is about more than watching him. Seeing Jesus is about letting his life become the pattern for our life. Seeing him is about becoming one of his disciples. Jesus offered an illustration: "Very truly, I tell you, unless a grain of wheat falls into the earth and dies, it remains just a single grain; but if it dies, it bears much fruit" (v. 24).

This illustration referred to the circumstances of Jesus's own death, resurrection, and ascension. Up until now, Jesus had been saying that his hour had not yet come. Now he says that the hour has come for the Son of

Man to be glorified (v. 23). "Glorified" is the word Jesus uses in John to talk about his crucifixion and the resurrection.

So Jesus is the kernel of wheat that falls to the ground and dies. Until the kernel dies, it remains only a single seed. But if it dies, it produces many seeds. There is life in the seed, but the life does not emerge from the seed until the seed is planted and dies.

Jesus said this, not only to preview his death, but also to say that anyone searching for more, anyone who wants to see him, must be willing to die. His life must become the pattern for our life. Jesus's death will be a literal death. The death we must die is the death of letting go. The death of surrender. This is the only way that leads to life. Whenever we let something die, something new will live.

All of the Gospels say something about the connection between death and being a disciple. The main barrier to spiritual development is that we are not willing to die. Jesus says, "Those who love their life lose it, and those who hate their life in this world will keep it for eternal life" (v. 25).

Loving something involves clinging to it. Hating something involves resisting it, rejecting it, or letting it go. To love one's life means that we love our own will, our own plans, our own priorities, and our own wants so much that we cannot let them go. We choose the way that seems right to us.

Hating one's life means that we put down our will, our plans, our priorities, and our wants. Jesus says that anyone who loves their life will eventually lose it, but anyone who hates their life will keep it. This is his way of saying that death is the only way to life. We are like that kernel of wheat. What God wants to bring out of us will not come forth until we fall to the ground and die. We do not need to become doormats for people to walk over us or abuse us, but we have to find the way of humility if we are going to see Jesus.

False ego has to die.
Pride has to die.
Guilt has to die.
Unresolved anger has to die.
Any unhealthy longing to be needed has to die.
Insensitivity has to die.
Habits that hold us back have to die.

Only when the kernel of wheat dies can it bring forth life. The Greeks wanted to know if they could see Jesus, but Jesus wanted to know if they were ready and willing to die. Inevitably, the search for something more in life will bring us to the point where something within us has to die for something new to live.

But seeing Jesus is not merely an internal and spiritual transformation, moving from death to life. According to John 12, seeing Jesus is also an outward and visible expression. The disciple is not the person who sits around thinking about how great God is while the world passes by. Jesus says, "Whoever serves me must follow me, and where I am, there will my servant be also. Whoever serves me, the Father will honor" (v. 26).

Among the many ways we can describe Jesus, we can call him a true servant. The word for serve in verse 26 is the word *diakoneo*, which means to wait upon, to minister to. Literally, it is someone waiting on tables, preparing food, providing necessities, taking care of the needs of someone else. Jesus says that the Father will honor the one who serves him. Jesus knows something about being a servant. He gave freely of himself to others. When he saw children, he blessed them. When he encountered the ill, he healed them. When he heard desperate prayers, he answered them. On more than one occasion, he said he had not come to do his will. He only wanted to do the will of the Father.

But now his resolve is about to be tested. The mood shifts at this point in the Gospel of John. From here on out, there will be no more crowds cheering Jesus's name in the streets. Jesus could sense death in the air. He had a decision to make. Would he continue to serve or would he turn back?

We sometimes act as if Jesus was on autopilot and did not have a choice in his suffering and death, but he had a choice. Because the relationship he had with the Father was based on love, he had to have a choice. Love always has a choice. Jesus said that his soul was troubled. He knew he could ask God to save him from the coming crucifixion or could continue to serve, knowing that it would lead to agony, suffering, and death. He made a choice. Jesus made up his mind. He would serve the Most High God. "No, it is for this reason that I have come to this hour," he said. "Father, glorify your name" (vv. 27-28).

He knew that the glory coming to him would not end with a rousing rendition of pomp and circumstance. The glory coming to him would be the glory of the cross. Disciples would abandon and betray him. Crowds would condemn him. But Jesus made up his mind. He did not need to be a royal king. He wanted to be a faithful servant.

And so I wonder if, since Jesus knew he would not be on earth much longer, he was going on record to say that if anyone really wanted to see him, they did not need to look for him at the center of a parade. They did not need to look for him in a palace being waited on by servants. But, if they chose to serve others as he served the Father, they would see him.

To see Jesus, we only have to go to the places he would go. To see Jesus, we only need do the things he would do. To see Jesus, we only need to stay so close to him that where he goes, we go. Where he works, we work. Where he is, we are.

If we go to the prison or the jail, we will see Jesus. He'll be there. If we serve the sick, we will see Jesus. He'll be there. If we stop by the hospital, we are definitely going to see Jesus. He'll be there. If we build a Habitat for Humanity house, he'll be there. If we check on our lonely neighbor, he'll be there. And this is how we know he will be there: Jesus said that when you visit the sick, clothe the naked, feed the hungry, whatever you have done for these, you have done it to him. (Matt 25:31-46)

Jesus said that the Son of Man did not come to be served but to serve and to give his life as a ransom for many.

The apostle Paul said Jesus was "in very nature God, and did not consider equality with God something to be grasped; he made himself nothing, by taking the very nature of a servant, being made in human likeness and being found in appearance as a man, he humbled himself, becoming obedient to death—even death on a cross" (Phil 2:6-8, translation mine).

And this same Jesus now says to you and me, " Whoever serves me must follow me, and where I am, there will my servant be also" (v. 26).

Once we are where Jesus is, we will see that he is everything we have been searching for and so much more. He is the answer to our prayer. He is the fulfillment of our deepest desires. He is the realization of our highest hopes. He is balm for our incurable wounds. He is the Lamb of God who takes away the sin of the world. He is light shining in darkness. The search is finally over. We have found the One we have been looking for. Jesus is living water who truly satisfies. He is bread that feeds us until we want no more.

So tell me, what more are you searching for?

21

Training Day

John 13:1-30

While driving in Kernersville, North Carolina, recently, I stopped in a popular fast food restaurant to get something to curb my afternoon appetite. As I walked through the restaurant, I went past one of the booths and overheard a conversation between two male employees.

One employee was a manager and the other person was a young man who appeared to be in his first day on the job. It's exciting when we make it through the application and interview process and arrive at the place where we are trained to do a new job.

The manager probably understood what any good manager should know. Everything his new employee heard that first day on the job was going to set the tone for the employee's tenure at the company. The employee may not have known how crucial that conversation was, but the manager, no doubt, knew. The manager probably understood that whatever he said to new employees on their first day profoundly shaped their idea of what it meant to be a part of the staff, how they interacted with the customers, and ultimately whether they succeeded or failed. This was training day.

Some of us have worked in restaurants. While I do not know how you feel about that kind of work, when I heard the enthusiasm in the manager's voice, I almost decided to put in an application myself. The manager talked about how great it was to work in the company and mentioned the difference employees made in customers' lives not just by serving food but also by showing courtesy. Eventually someone was going to show the employee how to make lemonade, blend shakes, and work the cash register, but at that moment the conversation was not about the lemonade, shakes, or registers. The conversation sounded like it was about how to treat people. From what I overheard, this was one of the critical lessons on the new employee's training day.

When you read John 13, it's like a transcript of a training day for people who want to be like Jesus. Training is usually provided on the first day of the job. John 13 marks the beginning of the last day of Jesus's earthly life. Jesus saved his most crucial lessons until the end. We are still hours away from the crucifixion, but the clock is ticking. As Jesus prepared for the worst, he sat down with the disciples in chapters 13–17 to tell them what he wanted them to know about being his disciples. He did not give them a class on preaching. He did not offer lessons on religious etiquette. Jesus spent the most time (nearly all of chapter 13) teaching and showing them what God had done for them and, consequently, how they should treat one another.

The context for this conversation is just before the Passover festival. John has been careful to tell us all along which of Israel's major festivals was taking place as a way to help us keep time and anticipate changes in the plot of the Gospel. In scary movies, when we hear the hair-raising chords of the macabre theme music, we know something terrible is about to happen. Whenever there is a festival in John, that's our cue that something major has just happened or is about to happen.

When John says that it was just *before* the Passover festival at an *evening* meal, we learn that everything that takes place in chapter 13 happens on the Thursday before Jesus was crucified on Good Friday, the first day of Passover. Keep in mind as we read John 13–17 that everything in these five chapters—the meal, the teaching, the betrayal, and Jesus's prayer—takes place between Thursday evening and Friday morning. It will seem like a long time to us, but it was only a matter of hours for Jesus and the disciples.

For one final time before the crucifixion, Jesus gathered with his disciples for a meal. It seemed like an ordinary meal, but Jesus soon turned it into a training exercise. Right in the middle of dinner, Jesus rose from the table. He took off his outer garment, picked up a towel, and wrapped it around his waist. Next, he poured water into a basin and began to do the unthinkable. Without any warning or introductory remarks, Jesus began to wash his disciples' feet, drying them with the towel that was wrapped around him.

Jesus's behavior did not make sense. Servants washed feet. Rabbis, teachers, and certainly saviors did not wash feet. Lower-ranking people washed the feet of higher-ranking people. That was the way of the world. Jesus was the Son of God. So why was he washing his disciples' feet?

Most of the disciples had been tolerant when Mary poured perfume on Jesus's feet and wiped his feet with her hair (John 12). They did not deny that Jesus deserved such extravagant honor. These disciples knew their place. They were tax collectors and fishermen, ordinary people following an extraordinary Messiah. Jesus may have deserved to have his feet anointed, but how could they deserve to have their feet washed by Jesus? Jesus had gone too far.

Please understand that foot washing in first-century Israel was not a luxury. It was a necessity. The dusty roads and open sandals meant that whenever someone arrived at a destination, his or her feet were certain to be covered with the dust, dirt, and grime of the village streets. Anyone hosting a dinner would have been sure to have foot-washing services available. Often, a host would hire a servant to do this menial, lowly job. But Jesus, who had just come into Jerusalem being celebrated as Israel's king a few days earlier, took this humble task upon himself. He was the host, but because this was training day, he willingly took on the role of the servant.

Jesus rinsed sweaty feet in a basin until they were clean. He dried calloused feet with the towel he wrapped around his waist. Jesus did this not so much to remove the dirt from their feet as to show his disciples once again who he was, what he came to do, what God was like, and what he called them to do for one another as his disciples. This was training day.

Days, weeks, or years later, when the disciples looked back on this moment, there were many lessons they could have gleaned from the experience.

Quite possibly, one of the lessons Jesus may have wanted to share with the disciples is how to deal with opposition when doing the work of God. John says the evening meal was in progress, but the devil had already prompted Judas, the son of Simon Iscariot, to betray Jesus. Food was being shared. Cups were being passed, but the devil had already prompted Judas to betray Jesus. John does not say that the devil was *about* to prompt Judas. He says the devil had *already* prompted Judas before Jesus washed the disciples' feet. Jesus knew what was lurking in Judas, and yet he kept moving forward by faith.

"Betray" translates to a word that means to give into the hands of another. Theories abound as to why Judas betrayed Jesus. Speculation aside, Jesus knew that the devil was using Judas, and he also knew exactly what he was going to do about it. Jesus decided to keep doing what God called him to do despite what the devil prompted Judas to do. If you are going to do the work of God—in the church or in life—it is important to know how to deal with opposition and evil.

Make no mistake about it, evil is at work in the world. Evil forces—what the New Testament calls powers and principalities (Eph 6:12)—were at work to stop Jesus from the very beginning. Herod tried to kill him when he was a baby. The devil tried to tempt him with wealth and power after forty days of fasting. At every turn, Jesus faced evil obstructions, so it should not surprise us that doing the Lord's work does not turn out to be easy. Greed, hatred, oppression, injustice, and inhumanity are merely the offspring of evil. The good news for us is that as pervasive as these powers are, the reality of evil does not tell the whole story. Jesus knew how to deal with the devil.

Jesus dedicated his entire life to doing the work of God. It never seemed to surprise him when he faced difficulty or demons while doing God's work. When he preached, some people did not believe, but he preached again. When he forgave sinners, people condemned him, but he continued to forgive. When he healed on the Sabbath, some people persecuted him. When he made claims about his divinity, some accused him of blasphemy. When he fed the multitudes, they came back the next day and said they were still hungry, but he continued to do good.

We know this because after the devil prompted Judas to betray Jesus, Jesus kept moving forward in the faith that his life was in God's hands. His life was not in Judas's hands. His future was not determined by anyone or anything working against him. His future was in God's hands.

Judas, as misguided as he may have been, was not ultimately in control of Jesus's life. Jesus lived by the faith that the Father was leading his life, guiding his life, and directing his life. He had learned to rely on the ever-present guidance and presence of the Father. Right up to the very end, Jesus held on to the conviction that only God had the final word about his life. So even after he sensed that something sinister was stirring within Judas, Jesus got up from the table and started washing the disciples' feet.

Jesus knew it was about to get messy and miserable, but he was not about to change course now. His life was in God's hands. John put it like this: knowing that the Father had put all things under his power and that he had come from God and was returning to God, Jesus got up from the meal, took off his outer garment, wrapped a towel around his waist and washed twelve pairs of feet. The knowledge that he had come from God and was returning to God was more influential than the fact that Judas was no longer on his side. And sooner or later, we have to decide that no matter what is working against us, we will trust that God is working for us.

Paul said it this way: "No, in all these things we are more than conquerors through him who loved us. For I am convinced that neither death, nor life, nor angels, nor rulers, nor things present, nor things to come, nor powers, nor height, nor depth, nor anything else in all creation, will be able to separate us from the love of God in Christ Jesus" (Rom 8:37-39).

Every servant of God has to know that God can work with and through and in our messes and our misery. He can take what is bad and transform it into something for our good. He can take what is hard and turn it into a triumphant testimony. Jesus knew the disciples were going to meet challenges ahead, so his first training exercise was to keep moving forward by faith even if the devil himself was out to get him. Jesus knew that if God is for you, it matters not who is against you (see Rom 8:31).

The hour for his crucifixion was upon him, but he was not going to turn around. He knew where he came from. He knew where he was going. John says that after wrapping the towel around his waist, Jesus poured water into a basin. He stooped down and one by one began washing his disciples' feet and drying them with the towel. Jesus was setting the example for what disciples were called to do for one another. This was part of the training. Jesus wanted to remind the disciples of how to live in the kingdom of God, a lesson that we will continue next week in the second half of John 13.

John told us in his first chapter, "In the beginning was the Word, and the word was with God, and the word was God." A few verses later, John wrote, "The Word became flesh and made his dwelling among us. We have seen his glory, the glory of the one and only Son, who came from the Father, full of grace and truth" (1:1, 14). But now the Word is washing feet. The man hailed King of Israel is carrying out the work of a humble servant. This is how to live in the kingdom of God. The kingdom of this world praises people who climb to the top. The kingdom of this world measures success by how many people work for you. But Jesus acted out a scene with water, a towel, and a basin that cast humility in the starring role.

Jesus has shown us the way of humility from the day he came into the world. He was born to a poor, teenage girl. He was delivered in a manger used for feeding animals. He was raised in an out-of-the-way village called Nazareth. Though he knew no sin, he submitted to baptism by John the Baptist. Although he was the firstborn of all creation, he lowered himself and became like us to redeem us. He alone wears the title "Alpha and Omega," but he was willing to put on a towel and clean his disciples' dirty feet. Washing feet is a visible reminder of how we live in the kingdom of God.

Luke's version of this incident tells us that at this meal, the disciples were arguing with one another about which one of them was the greatest. Maybe this is what prompted Jesus to get up and wash their feet. Jesus wanted to go on record saying that none of his disciples should think themselves better than any other disciple. Life in Christ is not a competition of who can outdo, out-quote, outsing, outpreach, out-cook or outdress someone else. Life in Christ is not about standing up to be seen. It is about bending down to serve.

Our world is marked by so many signs of self-absorption and self-importance. You can buy a telescoping pole to hold your cell phone at a distance so that you can take better pictures not of other people but of yourself. It's called a selfie stick and allows you to take better selfies. But in the kingdom of God, there are no selfies.

Jesus took off his outer clothing and put a towel around his waist. He traded the garments of a host for the attire of a servant. When Jesus took off his robe, he humbled himself to serve others. When Jesus took off his robe and knelt down, he reenacted the humility that brought him down from right hand of the Father to be born of a woman. So when Jesus washed his disciples' feet, it was an affirmation of how far down God stooped to be with you and me.

Jesus could serve with such humility because he knew who he was. Verse 3 says Jesus knew that the Father had put all things under his power and that he had come from God and was returning to God. When you know who you are, you can do whatever needs to be done whether large or small. When you know who you are, you can walk with kings and queens just as easily as you can with the common person. Jesus was free to serve with humility because he was not looking for anyone to validate who he was. The Father had already told him, "You are my beloved Son; with you I am well pleased" (Mark 1:11, ESV).

So, Jesus washed feet. He wanted his disciples to see that the way up in the kingdom is down. The way to go higher in the wisdom of God is to stoop low enough to serve others with a Christlike attitude, which was what he had being saying all along. "The first shall be last and the last shall be first. Bless the children and let them come to me for such is the kingdom of heaven. Blessed are the poor, for they shall inherit the earth" (see Matt 20:16; 5:5). Everything in the kingdom is upside down.

When he finished washing their feet, he put on his clothes and returned to his place. Then he asked,

Do you understand what I have done for you? ...You call me 'Teacher' and 'Lord,' and rightly so, for that is what I am. Now that I, your Lord and Teacher, have washed your feet, you also should wash one another's feet. I have set you an example that you should do as I have done for you. Very truly I tell you, no servant is greater than his master, nor is a messenger greater than the one who sent him. Now that you know these things, you will be blessed if you do them. (John 13:12-17, NIV)

In other words, this is not only a pattern of what Jesus has done for us—divinity humbly coming down to humanity to serve—but is also a pattern of what we, as his disciples, will do for one another. This is the training for a life of faith. Now that we know these things, we will be blessed if we do them. Jesus said we will be blessed . . .

when parents serve children and children serve parents.

when husbands serve wives and wives serve husbands.

when friends serve friends, neighbors serve neighbors, and the rich serve the poor.

True faith is not measured by the spectacular signs we can do. True faith is not verified by the impressive spiritual heights we can reach. True faith is not measured by the size of our Bible but by the dirt on our towels. True faith is not measured by how popular we become but by how many feet we wash. True faith is measured by the way we imitate the One who washed feet. It is training day, so grab your towels and do for others what Jesus has done for you.

22

A New Way to Love

John 13:31-38

First Corinthians 13 has been labeled the "love" chapter in the Bible. We read this chapter at weddings and other occasions when we want to highlight the depth and breadth of Christian love. The words of 1 Corinthians 13 are poignant and powerful no matter how many times we hear them:

> If I speak in the tongues of [humans] or of angels, but do not have love, I am only a resounding gong or a clanging cymbal. If I have the gift of prophecy and can fathom all mysteries and all knowledge, and if I have a faith that can move mountains, but do not have love, I am nothing. If I give all I possess to the poor and give over my body to hardship that I may boast, but do not have love, I gain nothing. (vv. 1-3, NIV)

The chapter closes with the statement, "And now these three remain: faith, hope and love. But the greatest of these is love" (v. 13, NIV).

If 1 Corinthians 13 is the love chapter in the Bible, the Gospel of John could be considered the love book in the Bible. Some of the New Testament's strongest statements about God's love are found in the Gospel of John.

"For God so loved the world that he gave his only Son, so that everyone who believes in him may not perish but may have eternal life" (3:16).

"The Father loves the Son and has placed all things in his hands" (3:35).

Speaking to Pharisees, Jesus once said, "If God were your Father, you would love me, for I came from God" (8:42).

The best way for John to capture the relationship between Jesus, Mary, Martha, and Lazarus was to say, "Jesus loved Martha and her sister and Lazarus" (11:5).

Jesus will tell the disciples in chapter 15, "As the Father has loved me, so I have loved you; abide in my love" (v. 9).

And what about the life-altering question Jesus asked Peter after the resurrection: "Simon Peter, do you love me?" (see John 21:15-17).

Love is a prominent theme not only in John but throughout Scripture. The Bible from cover to cover is the story of the love God has for the world and everything and everyone in the world. God put Adam and Eve in a garden and gave them everything they needed for life and joy. God did so out of love.

Adam and Eve chose to go their own way rather than God's way, but God did not abandon them. God stuck with them because of love. God delivered Israel from slavery in Egypt and claimed Israel as God's chosen people. Deuteronomy says that God did not choose Israel because they were more numerous or better than other nations. God chose them because of his love (Deut 7:7-8). The prophets preached about God's love. The psalms are songs and prayers about God's love.

Yet the way Scripture speaks about love and the way we use the term in everyday language seems to be quite different. We use love when we really mean "like" or "enjoy." We love a restaurant. We love our houses. Commercials for a popular hamburger chain use the tag line "I'm Lovin' it." Subaru sells cars with the slogan, "Love. It's what makes a Subaru a Subaru."

What we have in mind when we talk about love in this way is a feeling of emotional attachment or enjoyment. And if this is the full extent of our definition, then yes, it is possible to love a car. At least for a little while. As long as the car is reliable and clean and the repairs do not cost too much money, we will have positive emotions about the car. But as soon as the timing belt has to be replaced or it is damaged in a fender bender, we may find ourselves falling out of love with the vehicle, wanting to trade it in or even abandon it on the side of the road.

So it is not clear what advertisers have in mind when they use the word "love," but we can be sure that it must be something different than what Jesus had in mind when he said to his disciples, "love one another" (v. 35, NIV). Jesus was not limiting his definition of love to feelings of affection. Affection certainly has its place, but Jesus came to show us a new way of love that involves action and commitment.

Washing the disciples' feet was love in action. On the last night of Jesus's earthly life, it was not enough for him just to say he cared about the disciples. Loving them meant showing them how he felt through action. So he took off his outer garment. He wrapped a towel around his waist. He poured water into a basin. He washed their feet. Notice all the verbs John used. Jesus "took off." Jesus "poured." Jesus "wrapped." Jesus "washed." Jesus's actions confirmed the authenticity of his love. Love is an action more than it is a feeling. (13:3-5, NIV)

As we follow along in the story of Jesus's final hours before the crucifixion, Jesus, having demonstrated love to his disciples, explained what the disciples must do for one another. He told them, "I give you a new commandment, that you love one another" (v. 34).

Jesus uses the word "command." He says his command to love one another is new. What made him say this command was new? The command to love one another was not new in the sense that the Old Testament lacked such an imperative. Leviticus 19:18 says, "you shall love your neighbor as yourself." To see what Jesus meant by *new*, we have to take a closer look at the word "as" in the phrase "as I have loved you" (13:34).

In English we use the word "as" to compare things. When someone is learning to play the piano, the teacher may play notes on the keyboard and expect the student to play those same notes *just as* the teacher played them. Of course, the student does not have the same ability as the teacher, so it is difficult at first for the student to play just as the teacher played. The teacher can only show the student how to play; she cannot give the student her years of training and experience. The student must practice and practice and practice and become better on their own.

John likes to use words with double meanings, and the Greek word he uses for "as" is one of those words. So it may be that Jesus was not telling his disciples to imitate him. He may not have been using "as" in that way. After all, do you know how hard it is to imitate Jesus? Peter tried to imitate Jesus walking on water, and that didn't last long.

The word translated "as" does not merely compare things; it also refers to the source, the cause, or the point of origin of something. So when Jesus said, "as I have loved you," he was telling the disciples that his love for them would be the source or the power that enabled them to love one another. Now that he had freely loved the disciples and they had willingly accepted his love for them, they could draw from the abundance of his love when they loved each other. This is why Jesus's command was "new." From now on, there would be a new source for our love. Jesus's love for us is the strength behind our love for one another.

We all know that if it were not for the power of Jesus, we simply could not love some people. Only as we sense how much God loves does our capacity to love one another increase. When I know how merciful God has been to me, I am more inclined to be merciful to others. When I know how low God had to reach to rescue me, I am more patient with those who have lost their way. When I know how amazing God's grace has been toward me, I am more willing to offer grace to someone else. The more we sense how much God loves us, the greater our capacity to love one another. "As I have loved you" means that Jesus's love for me will give me the strength to love others.

This is why Jesus had to correct Peter's misunderstanding about foot washing. Initially, Peter objected to having his feet washed. He did not quite understand what Jesus was doing. He asked Jesus, "Lord, are you going to wash my feet?" (v. 6). As far as Peter was concerned, Jesus was not going to wash his feet. Peter did not intend to let Jesus wash his feet that night or ever in the future. But Jesus had to wash them. Why? Because Peter would not have the strength to love others if he did not first receive God's love for himself.

If this is true, I wonder if being able to accept goodness from God and from others is just as important to our spirituality as being able to show goodness and kindness to others.

Sometimes it is a struggle to accept goodness and grace from God and from others because, at some point in life, we were made to feel like we are unworthy. We were told in subtle and not so subtle ways that we were not good enough. Past failures brought guilt and shame, causing us to resist goodness from God or from other people.

Peter did not think he deserved to have his feet washed by Jesus. So Jesus told Peter, "Unless I wash you, you have no part with me" (v. 8, NIV). It's like Jesus was saying, "Unless you let me put my hands on you, you cannot fully experience the grace of God, goodness of God, and mercy of God. Until you experience and accept the love of God, you cannot freely share the love of God." We have to accept how much God loves us so that we can in turn love others.

At this point in the meal, Judas has already gone out to betray Jesus. It will not be much longer before Jesus goes with the remaining disciples to the Garden of Gethsemane to pray. In the next few chapters, we will hear Jesus telling the disciples over and over again that he will only be with them a little longer.

If we think about the original audience for the Gospel of John, one of the questions they must have had is how they could continue in the way of faith when Jesus was no longer with them. He was not going to be around to perform miracles. He was not going to be with them to deliver sermons. Movements often die out when the leader dies or is taken away.

Jesus wanted to be sure that did not happen with his disciples. This may be one more reason he gave this new commandment to love one another. The call to love one another was a call to be in community with one another. "Just as I have loved you, you also should love one another" (v. 34).

One of the hurdles to being Christians in contemporary North America is that we place such a premium on independence and individuality that we become consumers instead of disciples. As a consumer, I go into the store and get what I want. I do not have to pay attention to or get involved with anyone else in the store. I don't have to work with any of the other customers. As a consumer, I am only there to get what I want or what I need. All I have to do is find what I like, get as much as I want, pay my money, and leave. The store does not owe me anything, and I do not owe the store anything because I am a consumer.

Jesus had something different in mind for his disciples. He did not want them to be spiritual consumers. He called them to be his disciples. As disciples, Jesus invites us to stretch beyond independence and move into the realm of interdependence and real relationship. Remember the context. Jesus is having a private conversation with his disciples in John 13. He is telling them to love *one another.* He is calling them to be a community of disciples who share in real relationship with each other. God's love works in us to help us become a community with one another.

A well-known children's story, *The Velveteen Rabbit,* has something to say about this. The book describes a young boy who receives a new stuffed rabbit one Christmas. At first, the new, furry toy is the boy's favorite. But quickly the boy forgets about the rabbit and plays with his mechanical toys.

All the boy's toys have the power to talk to one another when no one is looking. The trucks and trains often intimidate the Rabbit because he doesn't have their gears and abilities. But the Rabbit makes friends with one of the oldest toys in the collection, the Skin Horse. The Skin Horse is falling apart. He had bald patches, and the hairs on his tail are nearly pulled out.

One day the Rabbit hears the other toys talking about becoming "Real," so he asks the Skin Horse what the other toys mean by this. The Skin Horse replies, "It's a thing that happens to you. When a child loves you for a long, long time, not just to play with, but REALLY loves you, then you become Real."

The Skin Horse goes on to add,

It doesn't happen all at once. You become. It takes a long time. That's why it doesn't happen often to people who break easily, or have sharp edges, or who have to be carefully kept. Generally, by the time you are Real, most of your hair has been loved off, and your eyes drop out and you get loose in the joints and very shabby. But these things don't matter at all, because once you are Real you can't be ugly, except to people who don't understand.[1]

I wonder if Jesus would say that Real is what happens when disciples love one another. Sometimes community is not easy, but is there any other way to love one another? We cannot love one another if we have sharp edges or have to be carefully kept or break easily. Jesus's love is not the kind of love written into the script of a romantic movie. The symbol for his love is the cross. This is what he meant when he said, "Where I am going, you cannot come" (v. 33). But once we love one another, we are never alone.

Disciples are not a group of individuals who happen to meet at the same place for worship each week. We are sons and daughters, sisters and brothers, mothers and fathers, husbands and wives whom God has called to be one caring, Christ-centered community.

We speak words of wisdom to one another. We speak the truth in love to one another. We are partners striving to raise our children in faith. We pray with one another through the rough patches of life. And as we do this, we make each other real. When someone mourns, we stand beside them. When someone rejoices, we celebrate with them.

As Baptists, we have even captured this kind of love in our church covenant:

> Having been led by the Spirit of God, to receive the Lord Jesus Christ as Savior, and on the profession of our faith, having been baptized in the name of the Father, Son and Holy Spirit, we do now in the presence of God, angels and this assembly, most solemnly and joyfully enter into covenant with one another as one body in Christ. We engage, therefore, by the aid of the Holy Spirit, to walk together in Christian love.

When Jesus used the word "love," he meant acting in good will toward one another, considering the preferences of one another, being unwilling to abandon one another, and welcoming one another. This is how we love one another.

The command to love one another was a call to be in relationship with each other. Isn't love what every human being wants? Love is what we all truly need. Whether we are red or blue, black or white, male or female, liberal or conservative, young or old, wealthy or trying to make it, every human being desires to be loved and to love.

Love is a powerful force for good. Sometimes it does not matter how much faith we have. If we do not have love, faith has no place to grow. Sometimes it does not matter how much knowledge we have. If we do not have love, knowledge can become pride. So Jesus lifts up one last time what it means to be his disciple. Love one another.

Do not repay evil for evil. Love one another. If anyone forces you to go one mile, go with them two miles. Love one another. Do not speak harshly against each other. Love one another. Do not spread rumors. Love one another. Strive to avoid a contentious spirit. Love one another. Maintain family and personal devotions. Love one another. Be kind and just to those in your employ. Love one another. Watch over, exhort, and pray for your brother and your sister. Love one another. Guard each other's reputations, not needlessly exposing the infirmities and frailties of others. Love one another. Participate in each other's joys and with tender sympathy bear one another's burdens and sorrows. Love one another. Be slow to give or take offense. Always be ready for reconciliation. Stir up each other into every good word and work. Love one another.[2]

When we love one another, love does more than build relational bonds; love also sends an evangelistic message to the world. Jesus said to his disciples, "By this everyone will know that you are my disciples, if you have love for one another" (v. 35).

Jesus is telling us, "You may be able to walk on water, but that is not how the world will know you are my disciples. You may be members of a church, but that is not how the world will know you are my disciples."

The world will know we are disciples by our love for one another. If we pray for each other, everyone will know. If we show compassion toward one another, everyone will know. If we build up one another, everyone will know. If we share with one another, everyone will know.

They will know that we believe that Jesus is the Son of God. They will know that we have been forgiven of our sins. They will know that our name is written in the Lamb's book of life. They will know that God loves us, and when they see our love for one another, they will know that we love God. By God's grace, they will see how much God loves them.

Notes

1. Margery Williams Bianco, *The Velveteen Rabbit* (New York: George H. Doran, 1922) 4.
2. These imperatives are taken from the Baptist Covenant. See that of Calvary Baptist Church in Denver, Colorado: http://www.thecalvarybaptistchurch.org/covenant.html.

23

Living above Our Fears

John 14

Do you remember a time when you were afraid? Not slightly startled, but really afraid. I remember when I was about five years old being chased home by a neighbor's dog. I do not remember how big the dog was, but I remember how fast I ran. I was terrified. Surprisingly, I actually like dogs today.

Human beings have always grappled with fear. Some fears have helped humanity survive real dangers like snakes or lions or bears. When we are afraid, our body responds psychologically and physically. Our palms sweat. Our heart rate increases and adrenaline floods our system. Our body readies itself for fight or flight.

Fast-forward to today and fear has become big business. Haunted houses, scary movies, and television shows about zombies draw scores of fans and top the ratings lists week after week. Critics have already given glowing reviews to Steven Spielberg's latest movie about resurrected dinosaurs taking over the world. We seem to enjoy this kind of fear. We pay good money to be afraid. But there are also fears we do not like at all.

When I was nine or ten, one of the scariest times was during the unsolved missing and murdered spree in Atlanta. Young African-American boys, all around my age, were being abducted. The tragedy of the mysterious and heinous crimes evoked widespread panic. The city residents felt powerless, and parents of young black boys were gripped by fear. No one knew when or where the attacker might strike next. Although we were only children, my friends and I were well aware of what was going on, and it was definitely a time of fear.

Some fear is personal. Psychologists use the word "phobia" to describe the kind of fear that is an extreme or irrational aversion to something. Arachnophobia is what we call the fear of spiders. Claustrophobia is the fear of being in small spaces. People who are afraid to fly pace nervously back and forth in the airport terminal to cope with the preflight jitters. The second most common fear, right behind the fear of flying, is the fear of public speaking. Acrophobia is the fear of heights. It is not uncommon for grownups to sleep with a night-light because they fear the dark. And the fear that may lie beneath the elusive quest to stay forever young is the unspoken and almost universal fear of death.

Fear is everywhere. If we watch the financial news, the rumors of disappointing economic growth leave us feeling unsettled about our money. If we watch the world news, the cruelty and relentlessness of extremists lead us to feel afraid of crowded public spaces. When we consider our personal circumstances, mounting debt and concerns about the well-being of people we love may also be convincing and compelling reasons to be afraid.

But what if it were possible to live above these fears? There will always be threats, dangers, and hazards in life. But what if we did not feel paralyzed by them? What if, instead of fear, we had a profound sense of peace? During the late-night conversation between the disciples and Jesus in the last twenty-four hours of his earthly life, Jesus's message to the disciples was clear. No matter what happens to me or to you, you do not need to live in fear.

It is hard to know exactly what the disciples were thinking or feeling after the dinner and the foot washing, but fear is a pretty good guess. Jesus dismissed Judas early; Judas had been agitated all night, and right before he left Jesus gave him instructions to do quickly whatever he planned to do (John 13:27). Jesus knew where Judas was going, but except for the disciple whom Jesus loved, no one else realized that one of their own was on his way to betray their friend and teacher.

Jesus added to the mystery of the moment by telling the disciples, "My children, I will be with you only a little longer . . . . Where I am going, you cannot come" (13:33, NIV).

Peter was confused by what Jesus meant about going somewhere they could not come. He asked Jesus, "Lord, where are you going?" (13:36). It did not make sense to him that Jesus was going somewhere he could not go. Peter, James, and John were the three disciples Jesus took with him on those occasions when he left the other nine disciples behind. Peter was in Jesus's inner circle and among his most trusted disciples. And yet Jesus was going to a place Peter could not go? Where was this mysterious location?

The disciples had been everywhere with Jesus for the last three years. They left behind friends and family in order to follow him. It is true that as a disciple Peter did not always give Jesus the right answer to every question, but he had always been willing to stand with Jesus.

For example, in John 6, Jesus taught a large crowd that to be truly satisfied, to have real life, they needed to eat his flesh. Jesus used the metaphor of eating to speak about entering into his way of life. Eating his flesh meant entering into relationship with him based on the faith that he was God's divine Son.

The crowd did not understand Jesus so they argued among themselves. "How can this man give us his flesh to eat?" they wondered (6:52). Most of the people were so offended by Jesus's claim that he was divine that they quit following him that day. Seeing the crowds walk away, Jesus turned to his twelve disciples and asked, "You do not want to leave too, do you?" (6:67, NIV). And it was Peter who answered for the group, "Lord, to whom can we go? You have the words of eternal life. We have come to believe and know that you are the Holy One of God" (vv. 68-69). Peter had been with Jesus through thick and thin.

But now Jesus said that he was going somewhere Peter could not come. Peter didn't realize Jesus was talking about the cross. When Peter doubled down on his commitment, Jesus said that Peter was not going to be as reliable as he thought he would. "I will lay down my life for you," Peter insisted (13:37). Jesus answered, "Will you lay down your life for me? Very truly, I tell you, before the [rooster] crows, you will have denied me three times" (v. 38).

Surely the disciples must have been at least a little afraid when they heard Jesus talking this way. Judas walked out into the darkness, Jesus was going somewhere they could not come, and Peter—whose nickname was Rock—learned that he would deny knowing Jesus three times before the sun rose. Things did not look good.

Thankfully, Jesus did not hesitate to give the disciples a word of encouragement. He saw exactly where they were and knew exactly what they needed. He knew they needed a word of faith to overcome their fears, of which there were at least two.

The first fear Jesus wanted to calm was the fear of what to do in a crisis. Jesus said, "Do not let your hearts be troubled. Believe in God, believe also in me" (14:1). John 14 is part of what is known as the farewell discourse. Jesus was saying good-bye to his closest companions. He would soon lay down his life for his friends, but first he wanted to prepare them for life without his physical presence.

In a few hours, Jesus would be crucified on a cross. All the disciples' hopes would appear to be crucified with him. Jesus showed them so much power in his life, but in his death the disciples saw only weakness and suffering. They had a crisis of faith like they had never known before. And Jesus knew that when a crisis or calamity comes into our lives, it can trouble our hearts.

In the New Testament, the heart is the center of everything that makes us alive: our feelings, our passions, our joy, our understanding, and our thought. The heart represents the center of our inner being. Jesus knew that the real danger of a crisis is what it can do to us from the inside out. Do not let your hearts be troubled, he said.

Troubled means agitated, trembling, inwardly disturbed, restless, stirred up, or anxious. Troubled is the natural and typical response to a crisis, so what Jesus said to the disciples was what every fearful soul needs to hear. He told them that the remedy for a troubled heart is a trusting heart. "Do not let your hearts be troubled. Believe in God, believe also in me" (v. 1). On Jesus's lips these words meant something like, "Hey, fellas, when the crisis comes, you already believe in God; keep believing in me."

"Believe" in the Gospel of John is a synonym for "trust." "Do not let your hearts be troubled," Jesus said. "You trust God; keep your trust also in me." This is how to handle the fear that arises in a crisis. Trust God. Trust that everything Jesus said about God and revealed about God is reliable. Trust what Jesus said. Trust what Jesus did. Trust what Jesus promised.

The encouragement to keep trusting, keep believing, is important because when the disciples see Jesus's lifeless body on the cross, it will feel like everything he told them over their three years together was a hoax or a fantasy. You know what happens when we hear something good on Sunday and then a storm comes on Tuesday. On Sunday, we are excited about the promises of God. But on Tuesday we may say, "I knew those promises were too good to be true." Jesus knew that the cross might push the disciples over the edge. The soldier's sword in Jesus's side would puncture the disciples' expectations for the future. The crown of thorns pressed down on his head would make them feel like fools for following and sacrificing for Jesus. So Jesus gave them a word in advance. I like the way Eugene Peterson says it in *The Message*: "Don't let this throw you. You trust God, don't you? Trust me."

In other words, when the worst happens, do not let Judas's betrayal distract you. Do not let Peter's failure make you lose hope. Whatever goes wrong from this point forward, at any time and in any place, for any reason, keep trusting in Jesus.

Keep trusting that he has come to give you life and life more abundant. Keep trusting that he is the good shepherd who promised not to lose a single sheep that belongs to him. Keep trusting that you are secure in the Father's hand. No one and nothing is strong enough to snatch you out. Keep trusting that Jesus gives new life. Keep trusting that your life matters to God. Not a sparrow falls to the ground that the Father does not know about. For even when we cannot control what happens to us, we can make a choice about whether we respond in fear or trust.

Jesus addressed a second source of fear that is expressed in the comments of Peter and Thomas: the fear that arises from uncertainty.

In some ways, this is a little like graduation day for the disciples. When students graduate, they move away from their teacher. There is excitement but perhaps also some uncertainty about what the next level has in store. We made it through high school, but what is it going to be like in college, the military, or your first job? Everyone knows me now, but who will know me then? Will I fit in? Will I choose the right major? Will I keep up my grades? What about graduating from college to the world of work or graduate school? Will I get a job in my field? Every new level brings a new set of questions, expectations, and hurdles to overcome. In Jesus's case, the students were not leaving the teacher. The teacher was preparing to leave the students. This gave rise to feelings of uncertainty.

If people crave anything in our times, it is certainty. We want certainty from political leaders. We want certainty from weather forecasts. We want certainty about our own future and the futures of those we love.

But sometimes when we want Jesus to give us certainty, he gives us something much, much better. Ask Thomas and Peter.

Peter was the first to go on record asking for certainty in this farewell conversation with Jesus. When Jesus told the disciples to love one another, Simon Peter jumped back to something Jesus said earlier about Peter not being able to follow him where he was going. "Lord," Peter asked him, "where are you going?" (13:36). Peter wanted a specific location. He wanted certainty.

Jesus kept to his normal method and didn't answer the question directly. Instead, he told all the disciples about his Father's house and how it has many rooms. He said he was going to prepare a place and then come back to take them to be with him. And then Jesus said, "you know the way to the place where I am going" (v. 4).

I can almost imagine Thomas and Peter looking at each other when Jesus told them they knew the way to the place he was going. Peter, after all, had just asked Jesus where he was going, so why did Jesus think Peter knew the way? If he knew the way, he would not have asked where Jesus was going.

So Thomas spoke up. Thomas was the skeptic in the group. He wanted hard evidence. He liked certainty. He wanted directions. He wanted Jesus to unfold a map and put an X on the spot where he was going so that he could meet him there. "Lord, we do not know where you are going. How can we know the way?" (v. 5). In other words, Jesus, we want to follow you, but please tell us the destination. Give us certainty.

We can identify with Thomas. We want certainty about the path to take in life. We want certainty about the decisions we have to make. We want certainty about what God is calling us to do. We want certainty about how to raise children and how to relate to grown children. We want certainty about matters of ultimate importance, issues of life and death.

The appeal of some versions of Christianity, and other religions for that matter, is that they offer searching people certainty. Charismatic leaders often arise in times of social, political, and economic unrest and promise to solve everyone's problems. They have all the answers. They promise to extract all the questions and all the mystery out of life. Follow these simple rules, memorize these answers, and believe these doctrines and you will be blessed. But Jesus did not give Peter and Thomas the kind of certainty they were after. Jesus gave them something better. Jesus did not tell them where he was going or list directions to a specific location. Instead, Jesus promised to be their guide on the journey. "I am the way, and the truth, and the life" (v. 6).

Like most of you, I have always heard this verse used by Christians to explain how people get to heaven. Someone might ask, "If a person has never heard and believed certain ideas about Jesus, will they make it into heaven?" And the believer quotes this verse as an answer. Or sometimes this verse is selected when someone has a question about people of other faiths. "No one comes to the Father except through me," the believer says with certainty (v. 6). Here, then, is where the sermon gets interesting; Jesus may have more to say in these verses than what we have always heard. It seems that, at this point, he is still talking to his disciples about not being afraid. He has not changed the subject to heaven or to people of other faiths.

One of the basic guidelines for interpreting any text is that first we have to understand the context of the text. Because of context, the word "bears" on the sports page means something different than the same word in a brochure for the local zoo. To get at the meaning of Scripture, we have to try to understand what the writer intended to say to the people in his own time. This is a way to avoid misusing the Scripture in our own time. Some of us may have been quoted by someone who heard something we said. And even though the quote was exactly what we said, it was not what we meant because they took our words out of context. This often happens with Scripture.

It can easily happen with John 14:6. We often treat it as a stand-alone verse: "I am the way, and the truth, and the life." But it does not stand alone. It is part of a conversation between Jesus and the disciples that takes place over several chapters. One of the most common interpretations for John 14:6 is that Jesus is talking about going to heaven. "I am the way, and the truth, and the life," he says. "No one comes to the Father except through me." We read this and assume he is talking about non-Christians. But let's look closely, because at no point before or after John 14:6 does anyone ask Jesus about going to heaven or salvation.

Jesus is answering Thomas's question: "Lord, we do not know where you are going. How can we know the way?" (v. 5). And Jesus answers Thomas, "I am the way, and the truth, and the life. No one comes to the Father except through me" (v. 6). Jesus is not answering a question about Buddhists or Muslims and how they could possibly get to heaven. Jesus is trying to address Thomas's uncertainty about what to do next. He is having a private conversation with his disciples about not being afraid when he leaves them.

But here's the challenge. In the Gospel of John, everyone, including the disciples, keeps having the same problem with Jesus. People hear what Jesus says but miss what he means. He speaks in spiritual terms, but they think he is talking about physical things. John 14 may not be any different. Note the pattern:

Chapter 3—Jesus told Nicodemus that he needed to be born again, but Nicodemus was baffled by how someone could reenter his mother's womb and be born a second time. Jesus, however, was talking about spiritual rebirth instead of physical rebirth.

Chapter 4—Jesus told the Samaritan woman that he could give her water that would make her never thirst again, and she told him that the well was deep and he had nothing to use for drawing water. Jesus, however, was talking not about well water but about himself as living water.

Chapter 11—Jesus told the disciples that Lazarus was sleeping and he was going to wake him. The disciples said that if Lazarus was sleeping, he would wake up on his own. Jesus, however, really meant that Lazarus was dead and Jesus was going to raise him back to life.

In John 14, Jesus tells the disciples he is going away. He tells them that his Father's house has many rooms and he is going to prepare a place for them. He says that the disciples know the way to the place where he is going. The disciples think he's talking about a location when he says "house," "rooms," "way," and "place." But is Jesus talking about a location, or is he using this language to describe a spiritual reality—specifically, the spiritual reality of the kingdom of God?

It is important to keep in mind that in John 14 Thomas is talking to Jesus about his own confusion and Jesus is talking to Thomas about the disciples. Jesus is trying to make sure his disciples stick to the plan even when they see him crucified.

So when Thomas asks for certainty about where Jesus is going, Jesus offers him something much better than information. Instead of telling him how to get someplace, Jesus says, "I am the way, and the truth, and the life" (v. 6). Or, as some have said, "I am the way because I am the truth and the life."

Jesus knew that his disciples would experience terrible things in the days ahead, but they need not cave in to fear. He is the way. He knew that they would question everything he ever taught them, but he promised that no matter what happened they could stand firm on everything he had told them. He is the truth. Jesus knew that when they saw him on the cross, death would appear to have the last word. But if they could wait on God to turn the crucifixion into a resurrection, they would see that Jesus is the life.

And if they still wanted to know why they could trust Jesus, Jesus told them, "Whoever has seen me has seen the Father" (v. 9). "I am in the Father" (v. 10), and you are in me, and I am in you. "I am going away" (v. 28). But "I will not leave you orphaned" (v. 18) . . . I will not leave you without help . . . I will not leave you all by yourself . . . Because even though they will crucify me, that will not be the end of me.

He is the way because he is the truth and the life. So keep trusting; keep hoping; keep waiting; keep serving; keep living; keep singing; keep moving; keep pressing; keep pushing; and keep reaching.

Do not let your hearts be troubled, and do not be afraid. Jesus is our way through, our way over, our way in, and our way out. Because of him, we can live above our fears.

24

Staying Connected[1]

John 15:1-17

The need to stay connected is evident in every segment of our lives. From Google eyeglasses to Apple watches, people are finding more and more ways to keep the lines of connectivity open. You will see icons for social media connections on almost any website today.

Staying connected is key in order for anyone or any group to accomplish just about anything. One of the strategic advantages an army tries to gain as quickly as possible is the ability to dismantle, disrupt, or intercept the enemy's communication. Every general knows that staying connected goes hand in hand with victory.

It was once the case that people stayed connected with friends, family, and colleagues by writing letters. I was thinking last week about my godmother who is getting along in years and lives a long distance away from where I currently reside. Although we have never lived close enough to one another to visit often, we managed to nurture a loving bond by staying connected through letters.

Every Christmas and every birthday, without fail, a gift box from her has arrived on time wherever I have lived for all the years of my life. My godmother always includes a handwritten note inquiring about my sisters and me. I read it and write back to thank her for the gift and to let her know how I am doing. Last week I felt the urge to reach out and connect with her for no reason at all. So I sat down and typed an old-fashioned letter. I caught her up on my life and filled her in on what's going on with the rest of the family. Staying connected matters.

When we talk about staying connected in the context of John 15, we are talking about a much deeper and more life-changing connection than what is possible through social media or even by letter. Jesus is talking to the disciples about staying connected to him. He is describing his connection to his disciples. He is explaining what being connected to him looks like and what is possible because of his connection to us.

Let us not forget that the hour is drawing near for Jesus to leave the disciples, which makes what he says so much more crucial and compelling. John does not tell us when this conversation took place, but perhaps it was now getting late in the evening. The disciples may have felt weary from all the things Jesus said that they did not fully understand. Jesus still had much more to say. In fact, one of the differences between John 14 and John 15 and 16 is that chapter 14 is a dialogue, but chapters 15 and 16 are a pure monologue. Jesus does all the talking. Can you imagine the disciples sitting around the table trying to absorb all that Jesus said to them? It must have been like trying to take a drink of water from a fire hydrant.

The importance of this moment is highlighted by the fact that Jesus uses one more of his "I am" sayings in this conversation. We have already come across six of these sayings in our series on John's Gospel. "I am the bread of life" (6:35). "I am the light of the world" (8:12). "I am the [sheep] gate" (10:9). "I am the good shepherd" (10:11, 14). "I am the resurrection and the life" (11:25). "I am the way, and the truth, and the life" (14:6). There are seven "I am" sayings in total and they are only found in the Gospel of John. The last of the seven sayings is right here in John 15: "I am the true vine, and my Father is the vinegrower" (v. 1). Let us walk through Jesus's words with three questions in mind. First, who is Jesus? Second, what is Jesus inviting us to do? Third, what difference will it make if we do what he says?

Who is Jesus? We do not notice many vines on a daily basis in our modern cities, so it may sound strange that Jesus would compare himself to a plant that many American homeowners consider a horticultural nuisance. But in the Jewish mind, vines were a common sight and essential to the agrarian economy. Grapevines are still plentiful in the Mediterranean region of the world. More important, the terms "vines" and "vineyard" are used in Scripture as spiritual metaphors to describe the people of God.

The Old Testament often refers to the nation of Israel as a vine. In Psalm 80, the psalmist says to God, "You brought a vine out of Egypt; you drove out the nations and planted it. You cleared the ground for it; it took deep root and filled the land" (vv. 8-9). The vine the psalmist is talking about is Israel when God brought them out of Egypt and eventually led them to settle in Canaan. The prophet Isaiah says in Isaiah 5:7a, "For the vineyard of the LORD of hosts is the house of Israel."

The image of the vine was deeply ingrained in Israel's identity as a nation, but the disciples may not have understood what Jesus meant when he called himself the true vine. Jesus had a way of using an image people already knew and redefining it to show how he fulfilled it in a different, better, and more complete way.

To say that he is the true vine is to say that he is authentic, legitimate, and real. As the true vine, he is reminding the disciples that he is not an imposter. He is not a magician. He is not a spiritual trickster trying to pull the wool over anyone's eyes, so to speak. He is the Son of God. He is the fulfillment of Israel's hopes. Throughout his three-year ministry, people wondered whether Jesus really was the Christ.

So before Jesus was arrested for impersonating a king, he went on record to say that he is who he says he is. "I am the genuine and authentic incarnation of God." This may be why he told the disciples in chapter 14 that anyone who has seen him has seen the Father. He is the true vine.

Maybe I can explain it this way. I enjoy watching the major horse races. Lately, there has been a great deal of hype around which horse might win the Triple Crown. The Triple Crown is when the same horse wins the three biggest American races in the same year: the Kentucky Derby, the Preakness, and the Belmont Stakes. Every year from May to June, the prognosticators speculate about whether any horse has a chance to beat the odds.

A favorite horse usually rises to the top, and everyone watches to see if the horse has what it takes to win the coveted Triple Crown. To give you an idea of how difficult it is to win this title, the last time one horse won all three races was in 1978. But in 2015 a special horse came on the scene.

American Pharaoh surprised a lot of people and won the 2015 Kentucky Derby without much effort. Then he won the Preakness with ease. But the Belmont Stakes is a much longer and more challenging track. American Pharaoh is not built like the horses that have won the Triple Crown in the past. So, on June 5, 2015, when the gates opened at the Belmont, the fans held their collective breath.

American Pharaoh went to the front of the crowd right from the start. He gained a small lead, but the question was whether he would hold on. The experienced jockey on his back waited as long as he could before he asked for all the effort the horse could give. In the final stretch, American Pharaoh lunged forward with power and grace as if he found a sixth gear. He pulled ahead to win the Belmont Stakes and capture the elusive Triple Crown. The crowd went wild. History had been made. American Pharaoh accomplished what no other horse had done since 1978. He will forever be regarded as an indisputable, undeniable, legitimate, champion racehorse. He's not some fly-by-night pony that got lucky a few times. He is the real deal.

This is what Jesus was saying about himself. When the soldiers come and arrest me, remember that I'm not just a kid from Galilee who had a few spiritual pranks up his sleeve. "I am the true vine" (15:1)! I am the authentic Son of the Living God. I raised the dead. I opened blind eyes. I walked on water. I miraculously fed a multitude. "I am the true vine" (15:1)!"

There comes a time when we cannot make progress until we know who we are. At every turn, people tried to tell Jesus who he was not. "You cannot be the Son of God. You are Joseph's son." "You are not the Messiah. You came from Nazareth." "You have no right to forgive sins. Only God can do that." "You do not have the authority to heal on the Sabbath. Who do you think you are, Jesus?" But Jesus's genius is that he knows who he is. Now he must make sure the disciples know who they are.

What is Jesus inviting us to do? "You are the branches" (v. 5). This is who we are, which is both challenging and comforting. The comfort comes from the fact that Jesus did not say that the disciples needed to make themselves into branches. He did not ask the disciples to fill out an application to see if they qualified as a branch. He did not say that if they worked really hard, he would promote them to be a branch. Jesus said that his disciples were branches as a statement of fact. He is the true vine. We are the branches. This is who we are, and we are such because he says we are. The good news is that if Jesus is the vine, the necessities for living flow through him to us because we are the branches. We just have to stay connected to the vine.

Self-help will only carry us so far because we are not the vine. We are branches. One of the great searches of life is to find something to hold on to that is strong enough, secure enough, and reliable enough to keep us from losing our way. What we need most for life and peace comes only from the true vine. So Jesus's word to the branches is simple: "Remain in me, as I also remain in you" (v. 4, NIV). This is what Jesus is inviting us to do.

"Remain in me" is rendered "abide in me" in the King James Version and others, like the New Revised Standard Version. To remain or abide means to "dwell, or to take up residence in, to stay with." Jesus makes it clear that his part is nonnegotiable. He will remain in his disciples. He was making it clear that he would not abandon them. He would not retreat from them. This is important to know in the tough places of life. Family and friends go with us as far as they can, but they are not always able to go with us as far as we wish. The great promise throughout the Bible is that God is so committed to us that God will not leave us.

Having established his commitment to the disciples, Jesus asked them for the same kind of commitment to him. "Remain in me. Abide in me" (v. 4). Jesus was not speaking to the multitudes. He was speaking to those who were supposed to know him best. Jesus knows that when trouble comes, the human tendency is to withdraw and hold back for self-protection. We disconnect and retreat into silos of self-preservation. In fact, the only way to inoculate ourselves against being hurt in this life is by not reaching out to others, not making room in our hearts for love. Of course, that only brings a different kind of pain, the pain of loneliness. So Jesus asked the disciples to do for him what he was willing to do and had already done on their behalf. "Remain in me. When you feel the sting of criticism, remain in me. When you endure the struggle of patience, remain in me."

It would be insensitive for Jesus to tell us to remain in him without saying something about *how* we remain in him. Jesus tells us how to remain in him beginning in verse 9-10: "As the Father has loved me, so have I loved you. Now remain in my love. If you keep my commands, you will remain in my love, just as I have kept my Father's commands and remain in his love" (NIV). We remain in Jesus when we continue in his love. Jesus's extravagant, radical love empowers us, fills us, and equips us to go out and be loving to others. This is the challenging part. Jesus's love is not sentimental. Jesus's love is costly and courageous. To love as Jesus loved, we bless those who curse us. To love as Jesus loved, we welcome the stranger.

This is an important lesson to remember, especially after the tragedy of last week. On Wednesday night, a twenty-one-year-old white male sat through Bible study at the historic Emmanuel African Methodist Episcopal Church in Charleston, South Carolina. When he left, nine people were dead, including the pastor, a servant-leader who had dedicated his life to the struggle for justice. We feel the horror of this racially motivated violence hanging over the nation like a gray, stormy cloud.

Jesus's words in John 15 seem to offer his disciples a strategy to deal with the persistence of evil, evil that he knew would result in his crucifixion. When evil brushes against our lives, it leaves a sticky residue. So before Jesus's enemies rise against him, he tells the disciples, "Remain in my love." He knew what was ahead for him and for his disciples. He knew the meanness they would face and the hostility they would encounter. So he gave them a countercultural command to remember. "Remain in my love."

We are called to remember Jesus's words whenever we are confronted by evil in any shape or form. This does not mean that we minimize or become complacent about injustice. But it does mean that we bear fruit by continuing to walk in his love. Jesus demonstrated the fruit of love even when it cost him everything. Jesus said, "Greater love has no one than this: to lay down one's life for one's friends" (v. 13, NIV).

What difference will it make if we do what Jesus commands? Thinking about the metaphors of vines and branches, it is clear that Jesus expects his disciples to grow. Growth is not a process that we make happen on our own. Those who abide in Jesus—those who remain connected to him through prayer, worship, and loving service—are the ones who bear much fruit. Apart from him, we do not bear fruit because apart from him we can do nothing.

The Father is so interested in fruitful disciples that when we do bear fruit, he prunes us to make us more fruitful. It isn't hard to understand why the Father would cut off a branch that does not bear fruit. But Jesus says that the Father prunes even the branches that do bear fruit. Every gardener knows that if a growing plant is not pruned carefully and intentionally, it will become an unmanageable mess. So the wise gardener prunes to produce more beautiful and bountiful fruit in the future.

It has been my experience that the closer I come to God, the more God reveals to me what God wants to remove from my life. The more I remain in God's love through the power of the Spirit, the better I am able to see what is not like God in my life. This begins God's pruning process. Every attitude we do not need, God prunes. Every thought that hinders our faith, God prunes. Every selfish ambition that is a stumbling block to ministry, God prunes. The closer we come to God, the more God prunes.

God can see the beauty within, so God prunes. God wants to develop the strength of our soul, so God prunes. God does not bring evil and sickness into our lives, but God does prune. God desires to see disciples bearing fruit, so Jesus gives us an open invitation: "Live in me. Make your home in me just as I do in you" (v. 4, *The Message*).

"Continue in my work and hold on to my words," Jesus says. "As you remain in my love, my presence will go with you. As you remain in my love, my joy will be in you. As you remain in my love, I will bear much fruit in your lives. Stay connected."

Note

1. The Emanuel AME church massacre occurred in Charleston, South Carolina, on June 17, 2015. Since that time, the killer, Dylann Roof, has been sentenced to death.

25

Courageous Faith

John 15:18–16:33

We need courage if we are going to flourish and thrive in this world. The list of things, people, circumstances, and failures we are told to fear grows longer every day. It requires courage just to get up in the morning and put one foot in front of the other, to face the day at hand. We need courage to work with the hand we have when we have not been dealt the hand we wanted. We need courage to find a way forward by faith when we are facing multiple possibilities and none of them are good.

One definition of courage is strength in the face of pain or grief. Another definition says that courage is the quality of mind or spirit that enables a person to face difficulty, pain, or danger without fear. I agree with everything in this second definition except the part that says "without fear." Courage is not the absence of fear. Courage is when we decide that fear is not going to tell us what to do or how to live.

Some of the greatest speeches in history have inspired ordinary people to act with extraordinary courage. Speaking at Brown Chapel AME Church in Selma, Alabama, in March of 1965, Rev. Martin Luther King Jr. told a packed church that a "man dies when he refuses to take a stand for that which is true. So we are going to stand up right here amidst billy clubs, amidst tear gas, amidst anything, letting the world know that we are determined to be free." With these words he rallied a city to pursue the courageous path of nonviolent civil disobedience.

Winston Churchill overcame a speech impediment to become a great orator and inspired courage among the British in 1940. In a speech to Parliament's House of Commons in June of that year, he said,

> Even though large tracts of Europe and many old and famous States have fallen or may fall into the grip of the Gestapo and all the odious apparatus of Nazi rule, we shall not flag or fail. We shall go on to the

end, we shall fight in France, we shall fight on the seas and oceans, we shall fight with growing confidence and growing strength in the air, we shall defend our Island, whatever the cost may be, we shall fight on the beaches, we shall fight on the landing grounds, we shall fight in the fields and in the streets, we shall fight in the hills; we shall never surrender, and even if, which I do not for a moment believe, this Island or a large part of it were subjugated and starving, then our Empire beyond the seas, armed and guarded by the British Fleet, would carry on the struggle, until, in God's good time, the New World, with all its power and might, steps forth to the rescue and the liberation of the old.[1]

Your spine straightens and your chin rises with every courageous word from Churchill's lips. This section of Scripture from the Gospel of John is Jesus's call for courage. Jesus had already predicted that Judas would betray him and Peter would deny him. The mood among the disciples was heavy and sad. As the night wore on, Jesus rallied them with a word of encouragement.

He told the disciples not to let their hearts be troubled. He promised to be the way, a guide leading them through the unpredictable paths of the future. His message to them was this: "Do not let your hearts be troubled, and do not let them be afraid" (John 14:27).

Jesus not only encouraged the disciples in this late-night lesson. He also challenged them. After they had been with him for these three years, Jesus now wanted them to do something for him. He wanted them to be ready for their next assignment. He told them that after he died, he expected them to testify about him.

"Testify" is a word that brings to mind a courtroom setting. John has been using legal images throughout the entire Gospel, especially the words "testify" and "witness," depending on the translation you read.

In fact, the Gospel of John is actually written as if Jesus is on trial. Is he or is he not the Son of God? John the Baptist was called as the first witness. John 1:32, 34 says, "And John testified: 'I saw the Spirit descending from heaven like a dove and it remained on [Jesus] . . . . I myself have seen and have testified that this is the Son of God.'" John the Baptist was the first witness to affirm Jesus's divine identity.

The Pharisees charged Jesus with a crime, the crime of blasphemy, when he healed on the Sabbath in John 5. So Jesus did what anyone charged with a crime would do. He called witnesses to testify on his behalf. Jesus told the Pharisees that John the Baptist testified that Jesus had come from God.

If by chance they did not believe John, he had a witness greater than John. Jesus said the works the Father gave him to do testified that the Father sent him. When you are doing the Lord's work, you do not have to tell everyone how great you and your works are. The works will testify on your behalf. Jesus then told the Pharisees that if they did not believe the works, the Father himself testified that Jesus had come from God. If they did not believe John the Baptist, his works, or the Father, they should at least believe the Scriptures, which also testified about him.

Jesus is on trial in the Gospel of John. But at the time of this text, Jesus was talking to his disciples. As he prepared for the crucifixion, which was only hours away, he knew that even when he laid down his life, many would not be convinced by his obedience and love that he was who he said he was. So he turned to the eleven remaining disciples. Judas had already left the place where they ate together. Jesus said to his disciples that he was sending them out to testify about him.

This was a definite change in plans. The disciples signed up to be students. They signed up to be followers. They came on board to be supporters. They signed up to soak in his wisdom, marvel at his miracles, and enjoy his teaching. They agreed to all of this as long as they could stay in the background. Now Jesus wanted to lift their discipleship to a higher level. Soon the time would come when they would be called to testify about him. They would need courage.

Have you ever wondered what next level of commitment God might be calling us to? This journey called faith is like a staircase where there is always one more step to climb. We never get to the top, but we keep moving up; otherwise, as Jesus says in John 16:1, we stumble. The next level for the disciples was to testify about Jesus. To testify is to affirm that one has seen or heard or experienced something. To testify is to give a report about what one has been taught or received by divine inspiration. To testify is to agree to the truth of something. This is what all the miracles, signs, and wonders have led up to. Jesus wanted the disciples to move from observation to participation, from student to teacher, from watchers to workers, from onlookers to leaders. "You also are to testify because you have been with me from the beginning" (v. 27).

Testifying about Jesus has always been and will always be at the center of the mission of the church. The primary task of the church is to be a witness, which is not limited to any one story about what God has done for us personally. Of course, every Christian should have a testimony of what God has done for us. But Jesus has put his finger on something else. To testify as John 15:27 suggests is to make it known by word and deed that Jesus is who he says he is. To testify is to do the work that Jesus did, to care as he cared, to live as he lived, and to love as he loved. To testify is to live by faith in the One who gives life—life that is more abundant—and to point others to him so that they too can experience the goodness of God.

Jesus is careful to warn the disciples that testifying about him will not be an easy assignment. It will require courage, because when we testify about him we will sometimes face the same resistance he faced. Jesus wanted to make it known that anyone who followed him would experience blessings and pay costs. This is why we need courage.

Go back to what Jesus said in John 15:18-19 (NIV): "If the world hates you [which it does], keep in mind that it hated me first. If you belonged to the world, it would love you as its own. As it is, you do not belong to the world, but I have chosen you out of the world. That is why the world hates you."

Sometimes it's hard to understand Jesus. When we want people to sign up for something, we don't offer as an incentive the promise that they will be hated for their efforts. We promise people recognition or fulfillment or a reward of some kind. We print their names in a program or give them special VIP treatment. Jesus does none of that. He has no time to give the disciples anything except the unfiltered truth. He has come down to the last few hours of his life on earth. If his disciples chose to love as he loved and care as he cared, if they want to live as he lived, they should know that the world hated him and there was a high probability that the world will hate them, too. This is why they need courage. And so do we.

Jesus was absolutely right. The disciples did not win friends by following him. They lost friends. They were expelled from synagogues. They were arrested, beaten, and even killed. Throughout the history of the church, Christians have willingly and unwillingly lost their lives as a result of their faith. But we do need to be careful when we read a text like this in the twenty-first century because it is tempting to see ourselves as victims who are being persecuted by a hostile world. We do not have time to talk about it today, but, sadly, history also tells us that the church has done too much persecuting of its own.

So what should we make of Jesus saying that the world will hate us? Why would anyone hate someone for following Jesus? Jesus preached and practiced love. Why would anyone become a target of people's animosity because they follow the Prince of Peace? One reason the world might hate a follower of Christ is because Jesus not only brings grace but also exposes sin and reveals guilt. We become a target not because of who we are but because of whom we represent. We may be hated by the world.

When Jesus said the "world," he was not talking about every person who lives on the earth. He was not focusing on how individual people may dislike us because we are Christians, although that does happen. In this passage, the term "world" is a spiritual term. "World" stands for every thought, institution, system, and power that is opposed to God. For example, Dylann Roof was not a lone wolf acting independently when he gunned down nine people at a Bible study at Emanuel AME Church in Charleston, South Carolina. He was a product of a system and culture that has systematically opposed the love of God in so many ways. The world represents the values and ambitions that maintain the status quo over and against the values and ambitions that embody the kingdom of God.

Jesus wanted the disciples to know in advance that even though they were going to live in the world, they would not always fit in with the world. They would not be able to go along with the systems, patterns, and institutions of the world when those were opposed to God—opposed to the love of God, opposed to the justice of God, opposed to the mercy of God, and opposed to the holiness of God. This was what got Jesus into trouble. When he saw a man who had been lame for thirty-eight years, he healed the man. The religious leaders did not like that Jesus healed the man on the Sabbath. Jesus was not able to go along with the Sabbath system when the system did not make room for compassion on a suffering soul.

So Jesus reminded the disciples, "you do not belong to the world, but I have chosen you out of the world" (15:19, NIV). He chose them out of the world's way of thinking. He chose them out of the world's way of living. He chose them out of the world's way of treating other people so that they might have the courage to live like they belonged to him. He has chosen us for the same. We need courage.

It takes courage to swim against the currents of convenience and comfort. It takes courage to overcome the daily distractions—some of them big and some so small we barely notice—that test our resolve to stand without compromise. It takes courage because there is always the risk of conflict with people, with institutions, and even within ourselves when instead of going along with the values and ambitions of this world, we choose the ideals of the kingdom of God.

The world says we are honored when people serve us, but disciples believe it is an honor to wash someone's feet. The world says "blessed are the powerful for they shall rule over the poor," but disciples believe the meek are blessed, "for they shall inherit the earth" (Matt 5:5, ESV). The world says "look out for you and nobody else," but disciples follow the One who says, "No one has greater love than this, to lay down one's life for one's friends" (John 15:13).

This is how we testify about Jesus. We live with courage even if we do not fit in, even if it is dangerous, even if we are misunderstood, even if we have to pay a price. Jesus knew that what he was asking was not easy, so he let the disciples know that living with courage was not something they had to do on their own. Since he was the one calling them and he was the One who chose them, he was not going to fail to help them.

Jesus already told them in chapter 14 about the help he would send them through the Holy Spirit. "But the Advocate, the Holy Spirit, whom the Father will send in my name, will teach you everything, and remind you of all that I have said to you" (14:26).

Here Jesus said even more about the soon-to-come Holy Spirit. This is where our courage comes from. "When the Advocate comes, whom I will send to you from the Father, the Spirit of truth who comes from the Father, he will testify on my behalf" (15:26). He says later in 16:7b (NIV), "Unless I go away, the Advocate will not come to you; but if I go, I will send him to you." The disciples will not have to do anything on their own that Jesus called them to do.

There will be testing and trials, but the disciples will not be on their own. There will be conflict and opposition as they continue his mission in the world, but they will not be their own. Some who follow him may lose their lives at the hands of misguided, misinformed, and malevolent people, but even in their darkest hour they will not be on their own. God will help them. Jesus intended to keep this promise by sending the Holy Spirit.

It is fitting that Jesus brings up the Spirit again now. The disciples must have sensed that something disturbing was about to happen, but they were not sure when, what, or where. The disciples now know they would be persecuted, but Jesus also said he was going to leave them. A burden is a little easier to bear if we do not have to bear it by ourselves.

It did not make sense that Jesus was going away. The disciples had given up so much to be with him, and now he was going away? If they ever needed courage, they surely needed it now.

If Jesus left them, who would be there to help them when the world was against them? If Jesus left them, who would be there to encourage them when they felt as though they could not continue one more step on the journey?

They did not understand it at the time, but it would be for the disciples' good that Jesus went away. Right now they had God with them, but when he sent the Spirit they would have God living inside them. Right now, Jesus could only be in one place at one time. When he was in Jerusalem he could not be with them in Galilee. When he was in Galilee he could not also be in Jerusalem. Jesus was limited by his humanity. He could not be on a mountain and also be with them when the storm was raging on the Sea of Galilee.

But do not fear, he told them. Be strong and courageous. Jesus and the Father had already worked everything out. The crucifixion would happen, but he and his Father would not leave the disciples alone. Jesus says in 14:16-17, 18, "And I will ask the Father, and he will give you another Advocate, to be with you forever. This is the Spirit of truth . . . . I will not leave you orphaned; I am coming to you."

Then in chapter 15, Jesus says, "When the Advocate comes, whom I will send to you from the Father, the Spirit of truth who comes from the Father, he will testify on my behalf" (v. 26). There was no doubt in Jesus's mind about what would happen when he left. The third Person of the Trinity was already in position. And once Jesus gave the word to the Father, the Father would send the Spirit.

It is easy to get disappointed when someone is sent to stand in for the person you were expecting. We may not be quite sure if a replacement can measure up to the standard we already know. But Jesus said the disciples had no need to think that when he went away they would be left with someone of lesser ability. When he says, "he will give you another Advocate" (14:16), "another" is the translation of a word that literally means another one of the same kind.

We need to know this about the Holy Spirit. The Father is God. Jesus is God. The Spirit is God. The Father is divine. Jesus is divine. The Spirit is divine. When the Holy Spirit is with us, we have the power of God with us.

Everything Jesus did he did by the Spirit, in the Spirit, through the Spirit, and with the Spirit. So when the Spirit came, the disciples would still have every bit of God with them that they had when Jesus was with them.

This is why Jesus could send the disciples to testify about him. This is why he could ask them to love those who hated them and love those they really did not like. They would not have to do it on their own. This is why he could say to them that they would grieve, but their grief would turn to joy. Once the Spirit came, the same God who was with them would be *in them*. This is the source of our courageous faith as well.

Jesus says, "In this world you will have trouble. But take heart!" (16:33, NIV). Don't let anyone fool you. In this world, we will have trouble. There will be obstacles and barriers, burdens and dilemmas, confusions and trials. There will be sickness and sorrow, grief and disappointment. But take heart. Jesus said he has already been through it. And not only has he been through it; he has already overcome. So "take courage" (v. 33)!

Jesus was not leaving because he had failed. He was not leaving because the pressure was too much for him. He was not leaving because doing the will of the Father was more than he could bear. Jesus's departure was not a sign of defeat. His leaving was going to be an act of completion. It was going to be an act of victory. This is why he said, "But take heart! I have overcome the world" (v. 33, NIV).

"I've overcome sin and suffering," he said. "I've overcome heartache and fear. I've overcome evil and injustice. I have overcome the world."

And if Jesus has the victory, then we have the victory because he is in us and we are in him. The power that enabled him to overcome is now available to anyone and everyone who puts their trust in him.

And that power is not only with us; that power is the Spirit of truth *within* us. So take heart. No matter how long the fight, take heart. No matter how long the night, take heart. Be strong and be of good courage, and God will strengthen your heart.

Note

1. Winston Churchill, "We Shall Fight on the Beaches," International Churchill Society (speech, House of Commons of the UK Parliament, June 4, 1940), retrieved from https://winstonchurchill.org/resources/speeches/1940-the-finest-hour/we-shall-fight-on-the-beaches/.

26

When Jesus Prayed

John 17

"After Jesus said this, he looked toward heaven and prayed" (v. 1, NIV). These simple words let us gaze at one of the most beautiful moments in Jesus's late-night session with his disciples. He has already been with them for many long hours. He has washed feet. He has warned Peter. He has even promised to send them the Holy Spirit, the Comforter, to be with them when he returns to the Father.

We may find it hard to believe, but it is important to remember that everything we have been reading since chapter 13 has taken place on one Thursday night. The exact span of time can be measured in hours, not days. At the end of his sobering conversation with the disciples, Jesus prayed.

Prayer was central to Jesus's life and ministry. Prayer was so much a part of Jesus's life that we could say he worked while he prayed and prayed while he worked. In the Gospel of Mark (chapter 3), Jesus prays before he chooses the twelve who became his disciples. In the Gospel of Matthew (chapter 26), Jesus prays when he is in the Garden of Gethsemane because his soul is overwhelmed with sorrow as the time of his crucifixion comes closer and closer. Jesus prayed so much and so well that in Luke, after he finishes praying, one of his disciples says to him, "Lord, teach us to pray, as John taught his disciples" (11:1).

I'm guessing that we are just like the disciples. We want someone to guide us and direct us in the arena of prayer. The disciples did not want to flounder in their faith. They wanted the kind of deep personal connection with God that they observed in Jesus. Sometimes we act as if prayer is something we should automatically or innately know how to do. Not so with the disciples. They asked Jesus to teach them how to pray.

What is prayer? Christian prayer is not a generic equivalent for mental relaxation. Prayer is the means of a spiritual connection between the Creator and the creature. Prayer is a dialogue between the human and the

Divine. Prayer is a conversation that takes place between God and the people of God. Prayer does not have to be complex to be effective. Prayer does not require a big vocabulary or a sophisticated theological background. But it is essential that the one who is praying has the desire to be in real fellowship and close communion with the God who hears and answers prayers.

Hannah struggled so deeply with her inability to bear children that her anguish drove her to deep, personal prayer. In her desire to hear from God, she prayed simply, "LORD Almighty . . . remember me" (1 Sam 1:11, NIV).

In Psalm 61, David starts out with the words, "Hear my cry, O God; listen to my prayer. From the ends of the earth I call to you, when my heart is faint. Lead me to the rock that is higher than I" (vv. 1-2). These heartfelt words of prayer may be why Richard Foster, the author of *Celebration of Discipline*, reminds us that prayer catapults us onto the frontier of the spiritual life.[1]

Jesus prayed often, but we know little about the content or mood of most of his prayers. Most of what we know about Jesus's praying comes from what we read in John 17. John 17 is sometimes called the "real" Lord's Prayer because what we usually call the Lord's Prayer is actually the prayer Jesus taught the disciples: "Our Father who art in heaven, hallowed be thy name . . . ." The prayer in John 17, on the other hand, is what the Lord himself prayed, making it the real Lord's Prayer. This prayer is also called the high priestly prayer because in it Jesus fulfills a priestly role by praying for himself and interceding for others.

However we want to describe this prayer, it easily divides into three distinct sections. The first section is Jesus's prayer concerning himself. The second is Jesus's prayer for the disciples. The third is Jesus's prayer for those who would come to believe in him in the future.

Consider what Jesus prayed concerning himself. John says in verse 1, "After Jesus said this, he looked toward heaven and prayed" (NIV). He had said everything to the disciples that could be said. He told them another Advocate was coming after he left. He told them that he had much more to say to them, but what he did say was all they could bear. He told them to stay connected and remain in him. He warned them that the world would hate them, yet he would never fail them. He then told them to take heart and be of good cheer because he had already overcome the world. After saying these things, he looked up to heaven and prayed.

If you don't already know it, there comes a time when human conversation has to end so that we can have a conversation with God. We all benefit from friends and loved ones we can look to for wisdom. But sometimes our conversations and brainstorming sessions can only take us so far. Our hearts will cry out in prayer for God. This was that time for Jesus.

His prayer was a personal, intimate, and sacred dialogue between the Father and the Son. What Jesus says in these twenty-six verses should be off limits to human ears.

I watched a woman sit down at a table in a restaurant this week. A waiter came out of the kitchen with part of the food she ordered. As he came closer to her table, he noticed that the customer had bowed her head to pray. Reverently and respectfully, he stopped, put the plate on the counter, and waited until she opened her eyes and raised her head before bringing the plate to the table. I do not know anything about the waiter's faith, but when he saw the customer praying he paused so as not to interrupt, disturb, or even overhear the woman as she prayed.

Truthfully, anyone who recognizes what was happening when Jesus prayed should tiptoe out of the room when they hear John 17. Who among us has the right to listen to what was said between the Father and the Son? This was a prayer like no one before or after Jesus has ever prayed. Who else can say that the Father granted them authority over all people that they might give eternal life to people? Who else can say, "Glorify me in your presence with the glory I had with you before the world began" (John 17:5, NIV)?[2] We have no right to hear these words, but once again Jesus gives us a gift better and bigger than we deserve.

A word that best describes the way Jesus prayed is "intimate." Jesus did not use the plural preposition "our" before Father. He addressed the Father in a much more personal way. He only said "Father." Our prayers are toothless and timid when we do not know to whom we are talking. Jesus was not praying to a frightening, demanding God. Jesus was not crying out to a harsh, angry deity. Jesus was not bowing before a critical and punitive personality. Jesus prayed to his loving, merciful, good, wise, and faithful Father. He said to his Father that his hour had come.

The phrase including the word "hour" first appeared in chapter 2 when Jesus changed the water into wine. At that time, he said his hour had not yet come. The hour referred to the moment of divine timing and to the crucifixion. When religious leaders tried to apprehend Jesus in chapter 7 because he claimed to come from God, John says no one laid a hand on him then because his hour had not yet come. The same thing happened in John 8. But now the hour has come. How did Jesus know that his hour had come?

One of the blessings of living in God, with God, and for God, is that it becomes possible for us to have insight not only into what God wants us to do but also into when the time has come to do it. Jesus knew that his time had come, and he was confident in facing his hour because of the fact that he finished the work the Father gave him to do. "I have glorified you on earth by finishing the work that you gave me to do," he prayed (v. 4).

Do we realize how few people can pray those words? "Father, I have completed the assignment you gave me." "Father, I have done the work you asked me to do." "Father, I have accomplished what you sent me to do." So many of our days are filled with unfinished tasks. There are too few hours in the day. There are setbacks and distractions. Our lives may end half-finished no matter how long or how well we live. Jesus is unique in that he can pray that he finished the work he was given to do.

His sense of completion and fulfillment might seem surprising given the barriers he faced along the way, not to mention the detachment of soldiers that was going to lead him to his death only moments after closing this prayer. What does Jesus mean when he says he finished the work? He is not talking about the cross since that has not happened yet. Besides, on the cross he says, "It is finished" (19:30). Here he says, "I have finished."

It may be that the work he finished is associated with the gift of eternal life. Just before he says he finished the work, he says that he gave eternal life to all those whom the Father gave him. Giving eternal life was what he came to do.

Eternal life sounds like a life that goes on forever, but Jesus had another thought in mind when he said "eternal life." Eternal life is not so much the quantity or duration of life as much as it is the quality or the character of life. John 17:3 gives one of the clearest definitions of eternal life in Scripture: "And this is eternal life, that they may know you, the only true God, and Jesus Christ whom you have sent." Eternal life is the life that results from knowing the only true God as revealed by God's Son, Jesus Christ. Eternal life is not memorizing creeds, doctrines, or dogmas. Eternal life is not earned by conduct or good works. Eternal life is knowing. Knowing is putting one's faith and hope and trust in God. Knowing is being in a spiritually growing relationship with God. Knowing is looking to Jesus as the giver of life. Knowing Jesus is different than knowing about Jesus.

People often ask me if I know certain people. Do I know this pastor or that pastor? Because I do not want to be the kind of preacher who claims a relationship with other pastors in order to boost my own status, I am always careful to say whether I know someone or just know *of* them. I know *of* many pastors. I know the names of the churches they serve. I know something about their ministries. But if I have never spent any time with them, if I cannot pull up their number in my phone, call, text, message, or email them and expect to get an answer, I will not go on record that I know them because we do not have that kind of relationship.

For three years, Jesus had been giving people the chance to truly know God through him. This was what he meant in verse 6: "I have made your name known to those whom you gave me from the world." Jesus will soon lay down his life so that those who seem unable to grasp the magnitude of God's love may see God, experience God, be drawn into relationship with God, and, through Jesus, come to know God the Father. Didn't Jesus tell Thomas in John 14 that if anyone has seen him, they have seen the Father?

Eternal life is knowing God through the One God sent. Eternal life is relationship. Jesus was sent to make it possible to come close to God. He came to open up the way for us to walk more closely with God. Because of the incarnation, God was no longer completely beyond the human imagination. In Jesus, God came near, opened wide his arms of unconditional love, and gave us the gift of personal fellowship and communion with God. This was the work Jesus finished. So in this prayer he asked the Father, "glorify me in your own presence with the glory I had in your presence before the world began" (v. 5). This is how Jesus prayed for himself. He prayed for the Father to glorify him now that his work was finished. The Father would do this for Jesus, but only through the cross.

Jesus was not thinking only of himself in this prayer. He remembered to pray for his disciples, too. Jesus made two main requests concerning the disciples. He asked the Father to protect them and to sanctify them and send them into the world.

Jesus prayed for the disciples' protection because faith in him is not meant to be an escape from the world. We do not put our faith in Jesus and then retreat from the world and hide from its problems. We cannot become so spiritual that we ignore brokenness that we encounter every day. Jesus's prayer acknowledged that he was going away, but the disciples would still be in the world. This is what it means to be a disciple. We are not of the world, but we are in the world.

We are in the world with its unemployment and injustice. We are in the world with its beauty and goodness. We are in the world with homelessness and war. We are in the world with its joys and triumphs. We are in a world gripped by inequality and poverty. Jesus prayed in verse 15 that he did not want the disciples to be taken out of the world. Why?

The world was where God needed them. If God took the disciples out of the world, it might look like God himself had abandoned the world. And John 3:16 says that God loves the world. So Jesus prayed for the disciples to go on living in the world. He wanted the disciples to stay in the midst of all that he dealt with in his life.

He wanted them to stay among sickness so one day they could build hospitals of care, stay among the hurting so they could offer words of hope, stay among the wicked so they could be representatives of God's righteousness, stay among the suffering so they could bring relief. Jesus did not want them to be taken out of the world, nor does he want us to disengage from this imperfect world. But he did pray that while the disciples were in the world, they would be protected from the evil one by the power of God's name.

This is the part of the prayer that should have given the disciples great comfort. Because of Jesus's prayer, the disciples now had the assurance of God's protection that they would not be defeated in this life. They were going to be protected by the power of God's name. Although they would have to remain in the world, they would be protected by the power of God's name when Jesus sent them out to continue his ministry. Every time the evil one came against them, they would be guarded by the power of God's name. Whenever an enemy tried to get the upper hand, they would be defended by the power of God's name.

We are sometimes able to get into places and get out of circumstances because we know the right name. We go for the interview, someone finds out that the CEO is a family friend, and we get the job because we know the right name. If we apply to a college and our parents went to the same school, our application may get special consideration because we know the right name. Jesus sent the disciples into the world protected by the name of God. And for what Jesus had planned for them, they needed the power of God's name.

The mission was not going to end when he returned to the Father. Just as the Father sent Jesus into the world, Jesus called the disciples to a mission in the world. Just as Jesus faced opposition and difficulty with the confidence that the Father was always with him, these disciples were called to go forth into the world knowing they would be protected by the power of God's name.

This is the faith that guides us in ministry and in life. When trouble comes, we do not have to rely on Peter's name. We do not have to put our trust in Andrew's name. In the words of David, "some trust in chariots and some in horses, but we trust in the name of the LORD" (Ps 20:7, NIV).

God's name is above every name. God's name is a strong tower. God's name makes powers and principalities tremble. God has many names because God's name represents God's character, God's ability, and God's identity. Since God is everything, God cannot be defined by a single name. If you are a disciple, Jesus prayed that you would be protected by God's name. Go into all nations making disciples, teaching them to obey everything Jesus commanded. We are protected by God's name. Face your upcoming mission with peace. You are protected by the Father's name. This does not mean we cannot be hurt, but it does mean that no matter what happens to us, God is still working for us. We are protected by his name!

What is God's name?

God's name is Eternal One. God's name is the Lord of our righteousness and the God of all comfort. God's name is Savior and Son, the ever-present God, and the great shepherd of the sheep; God's name is the Lord of glory, the only wise God, Alpha and Omega, the lion of Judah, and the King of kings. God's name is Yahweh and Elohim. God's name is Adonai. God's name is Spirit of truth and Light of the world.

Jesus prayed for himself. He prayed thankfully that he had finished the work of giving eternal life, which is relationship with God. He prayed reverently that the Father would glorify him, make it known who he was, through the crucifixion and resurrection. He prayed for the disciples to be protected by the power of God's name, and he also prayed for those who would come to believe because of the disciples' message.

In other words, Jesus prayed that the walls between human beings would come down so that we all might be one as the Father and the Son are one. He prayed for reconciliation to take place so that those who did not know him would come to know him through those that did know him. He prayed for hearts to change and minds to be transformed. He had done his work among Peter, James, and John, but he was looking ahead to the disciples yet to come.

Jesus prayed for the man who was disabled and sat at the gate of the temple in Acts 3. The man never met Jesus, but he came to believe because of Peter and John. Jesus prayed for the Ethiopian eunuch in Acts 8. The man never saw Jesus, but he came to believe because of the preaching of Philip. Jesus prayed for the jail guard in Acts 16. The man never encountered Jesus firsthand, but he and his entire household came to believe because of the testimony of Paul and Silas. Jesus prayed for the disciples to go out into the world because he knew there would be others to come.

And the New Testament says he was right. Three thousand joined the church when Peter preached on Pentecost. People came to believe in Ephesus, Lystra, and Derbe when Paul taught them that Jesus was the Christ.

Jesus said, "My prayer is not for my current disciples alone. I'm praying for those who will believe in me through their message, that all of them may be one, Father, just as you are in me and I am in you" (vv. 20-21, translation mine).

I like to think that when Jesus prayed this prayer, he was praying not only for the Ethiopian and the jailer and the 3,000 who came when Peter preached. He was also praying for you and me.

He prayed that somehow we would come into the kingdom. One day we would say yes to eternal life. One day we would accept his grace, be transformed by his love and sanctified by his word. We are not here on our own. We did not come to faith because we figured it all out. We are here because Jesus prayed. He prayed that we would be in him and he in us. He prayed that we would have unity with other believers. He prayed that we would see him as the light of our world and the bread of our life. He prayed that the love the Father had for him would be in us. He prayed that we would know him, trust him, serve him, follow him, wait for him, and belong to him. Aren't you glad Jesus prayed?

Notes

1. Richard Foster, *Celebration of Discipline* (San Francisco: Harper & Row, 1978) 33.

2. D. Moody Smith, *First, Second, and Third John*, Interpretation: A Bible Commentary for Teaching and Preaching (Louisville: Westminster John Knox Press, 2012) Kindle Edition, 196.

27

What Will We Do about Jesus?[1]

John 18:1–19:3

The four Gospels, Matthew, Mark, Luke, and John, tell us about the same Jesus but use different details. For example, we only read about the raising of Lazarus from the dead in John. We only read about Jesus healing a man who was possessed by demons and lived in a cemetery in Mark. One story shared by all four Gospels is the humiliating, painful account of Jesus's crucifixion and the conflict that precedes it.

Perhaps one reason for the variances we detect is there was so much story to tell that no one person could tell the whole of it. God enlisted four unique witnesses to testify about everything that took place on the three days that changed the world.

John has already proven to be different from the other Gospels in a few important ways. One of the key words in John is the word "believe." John has been saying this about Jesus all along. Believe. Believe that Jesus is the Son of God. Believe that Jesus is the resurrection and the life. Believe that Jesus is the way, the truth, and the life. Believe that Jesus of Nazareth came from God and is in fact God in human flesh, God incarnate. Most of the people Jesus encountered did not believe. The radical idea that Jesus was Divine was so scandalous to the religious leaders that Jesus eventually became public enemy number one.

From the day Jesus turned over the tables in the temple (John 2), people in positions of power sought to silence him. They did not believe. When Jesus said he was the Son of God, people accused him of lying. When Jesus made sick people well, people blamed him for healing on the wrong day. When Jesus forgave sins, people condemned him for saying he could do what only God could do. When Jesus raised Lazarus back to life, the high priest decided it was time to put a stop to Jesus once and for all. The high priest hatched a sinister plan to take Jesus's life to make sure no one else would believe in him.

Jesus's enemies waited for the right time. That time had finally come. Jesus had been in Jerusalem for almost a week by now. The city was crowded with pilgrims and a festive mood was in the air. This was the week of the annual Passover festival. Passover had been a yearly ritual since the days of Moses when their ancestors came out of slavery in Egypt.

The king of Egypt was so hardhearted that he would not willingly emancipate the Israelites, so after the sending of nine plagues to change the king's mind failed, God finally sent a plague of death that killed the firstborn son in every Egyptian household. Sadly, we have seen in our own time that sometimes things do not change until people die.

Celebrating Passover each spring helped ensure that the Israelites never forgot the cost of their freedom and the depth of God's love. Every Israelite who was able was expected to come to Jerusalem each year for the feasting, the remembering, and the ritual sacrifice of the Passover lambs.

Many of the pilgrims also came to Jerusalem with a sense of hope and expectation for the future. They wondered whether or not Israel's long-awaited king would finally come. The Old Testament prophets had spoken of a king who would come in the lineage of David. This king would faithfully lead Israel, as David had in his generation.

The prophet Zechariah declared, "Do not be afraid, Daughter Zion; see, your king is coming, seated on a donkey's colt" (Zech 9:9). John remembered this when he thought about Jesus coming into Jerusalem on Palm Sunday riding on the back of a young donkey. Jesus entered the city surrounded by crowds who praised him as a king, but in a few hours he would be treated less like a king and more like a criminal.

John tells us that when Jesus finished praying on Thursday night, he and his disciples went out from where Jesus had taught them and washed their feet, and they crossed the Kidron Valley. This valley was situated east of Jerusalem between the temple and the Mount of Olives. One thousand years earlier, David escaped the wrath of his son Absalom by crossing the Kidron Valley. Now Jesus and his disciples cross that same valley. They are on their way to the Garden of Gethsemane, which means "oil press." Perhaps this is the New Testament's way of foreshadowing what Jesus was about to experience. His soul was about to be crushed.

This garden was a place where Jesus had come many times before with the disciples. They knew it quite well. So when Judas conspired with the

Roman authorities to arrest Jesus, he had a pretty good idea where to find Jesus. He came right to the Garden of Gethsemane guiding a detachment of soldiers, the temple police, and the Pharisees. Some scholars suggest that there may have been hundreds of soldiers in the group. The soldiers marched through the darkness with torches and lanterns to find the man who said, "I am the light of the world" (8:12).

Can you imagine that? Jesus never lifted a finger against anyone. He always taught in public. He made sick people well and gave sight to the blind, but his teaching, his wisdom, and his devotion to God were so challenging to those in power that they came out to arrest him under the cover of darkness with a detachment of fully armed soldiers. In the story of the gospel, darkness is that which is not of God or is opposed to God. We also know from experience that darkness is a season through which every life eventually must pass. Darkness is that period when sorrow fills the chambers of our hearts. Darkness is what we feel when friends or family are not standing by us. Darkness comes because of the sting of rejection or the agony of defeat. Judas brought the soldiers to arrest Jesus at night because forces that opposed the presence and power of God wanted to avoid the light and hide under the cloak of darkness.

Jesus had three significant encounters in John 18 that deserve careful attention. First, he encountered the arresting mob. Then, he encountered the high priest. Finally, he encountered Pilate, the Roman-appointed governor of Judea. The more we take notice of these encounters, the more we are challenged by the same question that each person in the story had to answer: what are we going to do about Jesus?

The first group of people Jesus encountered had to decide what to do about Jesus's divinity. The Romans, chief priests, and Pharisees had already made up their minds about Jesus. The religious leaders sided with the Romans, probably because they thought they could get rid of Jesus more easily if they set him up to be an enemy of Rome. "[Jesus] came to what was his own, and his own people did not accept him" (John 1:11).

The crowd that came to arrest Jesus wanted to get rid of him because he kept insisting that he was from God and they should put their trust in him as the One God sent. Believing in him was clearly not something they wanted to do. They did not want some untrained carpenter from an insignificant place like Nazareth telling them how to live. So they decided to get rid of him.

Jesus even called himself equal to God. He told the people to eat his flesh and drink his blood. He told them they did not know the Father because if they really knew the Father they would know the Son. He told them that if they did not believe he was from above and not from this world, they would die in their sins (8:24). Jesus told them he could set them free, which implied that they were not already free. He healed a blind man so he could see, and he told the Pharisees, who could see, that they were blind. Jesus's message enraged the religious leaders.

The Pharisees and the chief priests did not believe Jesus was from God. They did not believe that he was the Word that became flesh and made his dwelling among us. They did not believe that Jesus was the Lamb of God who came to take away the sin of the world. They did not believe that when they looked at him, they were looking at the glory of the only begotten Son who came from the Father, full of grace and truth. Because they did not believe, they wanted to get rid of Jesus. That is what this crowd wanted to do with him. What about us?

Do we believe Jesus is who he says he is, or would we rather scheme and plot with our highly trained intellect to get him out of the way? We will tell ourselves that we are right no matter what everyone says. We will convince ourselves that if we want something, we should be able to have it. We will ignore the warnings that God gives us and keep going our own way. But every effort to eliminate God is doomed to fail. What John helps us see as Jesus encounters this mob in the garden is that no human plan or authority can eliminate God or control the power of God. Like it or not, God is here to stay.

The clue to this is the fact that the mob found Jesus in a place where he often met with his disciples. Jesus's arrest was not a surprise attack on an unsuspecting victim. He prayed in chapter 17 that his hour had come. The arrest of Jesus was an expected event. It was evil, but it was expected. It was an act of intimidation and violence, but it was completely expected.

Jesus sent Judas out of the room back in John 13 with instructions to do whatever he intended to do. When the soldiers, chief priests, temple police, and Pharisees arrived, John 18:4 says "Jesus, knowing all that was to happen to him, came forward and asked them, 'Whom are you looking for?'"

I think Jesus went out to meet his accusers because this was one more way for him to show by example that if evil is to be defeated, it must be confronted. We cannot wish evil away or hope it goes away on its own. There are some evils we must step up to and say, "Are you looking for me?"

John does not tell us about Judas kissing Jesus to signal which one was him. John wants us to know that Jesus was always in control. Nobody had to rat him out. He went out to meet his accusers and asked them who they wanted. Normally the police show up asking questions of the accused. But when the temple police and Roman soldiers showed up to arrest Jesus, Jesus went out to them and asked the questions. "Whom are you looking for?"

The crowd told him they were looking for Jesus of Nazareth. Jesus said two words to them that made them literally fall back in fear: *I am* (v. 5, NIV). He did not say, "I am he," as some translations have it. In the original Greek manuscripts, Jesus says, *I am*. What this crowd would do with Jesus was determined by what they believed about his answer. While it could be that Jesus was merely identifying himself as the one they were looking for (hey, that's me!), it is also possible that when he said *I am*, he was invoking the self-revealing name God uttered in Exodus 3:14: "I am that I am."

I am meant to alert this crowd that they were standing in the presence of God. *I am* signified that they were in the company of the Divine. This was what so many people did not believe. They took one look at Jesus and asked, "Is not this Jesus, the son of Joseph, whose father and mother we know? How can he now say, 'I came down from heaven'?" (6:42).

When the soldiers heard Jesus say "I am," they fell back in fear. Could it be that they caught a glimpse of his divinity and understandably dropped to the ground in reverent awe? Could it be that their ears heard the voice of God for the first time and they humbled themselves in submission? Could it be that the bright glory of Jesus made them cover their eyes and turn their faces?

Jesus asked them again, "Whom are you looking for?" This was a moment of decision. Would they believe in Jesus, or would they continue their plan to get rid of him and keep living in darkness? Jesus's question was the question we spend a lifetime trying to answer, isn't it? Who do we want? There are many paths we can take. Which one do we want? There are many gods vying for our allegiance. Who is going to be our God? Once we hear the good news proclaimed, we ask, "what will we do about Jesus?"

The authorities did not know what to expect when they confronted Jesus. Maybe that's why they showed up with temple police and Roman soldiers. They brought their most potent symbols of power to contain Jesus. Jesus, who had no army behind him, showed them that even when it looked like the world was gaining the upper hand, God was still at work for our good.

Jesus told the crowd a second time that he was the one they were looking for. Then he gave them a command: "if you are looking for me, let these men go" (v. 8). Jesus did not request that the disciples be released. He did not negotiate. He fulfilled what he prayed in John 17, that the disciples would be protected by the power of God's name. And just as he commanded, none of the disciples were arrested. Even with hundreds of soldiers, temple police, and the Pharisees surrounding Jesus and his disciples, Jesus spoke as only God could speak.

It did not look like it at the time, but God was at work. Jesus made so many wonderful claims about who he was and what he came to do. He opened the eyes of the blind and healed the sick, but he was unable to stop his arrest.

The soldiers brought Jesus to Annas, the father-in-law of the high priest, Caiaphas. John reminds us that Caiaphas was the one who had advised the Jewish leaders that it would be good if one man died for the people.

This was the second encounter with Jesus. The Pharisees did not believe Jesus came from God. Annas too did not believe Jesus had the authority to teach as he did. Annas questioned Jesus about his disciples and his teaching. Jesus did not try to talk his way out of trouble. He had made it known that he would not ask the Father to save him from this hour because this hour was the reason he had come.

Jesus replied to Annas, "I have spoken openly to the world; I have always taught in synagogues and in the temple, where all the Jews come together. I have said nothing in secret. Why do you [question] me? Ask those who heard what I said to them; they know what I said" (vv. 20-21).

Jesus did not respond to Annas like a fearful criminal. He did not respond as one who felt intimidated by someone who had power over him. He spoke like someone who knew he was doing the Father's will. His confidence offended the high priest so much that one of the temple police slapped Jesus in the face and told him to watch his tone of voice when speaking to the high priest. But that guard did not understand that one greater than the high priest was in his presence. The bound man standing before the high priest was the same one who said, "before Abraham was, I am" (8:58).

This is what some people do with Jesus. We treat him like he is less than the Son of God. We act as though we can move him around at our convenience and make him do what we want him to do. We approach him as if he is obligated to give us what we demand. We deny his authority over our lives. We partition areas of our lives so that we can give God control over a few areas and keep other areas private. We become our own gods. This was the mistake Annas made.

The truth of the matter is that Jesus is God. He came from God. Jesus told Annas to ask the people who heard him teach. They would have been glad to testify concerning Jesus's authority. Had Annas asked, people might have told him that Jesus said, "Very truly, I tell you, the Son can do nothing on his own, but only what he sees his Father doing; for whatever the Father does, the Son does likewise" (5:19). Annas would have heard testimony that Jesus said, "Very truly, I tell you, the hour is coming, and is now here, when the dead will hear the voice of the Son of God, and those who hear will live" (5:25). Only a man with divine authority can say that his voice will make the dead come alive. But Annas did not want to yield to Jesus's authority. He wanted to continue living as if he was in charge. So Annas sent Jesus, bound, to Caiaphas, the high priest.

The religious leaders took Jesus from Caiaphas for one final encounter. This encounter took place in the palace of the Roman governor with Pilate himself. Pilate had trouble with Jesus because he could not recognize the truth.

Evening had by now turned into morning. Pilate came out to meet the arresting mob and the handcuffed Jesus. He asked, "What charges are you bringing against this man?" (18:29, NIV). As if to say, why have you brought this man to me? The crowd insisted Jesus was a criminal. Pilate told them to judge Jesus for themselves. But the chief priests knew if they charged Jesus with a religious crime, they could not execute him. Only Rome could administer capital punishment.

John said that all this took place to fulfill what Jesus had said about the kind of death he was going to die. Jesus was not a victim. Just as he had said, "No one has greater love than this, to lay down one's life for one's friends" (John 15:13). Jesus's life was not being taken from him by force. He was laying it down in love.

Pilate questioned Jesus about being a king. He was confused about how anyone could think Jesus was a king. He had no army. He had no wealth. He relied on the hospitality of others and talked a lot about loving one another. That was not the way of a king. That was not the way of worldly power. Pilate knew that because he was an expert in the power of this world.

So Jesus did not answer Pilate's question directly, but he did say, "My kingdom is not of this world. If it were, my servants would fight to prevent my arrest. . . . But now my kingdom is from another place" (v. 36, NIV). Pilate took this to be an answer that Jesus was a king. Jesus replied, "You say that I am a king. In fact, the reason I was born and came into the world is to testify to the truth. Everyone on the side of truth listens to me" (v. 37, NIV).

Jesus was supposed to be the one on trial, but he was the one making all the judgments. It makes you wonder who the defendant was. It was supposed to be Jesus, but it seems like Annas and Pilate were the ones on trial. As far as Jesus was concerned, this was the single most important moment in Pilate's life. Jesus told him, "Everyone on the side of truth listens to me." So what was Pilate going to do about Jesus?

He did not see it, but truth was standing right in front of him. Pilate was used to thinking about truth as the world thought about truth. He only knew the truth that came at the end of a sword. But this was not the kind of truth Jesus had in mind. His kingdom and his truth were not of this world.

Jesus's truth is not something we can compute through mathematical formulas. His truth is not found in esoteric philosophies or learned from reading ancient scrolls. He is our truth. He is truth who came as a gift from God. Truth was not a principle but a person. Truth is our good shepherd. Truth fed a multitude. Truth raised Lazarus from the grave and healed a man's son long distance. Truth gave his life so we could have more abundant life. Truth gave himself to be arrested so we could be set free. And soon truth will go to the cross so we might have hope.

God's truth is Jesus of Nazareth.

Jesus said everyone on the side of truth listens to him. The only question that remains is what *we* are going to do with Jesus.

Note

1. This sermon was preached two Sundays after the Confederate flag was lowered from the Capitol in Columbia, South Carolina, as a response to the shooting at Emanuel AME Church along with other acts of racist violence in the country.

28

What Happened at the Cross?

John 19:3-42

Christian and secular historians alike find common ground on the fact that a man named Jesus of Nazareth was crucified. Where they differ is in their understanding of what that crucifixion means. St. Augustine, the African saint who was born in AD 354 and served as a bishop for thirty-five years in the country now known as Algeria, had this to say about those who witnessed the crucifixion:

> As they were looking on, so we too gaze on his wounds as he hangs. We see his blood as he dies. We see the price offered by the redeemer, touch the scars of his resurrection. He bows his head, as if to kiss you. His heart is made bare open, as it were, in love to you. His arms are extended that he may embrace you. His whole body is displayed for your redemption. Ponder how great these things are. Let all this be rightly weighed in your mind: as he was once fixed to the cross in every part of his body for you, so he may now be fixed in every part of your soul.[1]

Thomas Merton wrote in *No Man Is an Island,* "To know the Cross is to know that we are saved by the sufferings of Christ; more, it is to know the love of Christ Who underwent suffering and death in order to save us. It is, then, to know Christ."[2]

No object is more representative of Christianity than the cross. Steel crosses sit atop tall steeples. Wooden crosses stand in the ground in front of church buildings. Many people view the cross as a symbol of faith, but it was once a symbol of shame and humiliation. The cross was a violent tool for punishment used by the Romans not only to execute their enemies but also to strike fear in the hearts of every person who had the misfortune to witness a crucifixion. The cross was not used for the noble citizens, only for traitors, servants, rebels, or slaves.

Every year during Holy Week, we emphasize the cross. We do so because we cannot afford to lose sight of what happened on the cross. Theologian Dietrich Bonhoeffer said that the cross represents both suffering and rejection. We have to consider both because it would have been possible for Jesus to suffer without being rejected. Jesus could have suffered and attracted the sympathy of many, resulting in him being celebrated. But he was not celebrated. He was rejected and despised. His captors even had the audacity to slap him in the face.

This was the hour Jesus had been anticipating—the hour of his crucifixion. What actually happened on the cross? We could answer that question from historical or political perspectives and come up with worthwhile information. But if the cross will mean anything for our faith, it may be better to answer the question theologically. In other words, what does the cross say to us from God's perspective as given to us in the Gospel of John?

From God's perspective, it does not take much to see that the cross exposes the rebellion of the human heart against God. God came near and humanity said, "No, thank you. We can make it without you." The rebellion of humanity against God was evident from everything that happened leading up to the crucifixion itself.

After the religious leaders convicted Jesus of blasphemy, they sent him to Pilate to be crucified. Pilate was the governor of Judea, appointed by the Caesar of Rome. Unlike the religious leaders, Pilate acted like he did not want to get involved in punishing Jesus. He was not a disciple of Jesus, but he appeared to have no real interest in killing him.

Pilate would have preferred to have the religious leaders in Jerusalem handle their own religious disagreements without involving him, but they were persistent. The chief priests and Pharisees wanted Jesus dead, and only Pilate had the authority to administer capital punishment in a Roman territory.

So the leaders brought Jesus to Pilate. They refused to go inside the palace, or they would have been made unclean by entering the house of a Gentile. If they became unclean, they would have been unable to celebrate the Passover the next day. This was why they stayed outside. It is astonishing to think that they did not want to go into Pilate's house because they did not want to be unclean spiritually, while they were comfortable plotting to kill an innocent man and then going to worship the next day. Humanity comes up with strange ideas about what makes us clean or unclean, righteous or unrighteous, a sinner or a saint.

Because the religious leaders would not come inside, Pilate went back and forth from inside the palace to outside the palace. He came out and said to the leaders, "Look, I am bringing [Jesus] out to you to let you know that I find no case against him" (v. 4).

Jesus must have looked different by now. He was bloodied from the flogging, a punishment that involved being beaten across his bare back with a leather strap spiked with stone or metal fragments. Jesus must have looked weaker than when they arrested him in the garden. He was wearing a soldier's purple military robe meant to mock the distinguished purple robe worn by kings.

The soldiers stood Jesus up in front of the crowd and Pilate said, "Here is the man!" (v. 5). Some suggest that this was all Pilate thought he would have to do to Jesus. Teach Jesus a lesson and satisfy the religious leaders. But the leaders were not satisfied with seeing Jesus beaten. When wickedness overtakes the human heart, it is never satisfied. "Wickedness" may seem like a strong word, but it fits. There is something in us that does not always want to do what God wants us to do. We say things we should not say. We watch images we should not watch. We make choices we do not want others to know about.

Once selfishness takes root in the human heart, we will stop at nothing until we get what we want, no matter who else has to suffer in the process. The crowd shouted back to Pilate, "Crucify him! Crucify him!" (v. 6). Humanity's rebellion had kicked into high gear so that no one could see that Jesus was the true King. They could not see that he was the bread of life. To them he was someone pretending to be the Son of God. The cross reveals humanity's tendency to rebel against God. But this is not all that happened on the cross.

Have you ever met a celebrity in person whom you previously had only seen on television, in magazines, or in the movies? If this has ever happened to you, you know it is always a bit of a surprise to see people in person whom we have only seen through the lens of a camera or on a big screen. Sometimes they are taller than we imagined. Sometimes they are shorter than we expected.

This may be similar to what happened to Jesus. Humanity was used to God being far away, but now God was with them and no one recognized him. Human hearts had been overtaken by fear and rebellion. God was with them, but they did not notice. God came to dwell among them, and they rejected all of God's invitations. They mocked all of God's mercy. The cross revealed the grace of their true king. The crowd turned up their noses at God's forgiveness. I said *they* did this, but really I should say *we* do this.

Jesus was crucified 2,000 years ago, but he is crucified again and again. He is crucified whenever the shadow in our own hearts causes us to tell God, "No, thank you. I can make it without you."

He is crucified when the inhumanity in politics and policies causes the world to think it can find its way without its Creator. Rebellion against God always gives way to violence and suffering, which is partly why Jesus ended up on the cross.

When Pilate brought Jesus out one more time, the leaders insisted, "We have a law, and according to that law he ought to die because he has claimed to be the Son of God" (v. 7). Pilate went back once more to see if Jesus would defend himself. But Jesus was silent. The prophet Isaiah spoke of this when he said, "He was oppressed, and he was afflicted, yet he did not open his mouth; like a lamb that is led to the slaughter, and like a sheep before its shearers is silent, so he did not open his mouth" (53:7).

Pilate kept trying to set Jesus free, so the leaders threatened him with political blackmail. They shouted at him, "If you let this man go, you are no friend of Caesar. Anyone who claims to be a king opposes Caesar" (v. 12, NIV). In other words, if you let this man go, you are on the side of someone who challenges the kingship in Rome, and if you challenge the kingship in Rome, Rome will come looking for you.

Pilate had run out of options. According to verse 8, he seemed afraid that Jesus might be the Son of God, whatever that title might have meant to him. But he turned out to be more afraid of losing his power and privilege if the leaders reported him to Caesar. So Pilate brought Jesus out one final time. He sat on the judge's seat, a bench outside the Praetorium, and said to the leaders, "Here is your King" (v. 14). Some scholars think the text could also be translated to say that Pilate sat Jesus on the judge's seat. Then he said to the crowd, "Here is your king." In other words, the leaders brought Jesus to be judged, but in the end he was the one sitting in the seat to judge them.

The crowd ordered Pilate, "Take him away! Take him away! Crucify him!" (v. 15).

"Shall I crucify your king?" Pilate asked (v. 15, NIV). "'We have no king but Caesar,' the chief priests answered" (v. 15, NIV). If this sounds shocking to our ears, it should because choosing Caesar over Christ is the height of human alienation.

To say they had no king but Caesar was to reject the relationship God established with Israel when God brought them out of Egypt and chose them to be God's people. In the Old Testament, the Israelites came to the prophet Samuel and asked for a king, and Samuel told the people that God alone was their king (1 Sam 12:12). They did not need a king other than God. The psalmist once asked, "What can I return to the Lord for all his goodness to me?" (Ps 116:12, translation mine). And this was what the crowd said to Pilate: "We have no king but Caesar." They traded in a true God for a false god. We do too whenever we choose someone or something other than Christ to lead our lives.

Who is our king? Who or what gets more of our loyalty than God? Is it our emotions? Do we act on every feeling? Is it the pursuit of more material wealth? Is it the opinion of others? Who is our king? We have students going off to college soon. When you get on campus, who will be your king?

The crowds that crucified Jesus decided they did not want him to be their king. Thankfully, the cross reveals more than the rebellion of the human heart and our failure to recognize the true king. John also depicts the cross as a testimony to the power of God. This was one thing Jesus's accusers did not understand. Yet we can see the power of God shining through over and over again throughout John 18 and 19.

Jesus's opponents thought they had power over him. Soldiers slapped him in the face. The religious leaders ordered Pilate to hand down the sentence of crucifixion. They used their power to get Jesus out of the way so they could go on living their lives as they wanted.

Even Pilate thought his power was superior to Jesus'. After the chief priests and Pharisees demanded to have Jesus crucified, Pilate went back and told Jesus, "Do you realize I have power either to free you or to crucify you?" (v. 10, NIV). Pilate will eventually find out he does not have as much power as he thought. He wanted to let Jesus go, but he could not figure out a way to set him free. This is the irony of the crucifixion. When God looks weak, God is strong.

Jesus spoke up when Pilate mentioned the word "power." He knew that before long he would be crucified. He knew that the chief priests were aligned against him. But never for one moment did Jesus think that anyone had more power to do anything against him than God had power to do for him. Jesus told Pilate, "You would have no power over me unless it had been given to you from above" (v. 11). This is what we see on the cross—God's power on full display.

As far as Jesus was concerned, his fate was not in the hands of the chief priests or Pilate. It may have looked like they were doing with him what they wanted, but Jesus was not there by accident. He was there by choice. Evil had come against Jesus full force, but it was not going to be enough to defeat the power of God.

Verse 16 says that Pilate handed Jesus over to be crucified and the soldiers took charge of Jesus. The language of the soldiers taking charge of Jesus is John's way of contrasting the world's power and God's power. We should remember this in our own time. It may seem like the world has the power to take charge of us, but we belong to God. It may seem like circumstances can overwhelm us, but we are being kept by, sustained by, and preserved by the power of God.

Pilate, the man who was supposed to be in power, ran out of options. He handed Jesus over to be crucified. The soldiers took charge of Jesus. Jesus took the horizontal beam of the cross and put it on his bloodied shoulders to carry it to the place called Golgotha. There they crucified him along with two others.

Nails went into his wrists. He was hoisted upon a vertical beam, and a long spike was hammered into his feet. Pilate had a notice prepared and fastened to the cross. It read, "Jesus of Nazareth, the King of the Jews" (v. 19). This was Pilate's last act of defiance. Some wanted him to change the sign to say that Jesus *said* he was king of the Jews, but Pilate said, *"What I have written I have written"* (v. 22).

Jesus hung there, stripped of his dignity and his clothes since the soldiers took the garments he had. They gambled for the seamless undergarment (vv. 23-24). They took from him those clothes about which an infirmed woman once said, "If I only touch his cloak, I will be made well" (Matt 9:21). This was the Lamb slain for the sin of the world. This was the one who said, "No greater love has anyone than this: to lay down his life for his friends" (John 15:13, author's paraphrase).

And what does this show us? It shows us much more than a gruesome tale of a man's death. It shows us much more than a sad story of an innocent man suffering. When we see Jesus crucified, it shows us how much God is willing to suffer to be with us and for us to be with God.

The world tried to silence God, intimidate God, condemn God, and even crucify God, but it had no power to stop the love of God. This is what happened on the cross. This is also why when the soldiers gave Jesus wine vinegar to drink and when he tasted the sour, bitter vinegar on his lips, he said, "Te-te-les-tai" or "It is finished" (v. 30).

Finished does not mean over as in "unsuccessful." Finished means Jesus did everything he came to do. He completed his Father's mission. "It is finished" is not the cry of a defeated man fading off the scene. "It is finished" is not the surrender of a failed mission.

"It is finished" is the triumphant shout of a conquering King. Satan tempted him, but Jesus did not yield. Enemies opposed him, but he remained faithful. An army came out against him, but he did not back down. They twisted sharp thorns and made a crown for his head, but he did not quit. They cast lots for his clothes, but he did not leave his post. This is what happened on the cross.

On the cross, it looked as though Jesus lost. But Jesus did not lose. He finished the work he came to do. He finished letting us see the magnitude of God's love for us. "For God so loved the world that He gave His only begotten Son, that whoever believes in Him should not perish but have everlasting life" (3:16, NKJV).

He finished showing how much he loves the Father. "When you have lifted up the Son of Man, then you will realize that I am he, and that I do nothing on my own, but I speak these things as the Father instructed me" (8:28).

He finished showing the world who God is. As he said to Philip, "Whoever has seen me has seen the Father" (14:9).

He finished working out our redemption. Romans 5:8 says, "But God proves his own love for us in that while we were still sinners Christ died for us." This is what happened on the cross.

The cross means we can stop trying to save ourselves. The cross means there is no suffering we ever have to go through by ourselves. Jesus saw his mother and the beloved disciple at the foot of the cross and said, "Woman, here is your son" (19:26). And to that disciple, "Here is your mother" (v. 27). He meant for them to care for each other through their grief.

The cross means God is faithful. As John says, these things happened so that Scripture would be fulfilled (v. 28). The cross means Jesus was willing to go all the way to hell and back to rescue us, and once he claims us no one can snatch us out of his hand.

The cross means that we no longer have to stay the same. Even Nicodemus, who once seemed unable or unwilling to be a disciple in chapter 3, came to the cross. He came to give Jesus a burial fit for a king. He did not show up when the man born blind got his sight back in chapter 9. He did not show up when the physically disabled man started walking in chapter 5. He did not come around after Jesus fed the 5,000 or walked on water in chapter 6. We do not even hear about Nicodemus when Jesus raised Lazarus from the dead in chapter 11. But Nicodemus did come back to the cross (19:39-42).

Maybe this is why Jesus went to the cross. Some people did not believe the miracles. Some people were not convicted by his sermons. But Jesus knew what would happen if he went to the cross. Hearts would be made whole if he went to the cross. Sinners would be forgiven if he went to the cross. The friendless would have a friend if he went to the cross.

At the cross, we found hope we did not have before. At the cross, we saw love like we've never it seen before. At the cross, the bread of life was broken. At the cross, the Son of God died so that the children of God might live. "Just as Moses lifted up the snake in the wilderness, so the Son of Man must be lifted up, that everyone who believes may have eternal life in him" (3:14-15). The cross is foolishness to some, but to those who live by faith, it is the power of God.

Notes

1. Augustine quoted in Thomas C. Oden et. al., eds., *Mark*, Ancient Christian Commentary on Scripture: New Testament, vol. 2 (Downers Grove: InterVarsity Press) 224.

2. Thomas Merton, *No Man Is an Island* (Wilmington: Mariner Books, 2002) 92.

29

It Is a New Day!

John 20:1-18

We usually don't hear the words from John 20 until Easter Sunday. But because we've been following John's story for the last eight months, we have finally come to the good news of the resurrection. I welcome this liturgical chaos because the message of Easter should not be limited to one or two Sundays during the year. Easter is the reason Christians celebrate all year long. Without the resurrection, according to the apostle Paul in 1 Corinthians 15, our preaching is useless and our faith is in vain.

One detail that all the resurrection stories have in common is that a woman named Mary Magdalene was among the first to arrive at the tomb on Easter Sunday morning. And given what happened to Jesus just a few days earlier, she must have still been in disbelief and distress. Mary saw everything that Jesus suffered.

Mary saw Jesus struggling to carry his cross to the place of the Skull, which in Jesus's native language was called Golgotha (John 19). She saw the soldiers beat spikes through Jesus's wrists to hold his body on a wooden horizontal beam stretched across his shoulders. She watched the horizontal beam hoisted upon a vertical post in the ground and Jesus's body stretched out as the crowds jeered, "Crucify! Crucify!"

Mary Magdalene must have grimaced when the soldiers twisted Jesus's two feet, one on top of the other, and hammered a single spike to secure both of them to the cross. This was the way of a Roman crucifixion. Mary Magdalene saw everything.

By the way, Magdalene was not Mary's last name. Magdalene referred to her hometown, the village of Magdala near Tiberius. This Mary from Magdala had been one of the women who not only followed Jesus as a disciple but also financially supported him and the twelve apostles. Luke 8:2-3 tells us that Mary was among an inner circle of women who made monetary contributions to sustain Jesus's radical movement. It is a testimony to her faith that she used what she had to advance Jesus's ministry. She believed so genuinely in what Jesus was doing that she gave out of her wealth to ensure the success of the work. Mary acted on what Jesus taught in Matthew 6: "Where your treasure is, there your heart will be also" (6:21). It is one thing to say that we are in favor of causes and believe in institutions. When we are able to give and do not, we may not be as supportive as we think we are. Mary Magdalene and several other women did what they could for Jesus.

Therefore, it must have broken Mary's heart to see Jesus hanging on the cross. It must have been excruciating to see him gasping for breath when he had freely given life to so many others. Crucifixions did not kill a person quickly. Death usually came slowly, over a period of several hours. Sometimes it took as long as a day for the person to die. John told us in chapter 19 that as Jesus suffered, Mary Magdalene, Jesus's mother, Mary the wife of Clopas, and an unnamed disciple were at the foot of the cross taking it all in.

Men, I am sorry to report that it appears that all but one of the male disciples had scattered by the time Jesus was crucified, but the women hung around. Consequently, Mary saw it all. She saw when the soldiers broke the legs of the two criminals crucified next to Jesus. Breaking their legs quickened their death because a person being crucified had to push up with their legs in order to lessen the strain on their chest and take a breath. Mary was there when they came to break Jesus's legs. But by that time, Jesus had already bowed his head and given up his spirit. The soldiers confirmed his death by piercing Jesus with a sword until blood and water flowed from his side (see chapter 19).

Mary saw this and knew that Jesus was indeed dead. He had not fainted. He was not pretending. He was dead. Mary watched Jesus die and then stayed around long enough to see where Nicodemus and Joseph of Arimathea buried his body. Friday passed. Saturday came and went. By the time Sunday came, Mary knew what she had to do. "Early on the first day of the week, while it was still dark, Mary Magdalene came to the tomb . . ." (20:1).

She must have still been in shock and disbelief. Jesus had given Mary and others so much hope for life. Now he was dead. Mary and the other disciples believed that Jesus was Israel's Messiah, God's anointed servant. As far as she was concerned, the crucifixion and death of Jesus did not make sense. It did not make sense for a life filled with such hope and promise to end in bitter disappointment. It did not make sense for such a beautiful dream to turn into a terrible tragedy. Jesus was supposed to be their leader, but he was dead, and Rome was still in charge. He saved countless people with his miracle-working power, but the soldiers beat him and crucified him and he did not save himself. So Mary Magdalene went to the tomb while it was dark, early on the first day of the week, without any understanding of why Jesus had to suffer and die, or that he might once again be alive.

Mary's lack of understanding is what John is hinting at when he tells us that she went to the tomb when it was "still dark." Darkness is one of John's favorite metaphors for unbelief or a lack of understanding.

In chapter 3, Nicodemus came to Jesus at night and could not understand what Jesus meant by being born again. Jesus said in John 12:46 that he came into the world as a light so that no one who believes in him should "remain in darkness." John wrote in chapter 3 that with Jesus, "light has come into the world, and people loved darkness rather than light because their deeds were evil" (3:19).

Darkness is spiritual blindness. Darkness is where we end up when we choose any way that is not God's way. For Mary Magdalene, it was not only dark around her. She was also dealing with darkness within her because Jesus had been crucified.

When Mary arrived at the tomb, she saw that the stone had been removed from the entrance. She stumbled into the truth that God is always working before we even show up! When Mary saw the stone was moved, she did not think what we think today. We have probably heard the resurrection story so often that we assume an empty tomb means Jesus was raised from the dead. Not so for Mary. Mary ran to Simon Peter and the unnamed disciple and said, "They have taken the Lord out of the tomb, and we don't know where they have put him!" (v. 2, NIV). Mary is a lot like all of us, isn't she? Since she did not understand what God was doing, she came up with her own conclusions about what had happened. But maybe the resurrection means that it is time for us to change some of our assumptions.

When Mary saw that the stone had been moved, she assumed that if the tomb was empty Jesus's body must have been stolen. Mary assumed that Jesus's mission had been a failure at worse and a disappointment at best. She assumed that the way things ended on Friday would determine the way things started on Sunday. The entire Gospel of John has been about people assuming God was doing one thing when God was actually doing something else. People assumed they could see clearly, but they did not truly understand. So if Jesus has been raised from the dead, maybe we need to change our assumptions.

People Jesus encountered in John assumed he would act one way but he often surprised them. A group of Pharisees exposed a woman for an alleged act of adultery. They assumed that if they brought the woman to Jesus, he would quote the law and condone her execution by stoning. Instead, Jesus asked each accuser to examine his own life and then decide how they wanted to treat the woman.

Mary's guess that Jesus's body had been stolen puts us on notice that when God is involved, things are not always what they seem. We have to wait and see because sometimes what we assume is dead might not stay dead. We may assume God is absent, but God might be working behind the scenes. We may assume our efforts will fail, but sometimes failure is really success under construction. What we assume is human weakness might actually be the beginning of God's strength.

Mary was going to base her whole future on a false assumption. She was about to live out the rest of her days guided by the belief that Jesus's body had been stolen. We cannot blame her. Mary knew the facts. People lived. People died. They were buried. That was the end. There was nothing after the end. Mary assumed that Herod's word was the last word. She assumed that death was stronger than life. She assumed that the empty tomb was the result of human effort. She missed the signs of God's handiwork. "They have taken the Lord out of the tomb . . ." (v. 2).

It is possible to become so overwhelmed by disappointment that we don't notice the activity of God. We miss seeing the ways in which God is moving, guiding, nudging, warning, blessing, and revealing all around us.

This makes me wonder how many times we go through life building our beliefs on false assumptions about what God is or is not doing. A loved one gets sick. We assume God must have given them the illness. A tsunami destroys a village. We assume God did that. We fail and then we assume that we are a failure. We achieve great success and we assume it was because we did everything right. Someone rejects us and we assume that we are not worthy to be loved. These are the kinds of false assumptions that the resurrection can change.

The resurrection opens the path to a new day because if we believe Jesus was raised from the dead we have to reconsider some of our assumptions. The main assumption Mary needed to reconsider was that the emptiness of the tomb was the result of human effort rather than divine activity.

John says that all of this happened "early" and "on the first day of the week" (v. 1). These two time signatures tell us that although Mary thought the journey was over, in reality something new had already come to life.

"Early on the first day of the week" meant that last week was over. This was a new day. Yesterday had ended. This was the dawning of a new era. This meant that no matter what the past had been, the future would be different. This is no small thing in the Gospel of John or in our lives.

The gift to everyone who believes, who puts their trust in the risen Jesus, is that God can make all things new. Bringing the new out of the old has been Jesus's main work throughout the Gospel of John. In chapter 2, Jesus changed water into wine, signifying his ability to transform the old into the new. Jesus cleared the temple as a sign that the old order had passed away and that in him something new was taking place. In chapter 4, he offered a Samaritan woman a new start when he told her, "Everyone who drinks [the water I give] will never be thirsty again. . . . Indeed, the water I give them will become in them a spring of water welling up to eternal life" (v. 14, translation mine). That was a new beginning. In chapter 5, we learn of a man was physically disabled for thirty-eight years. Jesus gave him a new walk. In chapter 9, there was a man who was born blind. Jesus told him to wash his eyes in the pool of Siloam and he received new sight.

Mary had personal experience with Jesus's power to renew and recreate. The other Gospels tell us that there was once a point in her life when she was possessed by seven demons, but Jesus delivered her from their power and set her free. She had been made new once before, but, like us, she needed to be made new one more time.

She went to the tomb on the first day of a new week and discovered that things were not what they seemed. Mary ran back to Simon Peter and the unnamed disciple whom John called the beloved disciple. She told them about the theft of Jesus's body, so they both started running.

John says the unnamed disciple arrived first, but he let Peter go in the tomb ahead of him. Peter went straight in. He looked and saw the strips of linen that Nicodemus and Joseph had used on Friday to wrap Jesus's body. The strips were lying in the tomb. The cloth that had been around Jesus's head was lying in a separate place to the side. Then the second disciple came in. He looked around and saw what Peter saw—linen strips and no body. When Lazarus came out of the grave in John 11, he was still wearing his grave clothes. But when Jesus got out of the tomb, his burial clothes had been left behind. John says that the second disciple saw and believed (vv. 3-8).

We cannot say for certain what this disciple believed at this point since no one yet knew that Jesus had risen from the dead. He could have believed that Mary was telling the truth about grave robbers. What we do know is that he and Peter went back home. Even though the tomb was empty, life had not changed because they did not understand what had happened to Jesus. Likewise, our lives will not have the quantity or quality of joy God wants to give us without the resurrection. We will be weighed down by Good Friday without the resurrection.

Mary stayed behind at the tomb. She was still living in a Good Friday world. She was disappointed that she could not find Jesus's body. Perhaps she thought that Joseph and Nicodemus had not done a good job of burying Jesus and she wanted to do it right. Perhaps she just wanted to put her own personal touch on the burial arrangement. Whatever her reasons, she could not do anything but weep. Her weeping was a sign of her great love.

As she wept, John says Mary bent over to look into the tomb and saw two angels seated where Jesus's body had been, one at the head and the other at the foot. They asked why she was crying. Mary told them the same thing she told the disciples: "They have taken away my Lord, and I do not know where they have laid him" (v. 13). She was living in a Good Friday world.

At that point, Mary turned around, and a man was standing in front of her. Mary assumed this man was the gardener. The man asked her, "Woman, why are you crying? Who is it you are looking for?" (v. 15, NIV). Mary did not recognize this figure standing in front of her. John does not tell us why, but she was unable to see that this man was not the gardener. He was someone much greater. Mary was still living in a Good Friday world.

But that was about to change. Mary said to the man she thought was the gardener, "Sir, if you have carried him away, tell me where you have put him, and I will get him" (v. 15, NIV). In that moment, Mary heard one word that changed everything. The man called her name, "Mary" (v. 16). She did not recognize that she was talking to Jesus. He had spoken to her already, but she only took him to be the gardener. I wonder if there are times in our lives when we do not notice who is speaking to us. God shows up and we are so busy that we don't notice. Mary did not recognize that there was something different about this gardener until he called her by name. "Mary."

She had heard that voice before. John 10:4 says, ". . . the sheep follow him because they know his voice." Mary did not have the benefit of seeing wounds in his hands and side, but she knew that voice. The voice was the same voice that called Lazarus from the grave. It was the same voice that had said, "In this world you will have trouble. But take heart! I have overcome the world" (16:33, NIV). Mary's experience lets us know that the resurrection is not only powerful; it is personal.

When we realize that God knows our name, we can have faith we never thought possible. For Mary, hearing that voice call her by name could only mean one thing: Jesus was alive and not dead. And if Jesus was alive and not dead, she could live in hope rather than despair. So she turned toward the voice. And this is what Jesus is always waiting for when he calls our name. He is waiting for that moment when we turn to him in faith.

Mary turned and called Jesus by the title of teacher. Then Jesus said to her, "Do not hold on to me, because I have not yet ascended to the Father. But go to my brothers and say to them, 'I am ascending to my Father and your Father, to my God and your God'" (v. 17).

Mary tried to hold on to Jesus. Seeing Jesus, she thought things were going to be just like they were before. But this was a new day. Sometimes we cling and hold on when we need to let go because our clinging and holding keeps us from what's next. When we put our faith in Jesus who was raised from the dead, we have to let go of the old in order to enter the new. Jesus had not come to take Mary back to the way it was before. Now that he had risen from the dead, there was going to be a new kind of relationship whereby Jesus could be in every place at the same time through the Holy Spirit.

Jesus told Mary, "Instead of you holding on to me, I want to send you on a mission. Instead of wanting things to be as they used to be, I want to send you out on a new assignment. Instead of wanting to go back to the way things were, I want to show you how much better things can be."

"Go tell my brothers . . . ," Jesus said. He had never called his disciples brothers before. But he wanted Mary to tell them, "I am ascending to my Father and your Father, to my God and your God."

Jesus's relationship with the Father had been so special that it was off limits, but this is a new day. Jesus's resurrection makes a way for us to be in relationship with God that was not possible before the resurrection. Jesus opened the door to the kingdom wide enough for us to come in. The resurrection means it is a new day.

No more Good Friday. No longer is Mary weeping. No longer is Mary living in a Good Friday world. Her eyes have been opened. The Romans tried to use the cross as an ending. The chief priests tried to make the cross a finale. But God turned it into the beginning of new beginnings.

We can let go of our old assumptions and look for the possibilities of God. It is a new day.

We can let go of yesterday's despair and listen for the sound of today's hope. It is a new day.

We can be assured that Calvary's cross was defeated and Sunday's tomb is empty. It is a new day.

We can trust that no matter how hard or how long evil tries, it cannot conquer the Lamb of God who takes away the sin of the world. It is a new day.

We have proof that the weapons of this world are not able to win against the love of God. It is a new day.

We may get discouraged sometimes and start to feel like this world is helplessly under the influence of cold, heartless leaders. But today is a new day.

No matter how devastating our troubles, today is a new day. No matter how painful the heartache, today is a new day. This is why Mary went out to proclaim, "I have seen the Lord!" (v. 18, NIV). If he is alive, we do have a future. If he is alive, we do have hope. Every time we see the Lord, we can say that Friday was not final and today is a new day.

30

Four Words We All Need to Hear

John 20:19-31

The second part of John 20 is about what happens to the disciples *after* Mary reports that she has seen the Lord. It has to do with what Jesus gives to and does for the disciples when he returns. Ordinary people were changed after Jesus came back from the grave because of the difference resurrection made in their lives.

The first audience of the Gospel of John was a first-century community of believers who had finally separated from the synagogue of their birth and heritage. More likely, they had probably been kicked out of the synagogue for claiming that Jesus was the Son of God.

Some commentators suggest that by the time John was written, the church was in its third generation. This community had not seen Jesus personally. Consequently, false teachings sprouted up, presenting Jesus in a way that lessened his divinity or questioned his humanity. The church needed a clear vision of who Jesus was in order to continue living as faithful disciples. This is why we have the Gospel of John.

John presented the stories of Jesus's power and truth to renew faith and encourage trust in the Son of God. John could have included many other events in Jesus's life, but he selected what is in this Gospel with one purpose in mind, a purpose he explains in John 20:30 and 31: "Jesus did many other signs in the presence of his disciples, which are not written in this book. But these are written so that you may come to believe that Jesus is the Messiah, the Son of God, and that through believing you may have life in his name." What is in this Gospel was written so that we might believe.

What does it mean to believe? Believing, according to John, is not limited to intellectual acceptance of certain facts about Jesus. Believing is not a matter of whether we think it is true or false that Jesus existed. According to John, belief or believing is relying on, depending on, and trusting Jesus—trusting that Jesus is who he says he is, trusting that he is God with us, trusting that when we have seen him we have seen the Father, trusting him enough to follow his voice, and trusting him enough to do what he says.

Therefore, when John wrote about Jesus feeding the multitude, he did so hoping someone would trust Jesus to supply what is needed. When John wrote about being born again, he did so hoping the reader would rely on the Spirit to give a fresh start and a new life. When John wrote about the resurrection, he must have hoped that someone would hear it and believe and those who already believed would keep believing that Jesus was the Son of God.

Make no mistake about it: the resurrection was a life-changing experience for the disciples. Some days are so uneventful that they have little impact on our lives. We forget about them almost as soon as they are over. I cannot tell you where I was two weeks ago on Thursday at 11 a.m. But I can tell you exactly where I was at approximately 9:30 a.m. on Tuesday, September 11, 2001. Many of you could say the same about April 4, 1968, or other dates that are forever stamped on your mind. For the disciples, the resurrection was one of those unforgettable moments—not simply because Jesus came back from the dead but also because of what happened when he came back from the dead.

To keep our text in proper perspective, the first half of chapter 20 is about how Mary went to the tomb "early on the first day of the week" (v. 1). Verse 19 begins on the evening of the same day. At this time, Mary Magdalene was still the only one who had seen Jesus alive. After seeing him, she took off running, filled with joy and fear. She ran to the other disciples and announced to them, "I have seen the Lord" (v. 18). Her words were so unbelievable and unexpected that we have no evidence that any of the disciples took her seriously.

Can we blame them? The disciples did what was practical after Friday's crucifixion. They found a safe place to hide. Jesus was dead. Perhaps they went to the same upstairs room where Jesus had celebrated the Passover meal with them on the Thursday before his crucifixion. As is sometimes the case with us, the hurting and disappointed disciples may have returned to what was comfortable. They found somewhere secure, went inside, locked the doors, and hid.

The setting for the text may feel familiar to many of us. The feeling of being locked in or locked out is a common experience. I remember when my family first moved into our house in Winston-Salem before we learned how all the door locks worked. I was sitting on the porch before coming back to the church for one of our fall revival services. Our son was around eighteen months old. He came out on the porch to join me. My wife came outside, too. In the flash of an eye, our son ran back into the house and closed the door behind him.

My wife and I instantly shared a knowing look that something bad had just happened. Our fears were confirmed when we tried to open the back door and it was locked. Every door and every window was locked. And our firstborn child, who was just a toddler, was in the house with a flight of stairs less than fifteen feet away from him. He thought it was a game. We knew it was serious. At first we were shocked. Shock quickly turned to fear because our child was locked in, and we were helplessly locked out.

In our text today, the disciples were locked in, but thankfully Jesus was not locked out. "When the disciples were together, with the doors locked for fear of the Jews, Jesus came and stood among them . . ." (v. 19, translation mine).

Jesus did not have a key and the door was locked, but none of that mattered. Apparently, the One who could walk on water could also enter a room through locked doors. Jesus did say in chapter 10 that he was the "door" for the sheep.

This kind of home invasion is encouraging because it means there is nothing and no one who can stop Jesus from being with his disciples. Jesus entered the room and stood among the disciples. He did not stand over them like an angry tyrant, returning to punish them for their failures. He did not stand behind them or apart from them as if he did not want to be around them. Jesus stood among them as though he came to comfort them. This is when the resurrection became real for the disciples. They could now see the risen Jesus for themselves. Not only did Jesus come and stand among them; he also said four words they all needed to hear. He said, "Peace be with you!" (v. 19). We need to hear these words, too.

These four words are words of greeting and words of blessing. These four words are words of life and words of hope. Fear has the power to stop us in our tracks. Fear can keep us from moving forward when God calls us to take a leap of faith. We are afraid because we cannot turn on the television without hearing about another tragedy. The stock market goes down, and people are afraid because it is down. When it goes up people are afraid that it might go down again. The good news we need to hear is wrapped up these four words: "Peace be with you!"

Jesus's greeting meant that the disciples could finally live with joy.

Before Jesus came and stood among them, the disciples were filled with confusion about the past and doubts about the future. Jesus's greeting lifted them above their fears and filled them with hope. I wonder if the disciples had forgotten that before Jesus was crucified, he promised to give them peace. I wonder if seeing the crucifixion canceled out their hope that anything good would happen again. It really is the case that some experiences, some failures, and some breakups are so disappointing that we wonder if we will ever have joy again.

But Jesus made a promise to give the disciples peace, and not even death could keep him from fulfilling that promise. When Jesus taught the disciples on his last night with them, he concluded with this reminder: "I have told you these things, so that in me you may have peace" (16:33a, NIV). The peace he gives makes it possible for us to live with joy rather than hide in fear.

The peace Jesus gave to disciples was the same peace God promised throughout the Scriptures. This peace is described in the Hebrew word *shalom*. *Shalom* means that everything broken is whole again. *Shalom* is the ideal state of mind for living a full life. *Shalom* is safety. *Shalom* is a greeting that signals the intent to do no harm.

We can imagine how much the disciples needed to hear and receive *shalom*. They were hiding in fear behind locked doors. Their fears had grown to a level where they could not give themselves the peace they needed.

The disciples needed the peace of God. Only God's peace was going to be enough to guard their hearts and their minds. And Jesus wanted so desperately to give them this peace that he did not wait to be invited. He did not wait for them to open the door. He did not wait for the disciples to come looking for him. He came to them. This reminds me of what Scripture says in 1 John 4:19: "We love [him] because he first loved us." Just when the disciples must have thought that they would be locked in fear forever, in walked Jesus with the words they desperately needed to hear. "Peace be with you."

Jesus did not return with words of condemnation or criticism. He did not judge them harshly for not being able to stand and stay during the most difficult period of his life. He came to bring them peace. He came back to let them know that with God, it is not too late for a second chance. He came back to show them that God is always faithful.

This is our peace. And this peace brings us joy because the joy of the Christian is not dependent on our situation. The joy of the Christian is knowing what God has done for us in Christ. The disciples were overjoyed at the greeting of peace because those four words signified that all was well between them and God. "Peace be with you" meant that Jesus had indeed won the victory over death. "Peace be with you" confirmed what Jesus told them back in Bethany: "I am the resurrection and the life. The one who believes in me will live, even though they die; and whoever lives by believing in me will never die" (John 11:25-26a, NIV).

Therefore, whatever has you afraid today, hear the voice of Jesus saying these four words to you: "Peace be with you."

There are people who leave the house every day, yet they are living behind locked doors of uncertainty. What if I try this and it does not work? What if I ask and they say no? There are people living behind locked doors of anger, behind locked doors of emptiness and dissatisfaction, and behind doors locked with bitterness from the past that continues to strangle their happiness. They live in fear of something or someone, live behind questions that have no answer, and live in the shadows of yesterday's mistakes.

But Jesus is with us. He came all the way back from the grave just to give us peace. He came all the way back from the grave just to tell some worried parent, "Peace." He came all the way back from the dead just to slip his nail-scarred hands around the shoulders of someone who is successful but far too stressed and tell them, "Peace be with you." And we receive his peace by trusting that he is standing here with us, which lets our fears fade into the background and allows a new joy into our lives.

Lest we think that the peace of Jesus is only intended to make us feel good, what Jesus said next revealed that he did not bring the disciples peace so they could stay locked in the room. The story does not end with peace-filled disciples sitting comfortably inside a house. Jesus told them a second time, "Peace be with you!" (v. 21). The first peace was to comfort them. But the second peace was to commission them.

After the second "peace," Jesus went on to say, "As the Father has sent me, so I send you" (v. 21). And then he breathed on them. Jesus came back to empower the disciples to continue his mission. He did not intend to leave them in that locked room. Jesus never intended to leave us huddled together behind closed doors. Jesus did not come to create a spiritual country club. His resurrection was not just a reunion of old friends; it was also a renewal of mission. "As the Father has sent me, so I send you. . . ."

Everyone who believes in the resurrection is on a mission from God. Every church that affirms the resurrection is on a mission. Our mission is the same mission Jesus had while he was in the world.

Jesus commissioned the disciples go out into the world and share the joy of trusting in God. He said it this way: "If you forgive anyone's sins, they are forgiven; if you do not forgive them, they are not forgiven" (v. 23, NIV). Jesus was not saying that we are in the place of God in that we can forgive sins or deny the forgiveness of sins. Remember that in John, "sin" refers to unbelief (16:8) and blindness to the denial of the truth that Jesus is God in the flesh (John 9).[1] Jesus was sending the disciples out to share with the world what God had done in Jesus Christ so that all who heard the news could then decide whether to believe or not believe.

This is why the resurrection is not just an annual celebration. Resurrection is the renewal of our mission. Jesus came into the world sent by the Father to do the Father's will. Now he's sending the disciples to pick up where he left off.

"As the Father has sent me, so I send you . . ." (v. 21).

With his peace, we are sent out to our jobs, our schools, our families. As the Father sent Jesus to bind up the brokenhearted, so Jesus sends us to bind up the brokenhearted. As the Father sent Jesus to feed those who were hungry, so Jesus sends us to feed the hungry. As the Father sent Jesus to bless the children and care for the vulnerable, so Jesus sends us to be a church that reaches every generation and cares for the lonely. As the Father sent Jesus to reveal the kingdom of God, so Jesus sent Peter, James, John, Andrew, Philip, and now us to be the salt of the earth and the light of the world.

Isn't this incredible? God intends to use you and me to continue where Jesus left off. There are still people living behind locked doors. There are prayers that need to be prayed. Families that need to be blessed. Words of encouragement that need to be spoken. Jesus came back not only to comfort us but also to commission us. He came back not only to be present with us but also to send us to be a blessing to others.

He sends us to pray. He sends us to serve. He sends us into the city. He sends us into the prisons. He sends us into each other's homes and even into other countries. God is in the sending business.

And I am glad to report today that not only do we have God's peace but we also have God's power. Even though we may feel underqualified for the job we've been commissioned to do, Jesus both sends *and* equips us.

We know he equips us when he sends us because after Jesus said he was sending the disciples, he breathed on them. Both in Hebrew and Greek, the words for wind, breath, and spirit are the same word. So when Jesus breathed on them, he did more than blow breath on them. Jesus gave them the power of the Holy Spirit to do what he was sending them to do.

In other words, the reason they could have peace is because he endowed them with his power. When Jesus breathed on them, it was a supernatural enabling. When Jesus breathed on them, the Spirit that was upon him came to rest on them; it was a foretaste of the power that was to come in full on the day of Pentecost.

Let this be a word for us. Jesus came back from the dead not only to give us peace but also to send us on a mission. And to ensure the success of the mission, Jesus has breathed on us that we might have the power of the Spirit to do his work in the world.

God will never send us without breathing on us. And when God breathes on us, God prepares us. When God breathes on us, God equips us. When God breathes on us, God endows us. When God breathes on us, God preserves us. When God breathes on us, God fills us.

Jesus said, "Peace be with you" a third and final time in John (v. 26). This time he did not say it to the entire group of disciples. The third time, Jesus said it to one disciple in particular.

When Jesus first appeared to the disciples, Thomas was not with them. The disciples tried to share their excitement with Thomas about having seen the resurrected Jesus. But Thomas said to them, "Unless I see the nail marks in his hands and put my finger where the nails were, and put my hand into his side, I will not believe" (v. 25, NIV).

Thomas makes a lot of sense if you think about it. He was a realist. He was just like everyone else. Mary did not believe Jesus was alive when she saw the empty tomb. Peter did not believe Jesus was alive when he saw the linen strips lying around the tomb. Maybe Thomas simply did not want to be left out. He wanted to have the same experience and the same testimony that everyone else had. So he told everybody exactly how he felt. He would not believe unless he saw the nail marks in Jesus's hands and put his fingers where the nails were and put his hand into Jesus's side. Thomas did not just want to see Jesus. He wanted to touch Jesus.

Thomas needed to be sure that this person everyone claimed they saw was not a ghost. One day passed and Jesus did not show up. Two days passed and Jesus did not show up. Three days passed and still Jesus did not show up. I suppose it was not only Thomas who questioned what everyone else had seen; the other disciples might have been wondering by now if they had really seen what they thought they saw a few days earlier.

I think the appearance of Jesus to Thomas is but another reminder that Jesus is not only concerned about all of us collectively. He is also interested in each one of us personally. In a way, Thomas speaks for all of us who were not there at the earliest resurrection appearances.[2] Jesus did not ignore Thomas's request. John says that one week later, Jesus came back again. Everyone else had already seen him, but he came back for Thomas. He came in through locked doors again. He stood among them again. He said, "Peace be with you!" again (v. 26).

Despite his earlier protests, hearing those four words was enough for Thomas. Jesus invited Thomas to touch his wounds, but for Thomas, seeing was believing. Seeing the wounds was enough. Seeing the scars was enough. Seeing the Lord's face was enough. Seeing Jesus alive was enough.

Upon hearing those four words and seeing the Lord, Thomas declared what no one in John had been able to say about Jesus until now. He looked at the risen Jesus and said, "My Lord and my God!" (v. 28).

Once again, this only affirms that the resurrection does not become powerful until it becomes personal. Jesus came back then, and he keeps coming back so that you and I can say along with Thomas, "My Lord and my God!"

Every sign Jesus performed was to show us that he is our Lord and our God. Every miracle he made happen was to reveal that he is our Lord and our God. Every sermon he preached was an invitation for us to know that he is our Lord and our God.

So Jesus told Thomas, "Because you have seen me, you have believed; blessed are those who have not seen and yet have believed" (v. 29, NIV). Blessed are those like you and me and millions of others who were not there when Jesus walked on water, when he came through locked doors, when Mary saw him alive for the first time, or when he first appeared to the disciples. But because we have heard his voice and have experienced the renewal of his power, we too can say, "My Lord and my God."

Blessed are you!

Peace be with you! Amen.

Notes

1. See Frances Taylor Gench, *Encounters with Jesus* (Louisville: Westminster John Knox, 2007).

2. Ibid., 137.

31

When Jesus Shows Up

John 21:1-14

John sets the timeframe for this passage by beginning with the word "after." After Jesus appeared to Mary outside the empty tomb; after Jesus came into a room through locked doors; after Jesus told the disciples, "Peace be with you" (vv. 19, 21, 26); after Jesus breathed on them; after Jesus came back to appear again for Thomas who did not believe he was alive; and after Thomas confessed by faith, "My Lord and my God," Jesus appeared again to his disciples.

Jesus came back because he had unfinished business. He had already walked on water and fed multitudes, but there was still unfinished business. He had healed and brought the dead back to life, but there was still unfinished business. The victory of the resurrection would have been a good way to end the story. But Jesus came back one more time. Jesus came back to make sure the disciples were ready to do what he called them to do. He showed up to let them know what he could do for them. He came back to show them what they needed in order to be ready for their assignment. Consider how the text unfolds and see how Jesus blessed the disciples by coming back one more time.

John says that Jesus appeared again to the disciples by the Sea of Galilee. This is a rather unusual place for Jesus to show up. Remember that the disciples have already seen the empty tomb. They have already encountered the risen Lord. They have seen his wounds and received the Holy Spirit, but when we meet the disciples in John 21:1-3 they are fishing in the Sea of Galilee.

John said it happened this way: "Simon Peter, Thomas called the Twin, Nathanael from Cana in Galilee, the sons of Zebedee [James and John], and two other of his disciples" were together (v. 2). Peter told them, "I am going fishing," and they said, "We will go with you" (v. 3). Fishing is what the disciples had been doing before they met Jesus. In Matthew, Mark, and Luke, Jesus found the first disciples while they were fishing in the Sea of Galilee:

> And he said to them, "Follow Me, and I will make you fishers of men." (Matt 4:19, NKJV)

> As Jesus passed along the Sea of Galilee, he saw Simon and his brother Andrew casting a net into the sea—for they were fishermen. And Jesus said to them, "Follow me and I will make you fish for people." And immediately they left their nets and followed him. (Mark 1:16-18)

In Luke 5, the story is similar to what we read in John 21. Some say it is the same story inserted at the beginning of Luke but at the end of John. Some say these are two separate stories. Either way, both fishing trips take place at night. Both fishing trips end in failure. Both times Jesus tells the disciples how to catch more fish. Both times the catch of fish is abundant.

Sometimes the disciples have been accused of disobedience and backsliding for going fishing in John 21. They had seen the Lord and been empowered by the Spirit, but they went fishing. We do not need to assume, however, that the disciples went fishing because they were disobedient. After all, the disciples were ordinary people who needed to eat and work for a living. Fishing was not necessarily a sin, but fishing turned out to be an opportunity for Jesus to reveal himself to them.

Because of what happened that night, the disciples learned that the Lord will show up in ordinary places while we are doing our ordinary work. The disciples had returned to their homes in Galilee because the Passover in Jerusalem was over. They went back to get on with their lives. They went back to the place they knew as home. They returned to fishing, which is something most of them knew how to do quite well. Peter, Andrew, James, and John were fishermen before they became disciples. And while they were fishing Jesus appeared to them. He showed up in an ordinary place, the Sea of Galilee, while they were doing ordinary work, fishing.

The English word "appeared" comes from a Greek word that means "to reveal, to make known, to show oneself, or to manifest." The Lord chooses to work by revelation. This means that he makes himself known to us rather than waiting for us to figure out by reason alone where he is and who he is. Jesus came to the Sea of Galilee to make himself known once again, to reveal himself, while the disciples were doing something absolutely mundane. This may seem like a small detail, but it is one we should not overlook.

Jesus did not appear to the disciples on the top of a mountain with clouds swirling around his head while angels sang. Jesus did not appear to them in the synagogue where the scholarly rabbis taught. He did not show up at the temple in the holy of holies where only the sanctified priests could go. Jesus revealed himself to them at the Sea of Galilee, while they were fishing. Maybe we should take from this resurrection appearance the good news that we do not have to be in a church to have an encounter with the Lord. We can encounter the Risen Lord anywhere. As Frederick Dale Bruner wrote, "God chose to come down to us in his incarnate, crucified and risen Son to reveal himself by ordinary words, stories, fellowship, water, prayer and meals."[1]

We do not have to wait until Sunday morning to see Jesus. He shows himself to us at all times and in all places. We are just as likely to meet the Risen Lord at the grocery store as we are at a revival. We are just as likely to see the Lord in the face of a homeless person as we are in the work of a dedicated church member. We can just as easily encounter the risen Lord at our work as we can in worship. We can meet Jesus at our dinner table just like we can at the Communion table. God is not contained, limited, or confined to our special times of meeting together. We have a God who appears to us in the ordinary.

Jesus was born in a stable and laid in an ordinary manger. He was reared by ordinary parents. He grew up in an ordinary village. He had an ordinary job as a carpenter. He picked ordinary people to be his apostles. He died an ordinary death, like a criminal. And he came back to meet his disciples in an ordinary place while they were doing ordinary work.

This was a lesson the disciples would need in the future because the assignments Jesus had for them would eventually take them places where their only saving grace would be to trust that God could show up where they were. One day Peter even found out that Jesus could show up in a jail cell and post bond for him (Acts 12). Wherever we are and whatever we need, the risen, reigning, redeeming, reconciling, and ruling Lord will be with us.

It may be that Jesus showed up in this ordinary place to see if the disciples were ready to do what he called them to do. To be ready, they needed to confront their insufficiency, which may be why the fishing trip did not turn out so well.

Peter organized this nighttime fishing trip, and six of the disciples who were with him in Galilee said, "We will go with you" (v. 3). John says, "They went out and got into the boat, but that night they caught nothing" (v. 3). They were experienced, seasoned fishermen. They fished all night, but they caught nothing. By means of failure, they came to see their insufficiency. Insufficiency is hard to accept. We have too much pride for that. We like to believe that we have enough willpower to fight off any temptation; maybe some people do some of the time, but none of us do all of the time. We are insufficient. Like the disciples, we sleep when we should pray. Like Abraham, we have lied when we should have told the truth. Like Moses, we have let our anger get out of control. We are not bad people. We are merely insufficient.

This is why the disciples could not catch any fish. They fished all night and caught nothing. I probably do not need to say this, but "nothing" in Greek means the same thing as "nothing" in English. Nothing means they did not catch even one fish. The nets were empty. They caught *nothing*. Failure is an experience that no one enjoys, but this time failure became an opportunity for Jesus to let the disciples confront their insufficiency and see his sufficiency.

Verse 4 says that in the morning (John's spiritual symbol of a new day), Jesus stood on the shore, but the disciples did not realize that it was Jesus. Jesus called out to them, "Friends, haven't you any fish?" (v. 5, NIV). Jesus knew the answer, but he had a point to make. The disciples told him no and Jesus said, "Throw your net on the right side of the boat and you will find some" (v. 6, NIV). The disciples did not yet recognize that it was Jesus talking to them. But he was there. He saw their frustration. He saw their disappointment. He knew their insufficiency. And this is when he came to reveal himself to them.

Aren't you glad that Jesus does not wait until we have been recognized for our stellar accomplishments to come to us? He does not wait until the confetti is flying and the plaques are handed out. Jesus comes to us in our ordinary and even our most unpleasant experiences, especially in our failures. We may feel like our failures push God away from us, but when the disciples failed, Jesus came close to them. Jesus came to the disciples and told them how to turn things around. Now that they had confronted their own insufficiency, they were ready to see the Lord's sufficiency.

He asked the disciples if they had caught any fish. In other words, were their efforts working for their good? Since it was not, he invited them to try fishing in a new place: "Cast your net on the other side of the boat and you'll find what you're looking for." It is amazing how long we will keep doing things that do not work, do not bring us joy, do not give us life, and do not work for our good. It is remarkable how long we will try doing the same thing expecting different results. Jesus said, "Cast your nets on the right side and then you'll find what you're looking for."

They could not catch any fish without him, but they would catch an abundance of fish by casting the net where he told them. This was merely a preview of the rest of their lives. No matter how long or how hard they fished, they would not catch anything unless they were doing what Jesus told them. They were insufficient, but he is all sufficient.

This moment was a repeat of what Jesus taught them in John 15 when he explained that he was the true vine. Jesus wanted the disciples to remember that apart from him, they could do nothing. Yes, he had given them his peace. Yes, he had breathed the Holy Spirit on them. But if they did not listen to him, they would not ever catch any fish. He was preparing them to be fishers of men and women, but if they did not follow his voice, they would not catch anyone. Someone here today may be struggling with a long season of things not going well, relationships not working out, or health not getting better. Sometimes we go through these seasons because that's just the season we are in. Sometimes we go through these seasons because the Lord is waiting for us to do what the Lord has told us to do. God is waiting for us to realize that we are insufficient, and we need to cast our net where God tells us to cast it. As Jesus said in John 15, "No branch can bear fruit by itself; it must remain in the vine. Neither can you bear fruit unless you remain in me" (15:4).

And don't you know that when they cast their net on the other side, the haul of fish was so large they could barely bring it in? John has shown us over and over again that Jesus is able to supply every need. He is the Word that was with God and the Word that was God (1:1). "Through him all things were made; without him nothing was made that has been made" (1:3, NIV). Every time Jesus said, "I am" this or "I am" that, he was making it known that whatever we lack, he can supply.

If anyone is hungry, spiritually or physically, I am the bread of life.

If anyone is walking around confused, I am the light of the world.

If anyone is lonely, I am the good shepherd.

If anyone is searching, I am the door.

If anyone is going through the valley of the shadow of death, I am the resurrection and the life.

This explains why Jesus told them to cast their net where they could haul in a large catch of fish. Jesus did not let the disciples catch an abundance of fish so they could brag about their success. He filled their net so they could see who he was. John says that as soon as the disciples saw the abundance of fish in the net, the disciple whom Jesus loved said to Peter, "It is the Lord!" (v. 7).

He knew that man who spoke to them was not some stranger standing on the shore. It was the Lord. He has power over death and sovereignty over the fish of the lake. "He is the image of the invisible God, the firstborn over all creation; for in him all things in heaven and on earth were created, things visible and invisible, whether thrones or dominions or rulers or powers—all things have been created through him and for him. He himself is before all things, and in him all things hold together" (Col 1:15-17).

Jesus did not fill their nets because he needed their fish. John says that when the disciples came ashore, Jesus had already cooked fish on a fire of burning coals. Jesus did not need their fish, but he may have wanted to send a message about forgiveness.

The last time Peter saw a fire of burning coals like this one may have been when he was warming his hands after Jesus's arrest. A servant girl asked him, as he warmed his hands over hot coals, if he was a disciple of Jesus. Peter said he was not. Two more times that night Peter denied knowing Jesus, just as Jesus said he would (see John 18:15-18, 25-27).

So Jesus brought Peter back to burning coals to restore him and let him know he was forgiven. It is hard to convince someone else that they can be forgiven if we do not know that *we* have been forgiven. Jesus needed to restore Peter so he could use Peter. Jesus did so through the fellowship of an ordinary meal. He said, "Come and have breakfast" (v. 12). We joke about how often we eat in the church, but meals inside and outside the church can create meaningful moments and spiritual encounters.

Jesus took bread and fish and shared it with the disciples, similar to what he did when he fed the multitudes. He used an ordinary meal to communicate the extraordinary grace of forgiveness. He had already given his life for them, but he still had grace to share. Jesus invited them to come dine with him. He invited them to eat food he prepared for them. They had been working all night long without success to feed themselves. Jesus wanted them to trust that what he had for them was enough. They were insufficient, but he was sufficient because he was the Lord.

That's why we can trust him . . . he is the Lord.

That's why we can depend on him . . . he is the Lord.

That's why we can go to him, call on him, and wait for him . . . he is the Lord.

And because he is the Lord, what he feeds us will be enough to sustain us.

Sometimes we forget who wants to feed us, and we try to feed ourselves. But our food never lasts. So Jesus shows up, makes a meal, and says, "Come and eat with me." And beloved, when we come to this table every month, we do so to share bread and wine, to be reminded of how much God loves us.

We come not because we are worthy but because he invites us. We come not because of our merit but because of the Lord's grace. We come not because we have a right but because he has extended an invitation. "Come and eat with me."

And my, how it can change a person's life when they hear the Lord's invitation.

Two of John the Baptist's disciples came to Jesus and asked where he was staying. Jesus said, "Come and see" (1:39). After they came and saw, they realized Jesus was the Savior of the world.

In Matthew 11, Jesus said, "Come to me, all you that are weary and carrying heavy burdens, and I will give you rest" (v. 28). All who answer this call find out that his yoke is easy and his burden is light (vv. 29-30).

So when we have burdens, Jesus says, "Come, and my grace will make your load a little lighter."

When we have failed, Jesus says, "Come, and my forgiveness will let you start over again."

When we have lost our way, Jesus says, "Come, and I'll be the way, the truth, and the life."

When our spiritual well is empty, Jesus says, "Come, and I'll restore you and revive you."

When we need encouragement, Jesus says, "Come, and my word will stand you on your feet again."

That's why Jesus came—to let us know that there is still room at the table.

It is like the prophet Isaiah said: "Come, all you who are thirsty, come to the waters; and you who have no money, come, buy and eat!" (55:1, NIV).

Give ear and come to me; listen, that you may live. Jesus is still sufficient; he is still showing up in ordinary places; and he is still inviting us to come and dine with him.

Note

1. Frederick Dale Bruner, *The Gospel of John: A Commentary* (Grand Rapids MI: Eerdmans, 2012) 6.

32

Where Do We Go from Here?

John 21:15-25

At last we have come to the final verses in the Gospel according to John. The verses that claim our attention this morning are a continuation of the story that began at the beginning of chapter 21. Jesus had just appeared by the Sea of Galilee, showing himself to the disciples for the third time after he was raised from the dead.

Among the seven disciples who saw Jesus that day were James and John, brothers who went by the nickname "the sons of thunder." We are never told how they earned this holy handle, but it probably had something to do with their commanding and powerful personalities.

Thomas was there. He has unfairly been called "doubting Thomas." We should call him "sensible Thomas" or maybe "practical Thomas."

Nathanael from Cana in Galilee was there. We do not hear much about or from Nathanael, but his hometown is the place where Jesus turned water into wine. Nathanael became a disciple after realizing that Jesus knew more about him than he knew about himself. This discovery made him say to Jesus in John 1, "Rabbi, you are the Son of God! You are the King of Israel" (v. 49).

The seventh disciple present at the Sea of Galilee was Simon Peter. Peter became one of the most prominent disciples. He was clearly someone special to Jesus. When Jesus went on healing missions, he would often only take three of the disciples with him: James, John, and Peter. As far as we can tell, Peter was the only one of the twelve disciples whose name was changed by Jesus. At birth Peter was given the name Simon bar Jonah, which meant Simon son of John. Jesus gave Simon a new name, *Cephas*, which is translated as Peter and means "rock."

If we think about Peter's actions leading up to this point, a rock was probably not what he felt like by the time we arrive at John 21:15. Rocks are firm and reliable. Peter had been unreliable to the point of failure. He had not been as faithful under pressure as he said he would. He backed down after having promised that he would stand tall. He denied knowing Jesus after saying he would never do something like that.

So now Jesus was back. He came back and had breakfast with Peter and the other disciples. It should not be ignored that Jesus prepared food for the disciples. This says something about the way God cares for us. We have a God who understands hunger and relates to being thirsty. We have a God who knows what we are going through in this earthly life. Jesus knew the disciples were hungry. "Come and have breakfast," he told them (21:12). We have a God who can empathize with us when we are lonely or hurting.

The Lord is not just concerned about our souls without any regard for the bodies he created with such precision and purpose. He created hearts to send blood coursing through our arteries and veins. He created cells to carry nutrients through the bloodstream to supply what each organ needs to operate. He created bones, ligaments, muscles, and tendons to carry our bodies around on the earth that he made. He cares about every aspect of our being: our mind, our body, and our soul. So Jesus's first order of business was to give his disciples food and then have a talk with Peter about spiritual concerns.

Peter may have expected Jesus to have a talk with him. He probably anticipated words of rebuke or chastisement. Fortunately, Jesus is not like most people. He does not define us by our worst moments or even by our last failure. Jesus is always thinking of what we can become and not just how we have fallen down in the past. Peter had not been faithful, but Jesus still wanted to be in relationship with him. So he asked Peter a crucial question.

Consider some of the questions Jesus asks in the Gospel of John. Do you want to be made whole (5:6)? What do you want (1:38)? Do you believe this (11:26)? His questions were not merely a way for him to get information. Jesus asked questions to reach beyond the corridors of a person's mind and penetrate the chambers of the heart. His questions were intended to spark transformation. "Simon son of John, do you love me more than these?" (v. 15)

Why would Jesus ask Peter a question like this? Jesus asked Peter this question to help him with the one choice that makes us ready for the life of faith. Are we motivated by love? And not just any love but love for the Son of God, Jesus Christ? A lot of people love the church. We love the programs and the people. A lot of people love their ministry. We like the feeling we get from doing good work. But Jesus asked, "Simon son of John, do you love me more than these?" (v. 15).

It goes without saying that whenever someone calls us by our whole name, we know they mean serious business. This was not a good sign for Peter. Jesus called Simon both by his *whole* name and by his *old* name. Simon was the name he went by before Jesus changed his named to Peter. Since Peter had not lived up to the new name, which meant "rock," Jesus addressed him as Simon son of John. (It is a tragedy for a person to forget who he or she is. Don't forget who you are!)

Why was this such a crucial question for Peter? After all, Peter was the first one to go into the empty tomb. Peter was the first one to jump out of the boat and come to shore after the disciples caught 153 fish. Yet Jesus called Peter by his old name and asked if he loved Jesus more than these. Why? Because Jesus knows that the only way to follow him is to be motivated by love for him.

The question we are asking this morning is, where do we go from here? The answer has everything to do with love. Disciples do more than admire Jesus. Disciples love him. Admiration can fade, but love is persistent. The power of love drew Mary to come to the cemetery while it was still dark to find Jesus's body. The power of love made another woman named Mary take a pint of the most expensive perfume and pour it on Jesus's feet and wipe his feet with her hair. Love is what made Jesus weep outside of Lazarus's tomb. Love is why parents never stop praying for their children. Love is why parents stay up all night with sick babies.

This is the secret of discipleship. "Simon son of John, do you love me more than these?" Jesus did not ask if Simon respected him. A lot of people respect Jesus. Jesus did not ask if Simon fasted or if he preached. Jesus did not even ask if Simon knew more about him than the rest of the disciples. He asked if Simon loved him.

Love is the fire that keeps our faith from cooling off. Love is the way to keep our hearts from becoming calloused by cynicism. Love can keep us from quitting when serving the Lord turns out to be harder than we imagined. To follow him, we must love him. Love is our motivation as disciples. This is why we usher. We love him. This is why we do ministry. We love him. This is why we read to children as tutors. We love him. This is why we serve in the prison ministry and in the choir. This is why we check on each other, send cards, and offer encouraging words. We love him.

A good reminder for all who serve in Christian leadership is that we may have the skills to make us competent in what we do, but the one quality that is essential for discipleship is a heart motivated by deep love for Christ. It is not just the results that Jesus wants; Jesus also cares about the process and the relationships. Without love we can do nothing.

Perhaps someone is wondering why they should love Christ. There are so many reasons to love the Lord. Love him because he is the Lamb of God who takes away the sin of the world. Love him because he is the light of the world who leads us out of darkness. Love him because he is a shepherd who lays down his life for the sheep. Love him because he is humble enough to wash our feet. He was sovereign enough to say "before Abraham was, I am" (8:58). Love him because he prayed for us. Love him because he was arrested although he was innocent. He was wounded for our transgressions and bruised for our iniquities. Love him because he spoke a word of forgiveness from the cross. He died a real death and rose from the grave with true victory, so I love him. But perhaps the best reason to love him is that he made the first move to love us. First John 4:19 says, "We love because he first loved us."

It is not that we do not also love the people we serve or with whom we serve. We certainly should. It is just that sometimes doing what we do for other people does not always turn out to be adequate motivation. When the people we love do not love us back, will we sit down and stop serving? Jesus wanted Simon to go the distance as a disciple, so he had to begin with the right motivation. "Simon son of John, do you love me more than these?" (v. 15)

When Jesus said "more than these" he was not trying to stir up a competitive spirit within Peter. We do not need to know whether we love the Lord more than someone else. This question was a part of Peter's restoration. Scripture tells us that Peter once came close to boasting about how he loved Jesus more than everyone else. It happened when Jesus and the disciples ate the Passover meal together back in John 13. Jesus washed the disciples' feet and then told them, "Very truly, I tell you, one of you will betray me" (v. 21). The disciples were at a loss for words. None of them could imagine who might betray their leader and Lord. Jesus told them he was going away and that they could not go with him.

Peter asked, "Lord, why can I not follow you now? I will lay down my life for you" (13:37). Then Jesus answered, "Will you lay down your life for me? Very truly, I tell you, before the cock crows, you will have denied me three times" (v. 38). Laying down one's life was the epitome of love (15:13).

Peter was so sure he could lay down his life that Mark 14:29 adds the detail that when Jesus predicted Peter's denial, Peter said, "Even if *all* fall away, I will not" (NIV, emphasis mine).

Peter apparently saw himself as being much more committed, much stronger, and much more certain of his abilities than the other disciples. The other disciples might not be able to stand up under the pressure, but he was never going to let the Lord down. The other disciples might fall away, but he was never going to fall away. As it turns out, Jesus's prediction was correct. Before the sun came up the next morning, Peter denied knowing Jesus three times.

Asking if Peter loved him "more than these" (21:15) gave Peter a moment to think back on how sure of himself he had been a few weeks earlier and how much he had fallen short. We can be quite bold about what we would and would not do when we have never been in a real situation faced with that decision. It is easy to say, "If that had been me, I would have done this or that." We read the newspaper and watch the news. We hear stories about foolish mistakes people made and say, "I would never do what that person did." Maybe we would not do the same thing they did, but there are so many ways to mess up that if we have not made our own foolish errors yet, all we have to do is keep on living. Our day will come. Peter had a chip on his shoulder. He thought he would be the last person to deny knowing Jesus. It turns out he was the first.

Jesus wanted Peter to come to terms with his failure and lack of humility, so he asked Peter, "Do you love me more than these other disciples? Do you still think you are so much stronger than everyone else?" We cannot fully and freely love and serve God with arrogance or haughtiness gripping the heart. Peter needed to understand that he could not do anything on his own. He didn't even keep a promise he made to himself.

The experience of failure humbled him so much that when Peter responded to Jesus, he dared not say that he loved Jesus more than the other disciples did. He knew better than to try to fool Jesus. He stopped trying to make himself look spiritually superior to his friends. He stopped trying to boast about how much more faithful he was than the other disciples. He answered only for himself: "Yes, Lord; you know that I love you" (21:15).

Jesus probably asked Peter about his love three times in order to restore Peter after he denied knowing Jesus three times: "Do you love me more than these?" "Do you love me?" "Do you love me?" (vv. 15-17). Each time Peter said he loved Jesus. The text says that "Peter was hurt because Jesus asked him the third time, 'Do you love me?'" (v. 17, NIV).

Peter may indeed have been hurt. Sometimes God can't really help us until we no longer want to be like we are. But the good news is that the Lord did not write Peter off. The repetition was not designed to reject Peter but to restore Peter. Jesus was giving him another chance. The Lord did not kick Peter out of the group of disciples. He made him breakfast and then had a heart-to-heart conversation with him about his life. I'm glad to know that no matter how far we fall, the Lord can raise us up again.

- Lamentations tells us the Lord's mercy is new every morning.

- David prayed in Psalm 51:10, "Create in me a clean heart, O God, and put a new and right spirit within me."

- Psalm 103:8 says, "The LORD is merciful and gracious, slow to anger and abounding in steadfast love."

Peter now knows that the God he loves is the God of another chance. Peter failed, but the Lord came back to see him.

Where do we go from here? If we love him, we will answer the call to serve. Loving Jesus is always faith in action. Each time Peter said that he loved Jesus, Jesus gave him a command: "Feed my lambs," "Tend my sheep," "Feed my sheep" (vv. 15-17). One of the key words in the Gospel of John is "believe," but Scripture is clear that the measure of our belief in God is our Christlike love for others. In other words, once we have seen him, we answer the call to serve him.

> This is how we know what love is: Jesus Christ laid down his life for us. And we ought to lay down our lives for our brothers and sisters. If anyone has material possessions and sees a brother or sister in need but has no pity on them, how can the love of God be in that person? Dear children, let us not love with words or speech but with actions and in truth. (1 John 3:16-18, NIV)

> Religion that God our Father accepts as pure and faultless is this: to look after orphans and widows in their distress . . . . (Jas 1:27a, NIV)

> Dear friends, let us love one another, for love comes from God. Everyone who loves has been born of God and knows God. Whoever does not love does not know God, because God is love. (1 John 4:7-8, NIV)

And how did God demonstrate the depth of God's love? "For God so loved the world that he *gave* his only Son" (3:16, emphasis mine). According to Raymond Brown, a preeminent John scholar, love in the Gospel of John is not a theoretical idea that has nothing to do with community living or other people. Brown says that we need to believe that Jesus is the Word who has come from God because then we will know that when we have seen Jesus, we have seen what God is really like. Once we become a child of God, we are called to behave in a way that is worthy of God our Father and Jesus our brother.[1] This is why Jesus said "Feed my lambs," "Tend my sheep," and "Feed my sheep" (vv. 15-17). Our commitment to him is expressed in our compassion toward others.

This may be why Jesus called himself the good shepherd. To walk in love is to serve others in the same way God has served us. God has been our shepherd. God has looked after us. God has cared for us. God has led us to places of rest and renewal. God has watched over us and corrected us. God has been our defender and our provider. When we love God, this is how we are called to care for one another.

What the Lord does for me is not for me to keep to myself. If we have influence, we can use it to advance someone else. If we have power, we can use it on behalf of someone else. If we have time, we can spend it on someone else. God blesses us, and we then become a blessing to others. God blessed us with comfort so we can comfort others. God blessed us with grace so we can give grace to others. God gave us wisdom so we can share wisdom with others.

In other words, we cannot become so wrapped up in our own blessings that we neglect the call and the privilege to be a blessing to someone else. We are part of God's flock, and we are called to care for others in God's flock. When we love Jesus, we feed his lambs. When we love Jesus, we take care of his sheep. When we love Jesus, we feed his sheep.

Feed someone with the encouragement of an uplifting word.
Feed someone with hope by supplying their need.
Feed someone with joy by sharing your time and energy.
Feed someone with mercy by accepting them as they are.
Feed someone with truth by sharing the good news.
This is what we are called to do when we love Christ.

There is so much more we could say. John says that there was even more that he could have told us. But he figured that what he told us in these twenty-one chapters was enough. If he tried to tell us everything Jesus did, the whole world would not have room for the books that would be written.

He has told enough. He's told us enough to love him. He's told us enough to walk humbly before him. He's told us enough to serve him. But there is one more lesson for Peter: "If you love me, and you if you are going to serve me, from this point forward, you will have to trust me."

Jesus told Peter something about his future. He told Peter that when he was younger, he dressed himself and went where he wanted; but when he became old, he would stretch out his hands and someone else would dress him and lead him where he did not want to go. Jesus was referring to Peter's future death by crucifixion. This is what Jesus meant by Peter stretching out his hands and being led where he did not want to go. Then Jesus said, "Follow me!" (vv. 18-19).

Peter turned and saw that the disciple whom Jesus loved was following them. And Peter said, "Lord, what about him?" Jesus answered, "If it is my will that he remain until I come, what is that to you?" Again Jesus said, "Follow me!" (vv. 21-22).

Jesus did not tell Peter exactly how and when the future was going to take place, but Jesus wanted him to know that whatever questions Peter had, the answer was the same. If Peter was going to love Jesus, he was going to have to trust him. If Peter was going to serve the Lord, he was going to have to trust him. "Peter, don't worry about what I'm going to do in the other disciples' lives. Just trust me."

And when we look back on this glorious Gospel, Jesus has been saying the same thing to you and me on almost every page.

> I can turn water into wine. Trust me. I know things about you that you don't know about yourself. Trust me. I have authority given to me directly from the Father. If you have two fish and five loaves of bread, then give it to me. I can supply your needs. Trust me.
>
> I can walk on water. Trust me. I forgive sins and do not throw stones. Trust me. I am the light of the world. Trust me. I can open the eyes of the blind. I am the good shepherd and the door.
>
> Even though I have to go away, I will send you another comforter, the Holy Spirit, to lead and guide you into all truth. Trust me. I am praying for you. Trust me. My kingdom is not of this world. Trust me.
>
> Every Scripture about me has been fulfilled. I came into Jerusalem riding on the back of a donkey like Zechariah predicted. Soldiers gambled for my clothes like Psalm 22 predicted. I died and rose from the dead, just like I said I would. So come what may, you can trust me.

If you have seen me, you have seen the Father. Trust me. In this world, you will have trouble, but take heart; I have overcome the world. Trust me.

I think this what Jesus was saying to Peter, and it is certainly what Jesus is saying to us. As we close out this sermon series on the Gospel of John, let us remember what Jesus wants us to know:

> There may be some difficult days ahead. But trust me. Trust me in season, and trust me out of season. Trust me when life is good; trust me when life is hard.
>
> Because there is one thing you need to know: you may not know *how* you are going to make it, but you now know *who* is going to help you make it. Follow me.
>
> I am the bread of life. Follow me.
>
> I am the resurrection and the life. Follow me.
>
> I am the true vine. Follow me.
>
> I am the Son of God and the Word that became flesh. Follow me.
>
> When you are discouraged, I'll be your hope.
>
> When you are lonely, I'll be your comfort.
>
> When you are sad, let me be your joy.
>
> When you are in danger, do not fear. I will be your protection.
>
> When you are in need, remember to come to me.
>
> When you are broken, let me be your peace.
>
> When you are low on faith, look to me as your example.
>
> I am the first and the last, the beginning and the end. I am your God, the Word that was with God and the Word that was God, the Word that became flesh and made his dwelling among us.
>
> So if you love me, feed my sheep. If you serve me, you must also trust me. Believe this and you will live. That's a promise.

Note

1. Raymond Brown, *The Community of the Beloved Disciple* (New York: Paulist Press, 1979) 60–61.

Part 2

1 John

by Abby Thornton Hailey

Acknowledgements

Growing up, it never crossed my mind that I could one day be a preacher. I guess it should have: I had an uncle and a grandfather who were Baptist preachers. I loved to write, and to study the Bible, and to go to church. But I had never seen or heard anyone in the pulpit who looked like me or had a voice like mine.

So I publish these sermons with a sense of deep gratitude for those who, over time, drew that voice out of me and helped it find a place. For my professors in the Religious Studies department at the University of Virginia who taught me to read Scripture in new ways and nudged me toward seminary. For my peers at Duke Divinity School, in whom I could see God's giftedness, and who became a mirror that helped me identify God's giftedness in me. For Prospect United Methodist Church in Yanceyville, North Carolina, where my first sermon as a 22-year-old left me exhilarated and terrified by the sense of doing what God had created me to do. For the congregation that raised me, Winfree Memorial Baptist Church in Midlothian, Virginia, for nurturing and celebrating my calling, welcoming me home to preach, and ordaining me to continue this unexpected journey. For my husband, Victor, who I am so grateful to have beside me through the joys and struggles of this immense vocation that we share. And for Broadneck Baptist Church in Annapolis, Maryland, where an amazing group of people somehow consents to let me stand weekly in their pulpit, engaging in an ongoing dialogue about the story of God in Scripture and our lives.

My thanks are also due to the editorial team at Smyth & Helwys. Not only did they entrust this project to me, but they were the first publishers who trusted my gift for writing enough to hire me to do it. First Darrell in our work with *Formations*, and now Keith and Katie in our work with

Preaching the Word—thank you for your faith in me and your tireless efforts to make my voice stronger, clearer, and more resonant.

—**Abby Thornton Hailey**

Preface

As I note in my first sermon in this volume, letters make up 21 of the 27 books of our New Testament, yet I have always shied away from preaching on letters. I am a preacher drawn to narrative. I return again and again to the big stories of the Old Testament, and especially to the stories of Jesus. When it comes to preaching, I never felt the letters had as much to speak into my congregations' lives as a good story.

But working on this volume opened my eyes and heart to view to the letters of the New Testament in a new way. The Epistles, at their hearts, tell a story—the story of the first Christians who wrestled with the words of Jesus just as we do today, who had to figure out what to do with lives that had been turned upside down by the Gospel. These are not abstract theological documents. These are stories of people trying to figure out what Jesus meant and how to live with one another as Christ has called us to live.

This is why I chose "Letter to the Editors" as my theme for this series of sermons on 1 John, exploring the letter as written to a young community shaping how Jesus's message and meaning would be experienced by generations to come. I preached the series over nine Sundays immediately following Easter, the season in the Revised Common Lectionary when portions of 1 John appear as the Epistle reading. I then returned to the epistles in late summer to preach a two-sermon series on 2 John and 3 John entitled "Snapshots of Faith." The weeks we spent in 1 John prepared us to make sense of 2 and 3 John, which are hard to digest without recognizing their connections to their longer, more detailed predecessor.

Through both of these series, the congregation of Broadneck Baptist Church in Annapolis, Maryland sought to explore how the struggles these letters address in early churches are struggles our churches still face today. I was amazed how these texts again and again spoke to the seasons we found ourselves in, both in terms of the church year (Easter, Pentecost, Trinity

Sunday) and current events locally (the death of Freddy Gray in Baltimore police custody) and in our congregation (our ongoing conversations about racial justice and our mission partnership with a community in West Virginia). I sought to weave these things into my sermons whenever possible, letting voices from the past and the present mingle together. I am grateful for the gift of time with these books I might otherwise have neglected, and for my congregation's willingness to go on this journey with me. Together we came to a renewed sense that all Scripture does, indeed, have a word of grace and challenge to speak into our daily lives.

What You've Seen and Heard

1 John 1:1–2:2 (with John 20:19-31)

Letters are one of our oldest literary forms. Within this historic genre, the category of "letter to the editor" holds a special place. According to the great Wikipedia, a letter to the editor can have many different purposes: to support or oppose a stance taken by another writer; to comment on a current issue in an effort to sway the reader to one's viewpoint; to be critical of or praise ideas that have appeared previously; to correct a perceived error or misrepresentation.

Letters to the editor can be powerful things that rally people around an important cause. In the 1760s, a series of letters written by the Pennsylvania lawyer and legislator John Dickinson and published under the name "A Farmer" were reprinted throughout the thirteen colonies, helping unite the colonists against unfair British legislation, which helped spark the revolution to come. Just as often, however, letters are thinly veiled opportunities for people to rant about things that matter very little—or don't even make sense. I read letters to the editor this week that addressed everything from rage over cookies being placed in the wrong section at the grocery store to this brilliant suggestion submitted to the Munster, Indiana, *Times*: "A lot of deer get hit by cars west of Crown Point on US 231. There are too many cars to have the deer crossing here. The deer crossing sign needs to be moved to a road with less traffic." Yes, that's a real letter.

When I read the letters of the New Testament—and twenty-one of the twenty-seven books in our New Testament are classified as letters—I hear them as letters to the editor or, perhaps more accurately, letters to the *editors*. After the life, death, and resurrection of Jesus, after his ascension into heaven and the gift of the Holy Spirit at Pentecost that drew people together into diverse communities, congregations of Christ followers began springing up all over the place. These early churches had an awe-inspiring but difficult task: to take what they had learned about Jesus and translate it faithfully into their own contexts. They had to continue figuring out what his life and teachings meant for how they lived as individuals and communities. Their mission was to answer the question left hanging after the resurrection—"What next?" As they wrestled with this, early churches became the keepers, the tellers, the editors of the story of Jesus—those who would figure out how to pass the story on clearly and faithfully to those yet to come.

Not surprisingly, it seems like the first Christians almost immediately struggled with this responsibility. Over the next few weeks, we are going to be walking with one of those young Christian communities, the original audience of the Gospel of John. This particular story of Jesus's life, as we heard in John 20:19-31, ended with the hope that "you may come to believe that Jesus is the Messiah, the Son of God, and that through believing you may have life in his name" (20:31). Communities across the Mediterranean indeed came to believe, but by the time we meet them in today's text, they are facing big problems. Different community members had come to understand and interpret the teachings of the Gospel of John in different ways, and variations in interpretation threatened to tear churches apart. Best as we can tell, their differences were not over little things like where the cookies were shelved in the grocery store or what type of pita was best at the Lord's Supper. Their disagreements were over things that deeply mattered, over who Jesus was and what it meant to follow him, and over whether Christianity was just about knowing and believing the right things. Or does it also have something fundamental and transformative to do with the way we live.

So a wise person wrote a letter to these struggling young editors—to this church trying to figure out how to live the story of Jesus in a new day. And, as the letter we have come to know as 1 John begins, it doesn't start as a typical letter does, with a formal salutation. Rather, the writer jumps right to the heart of the matter. More than anything, the writer of 1 John wants to convey the soul of Christianity: what really matters in the midst of so many interpreters competing for allegiance and attention.

The letter's beginning instantly recalls the beautiful poetry that began the Gospel the community knew so well. We heard some of John's majestic prologue in our Call to Worship this morning: "In the beginning was the Word, and the Word was with God, and the Word was God. He was in the beginning with God. . . . What has come into being in him was life, and the life was the light of all people" (John 1:1-4). The beginning of 1 John helps the community reconsider the meaning of these words in light of the life, death, and resurrection of Christ. It brings these words out of the clouds and down to the earth where they live: "We declare to you what was from the *beginning*, what we have heard, what we have seen with our eyes, what we have looked at and touched with our hands, concerning the word of life—this life was revealed, and we have seen it and testify to it, and declare to you the eternal life that was with the Father and was revealed to us" (1 John 1:1-2, emphasis mine).

In this new era, rather than going back to the beginning of creation, before anything was seen or heard, this community must find its foundation in the word of life—otherwise known as the message seen, heard, and touched in Jesus's life. The Gospel of John's lofty words of a preexisting Jesus seem to have led some to think Jesus's embodied life was not all that important. Some interpreters maintained that perhaps Jesus was not actually human, that he was just a heavenly vision. What mattered, they argued, was not what happened in Jesus's life but that we now have some sort of otherworldly experience of God through him that gives us special knowledge.

The letter writer, however, wants to make it clear to this community that Jesus was more than words or an idea. He was flesh and blood, and the reality of who he was as a person matters deeply. His flesh and blood are what make the gospel not just about heaven but also very much about earth. It's far more than just subscribing to a set of ideas. It's the reason faith isn't individual but is something that draws people together to live a different sort of life in the flesh, alongside others to whom one can reach out and see and hear and touch. As Jesus walked with others, now this community has a new way of shared life—fellowship with each other and God (v. 3).

And what is that life together like? To add to the things dividing the community, apparently the same people who had been claiming that Jesus's flesh and blood didn't matter were also claiming that what they did in their embodied lives didn't matter. The only important thing, they argued, was that you knew the right things, the things Jesus wanted you to know—then you'd be as sinless, perfect, and pure as he was.

The letter writer can't shoot this idea down quickly enough. He grows increasingly forceful in his language as he reflects on these dangerous interpretations of the gospel, trying to snap the community out of these damaging beliefs: "God is light and in him there is no darkness at all," he reminds them (v. 5). How perilous it is, then—how destructive to community with God and others—to dally in the darkness: "*If we say that we have fellowship with him while we are walking in darkness, we lie and do not do what is true*" (v. 6); "*If we say that we have no sin, we deceive ourselves, and the truth is not in us*" (v. 8); "*If we say that we have not sinned, we make him a liar, and his word is not in us*" (v. 10). Each of these sayings is worded with increased strength, reminding the church that living in denial constitutes a dangerous road trip into the darkness. Interestingly, the fact that we still sin may not be the biggest problem. The writer, while discouraging any sort of sin free-for-all, seems to recognize that sin is still a struggle for each of us. Living in denial of it is the biggest danger, leading us fatally away from the healing light and into the paralyzing darkness.

I find it hard to imagine any of us claiming we are as sinless and pure as Jesus, like some in that community did; but I *can* understand denial. I mean, don't we all like to pretend that everything is okay? As I reflected on this passage after we celebrated the resurrection last Sunday, I really connected with the words of New Testament professor Audrey West:

> Easter is a week behind us . . . we have heard with our ears and seen with our eyes and touched with our hands this celebration of the empty tomb and a world forever changed by the resurrection of Jesus Christ. At the same time, however, our ears ring with the world's same old bad news. The joy of resurrection is flattened by political wrangling and the ongoing reality of home foreclosures and fruitless job searches, by despair and injustice and hearts broken open with jagged edges of grief. Is it not tempting to shut our eyes and our ears, to close our hands into fists of denial, to ignore those earthly realities? Don't we wish, at least for a moment, that the shining, bright holiness of a resurrected Christ would blind our eyes to the stains of this fleshy, painful world? Now that we walk in the light of Jesus, can't we just ignore the sin around us and especially our own complicity in it?[1]

No, the writer of 1 John says resoundingly—the death and resurrection of Christ have not just effected a blanket removal of all sin from the world, as perhaps we wish they had. That's obvious when we take a good look around. What Christ *has* done, however, is make a way to deal with it—to bring it into the light, where it can find the healing and redemption it needs, and demonstrate that sin no longer has the last word. This will be the first marker of a community living in fellowship with God, the writer says: you will not be afraid to bring sin into the light, to deal head-on with the things that threaten to break and divide and shatter. If we live our messy, fleshy lives in the light—not trying to hide what we are doing but living in open honesty before each other—we will find true fellowship. If we name the truth, confessing the places we are broken and have caused harm, then there's a chance for restoration. That's what Jesus made possible when he bore our sins on the cross for all to see, staring down shame, staring down defeat. Because of this, there's now a way for healing—not just for a few elite individuals but for the whole world. All of creation may now find the restoration it needs. This is the sort of life Jesus made possible—not a perfect one but one that's *real*. Isn't this a better way to live, the writer contends, than sneaking around in the darkness pretending everything is perfect? We can see things in the light as they really are and not be immobilized by the darkness. We can find a way to walk together with one another and with God into a future that Christ has opened wide before us.

It's amazing how so many of the things that plagued the first people seeking to live the gospel in their context continue to stalk us now. After all, with this faith passed down across generations, now it is we who are the editors, seeking to interpret the story of Jesus for a new time. Here we are, 2,000 years later, continuing to wrestle with the question of who Jesus is and how we live together in light of this understanding. This is, at least, what we wrestle with on our good days—when we're not scampering down the rabbit trails of things that don't matter.

In light of this, the reminders and reality checks the writer of 1 John offered that young church are the ones we need to hear as well. We need to be reminded to go back to the beginning, to what we have seen and heard and touched in the life, death, and resurrection of Jesus. Who is the God we have come to know in Christ? Where in our own lives have we seen and heard and touched this fleshy God who doesn't stay distant but is involved with us, present and living in relationship with us? And how does this experience change the way we live with others? Do we try to pretend that the ways we behave, the things we see and hear and touch in the world around us, don't matter anymore? Or do we name even the things that aren't perfect and bring them into the light, knowing it is only God who can heal them and restore not just our individual lives but also the life of our community and, indeed, our whole world?

These are big questions for these days after Easter, when we are once again trying to answer the question of "what next"—what will the continued story of Jesus be now that we are the ones living and sharing it with the world? It's an awesome responsibility. But as we come to the table this morning, where again we are invited to eat and drink, to taste and touch, to see and hear Jesus's words of promise, we are reminded that a flesh-and-blood savior has changed our flesh-and-blood lives, making a way forward even through the messes we continue to live in. There is so much yet to figure out, so many questions to ask and wrestle with—but as we begin our journey away from the empty tomb and into the world, we can know that Christ is among us, able to be seen and heard, making a way for us to walk out of the darkness of denial and into the healing light of truth.

Note

1. Audrey West, "Commentary on 1 John 1:1–2:2," *workingpreacher.org*, 15 April 2012, www.workingpreacher.org/preaching.aspx?commentary_id=1268.

What's New ... and Old

1 John 2:3-14 (with John 13:31-35)

"What's new?" It's a common greeting; when we see people we haven't seen in a while, we want to know what has changed in their lives, what's different, what's happening that might surprise us. We never—at least I never—greet someone by saying, "Hey, so what's the same as last time we talked? Tell me something I already know." No, our burning desire is to know what's new. It's an instinct that starts early—even babies and small children are quickly drawn to whatever is newest. And it remains true for adults. I was in the middle of working on this sermon when I took a break to check our mail. On top of the pile rested a catalog from one of my favorite stores inviting me to "come see what's new." Despite my best resistance, I wanted to do just that.

Obsession with newness might be perceived as both a manifestation and a cause of our cultural tendency to bounce along mindlessly from one thing to another. Yet, according to behavioral-science writer Winifred Gallagher, to be interested in what is new is also among our most natural and—if properly employed—most valuable human instincts. Our neophilia—what Gallagher and others have defined as our preference for and attraction to whatever is new—is what many people believe has enabled humanity to survive as a species in a changing world. "Our genius for responding to the new and different," Gallagher writes, "distinguishes us from all other creatures, saved us from extinction 80,000 years ago, and has fueled our progress from the long epoch of the hunter-gatherers through the agricultural and industrial eras into the information age." Yet, Gallagher warns, in a modern age where we are constantly surrounded by new ideas and stimuli, we face a new challenge: "to stay true to the evolutionary purpose of our neophilia," or affinity for novelty, "to help us adapt to, learn about, or create, the new things that matter, while dismissing the rest as distractions."[1]

Though Gallagher's observations are about modern society, I think they apply to struggles faced by the early church addressed in John's first letter, just as the things addressed in this ancient letter apply to our dilemmas as the twenty-first century church. As we talked about when we began our journey through 1 John, the writer of this letter addressed a community seeking to live out a new reality in a culture still ruled by an old story. The mission of those reading 1 John was to take what they had learned about Jesus and translate it faithfully into their own context, to figure out what it meant for how they lived as individuals and communities and how they would pass this new story clearly and faithfully on to those yet to come. A lot of questions accompanied this task: How was their relationship with God similar to or different from what it was before Jesus came? How were their relationships with one another the same or transformed? How were they to understand the old teachings of either their Jewish faith or their Gentile backgrounds—depending on where they came from—now that they were walking in the light of Jesus? What were they to hold on to, and what must they let go of?

As is true today, many in the community of 1 John seem to have been neophiles—lovers of the new. Throughout the letter, the writer seeks to address those in the community who were putting forth new ideas that threatened to tear the community apart. This group is mentioned in verse 4 of today's reading: the writer describes them as people who say, "I have come to know him," but then fail to obey God's commandments. New Testament professor Nijay Gupta speculates that these particular members of the community were among a sect "obsessed with new knowledge and special wisdom . . . they hungered for exclusive, unique knowledge, a privilege for the special few"—something new and fashionable that would help them get ahead.[2]

Instead of providing the sort of newfangled idea many were hungry for, the writer of 1 John takes them back to the roots of faith—in this case, the commandments. It is not some special magical level of understanding that shows people have knowledge of God, the writer argues, but rather the way people live out God's commandments. The word "know" is interesting here because at its heart it is not an intellectual word, not something that can be studied in a book or discovered in an abstract way—as we typically think of when we consider what it means to "know." Instead, it is a relational word. It is a word of intimacy. "How can intimacy with God be found and demonstrated?" the writer asks. Not through some fresh, trendy idea, but through the old, old pathway of living by God's commandments.

But what commandments is the author talking about here? After all, Judaism recognizes 613 different commandments just in the Torah—in the first five books of our Bible alone. Countless new commandments have been added or suggested since the Torah's composition. So of what commandment is the writer speaking? What leads to an intimate relationship with God, allowing one to abide or live in God, to walk as Christ walked? Well, there's a strong hint in the number of times John repeated himself. After the word "God," "love" is the most common word in John's letter. The word appears today for the first of a whopping fifty-two times in this letter.[3] As this word makes its debut here in conjunction with all the talk about commandments, the well-known words of Jesus from John's Gospel must have come flooding back into the reader's minds: "This is my commandment, that you love one another as I have loved you" (John 15:12); "I give you a new commandment, that you love one another. Just as I have loved you, you also should love one another. By this everyone will know that you are my disciples, if you have love for one another" (John 13:34-35).

The writer of 1 John, guessing the readers have made this connection back to the Gospel, then proceeds to become Captain Obvious—and Captain Anti-Neophile: "Beloved, I am writing you no new commandment, but an old commandment that you have had from the beginning" (v. 7). It's pretty evident that the commandment to love is no new thing: it is prominently featured in those 613 Torah commands: "You shall love the LORD your God with all your heart and all your soul and all your strength," reads Deuteronomy 6:5. Leviticus adds to it a second part Jesus was particularly fond of: "Love your neighbor as yourself" (19:18). Loving was old news to those with Jewish backgrounds. For those from Gentile backgrounds, love was part of their cultural ideals as well; "Love conquers all" was reportedly first spoken by the great Roman poet Virgil. And for all of them, Gentile and Jew alike, this love command would have been familiar from the teachings of Jesus. In John's Gospel alone, Jesus invokes the word "love" more than thirty times.

Yet here's the interesting thing: when Jesus first introduced love as a commandment on Maundy Thursday, at the table after washing the disciples' feet at the Last Supper, he spoke of it as a *new* commandment. And just after calling love an *old* commandment, the writer of 1 John performs an about-face and does the same thing: "Yet I am writing you a new commandment that is true in him and in you" (v. 8). How can a commandment be both old and new?

The key, I think, lies back in Jesus's words: to love one another "as I have loved you" (John 13:34). Love, now, is made concrete. Love is about acting toward and for each other in the same way that Christ loved—and continues to love—each of us. There is now a tangible model, a new definition of love. And this love is creating a new world where, just as Jesus's love connected us to God and one another, our love for one another now does the same. Jesus's love has created a new reality, a realm where "the darkness is passing away and the true light is already shining" (v. 8). And in that realm, everything is transformed—new possibilities burst forth. As blogger Dan Clendenin reflects, "When we love one another, the church becomes an exemplar of life out of death, a model of how the old can be renewed. We become a present-day sign of the future new heaven and earth, when God 'will wipe every tear from their eyes. There will be no more death or mourning or crying or pain, for the old order of things has passed away.'"[4] If we turn away from love, verses 9 and 11 of today's reading warn, the old continues to prevail; but if we choose to truly, radically love a brother or sister the way Christ loved us, the new possibilities are endless.

The poetic final three verses of this section show us some of these possibilities. The writer speaks repeated blessings over different segments of the community. There is a blessing for "little children," which could refer specifically to the youngest among them but could also refer to the whole community since that was a way the writer liked to reference them. Then there is one for "fathers" or elders, those old in the faith, and for "young people," those new in the faith. In his commentary on this passage, C. Clifton Black notes that this section, in some respects, resembles the household codes found in other New Testament letters—those passages spelling out specific roles and spiritual virtues for different members of the community according to their age and position.[5] But unlike those letters, 1 John doesn't distinguish between members. Rather, the letter addresses them as one community—young and old, parents and children, faith novices and those far along the way. They are a united family, connected by being loved by Christ and loving, in turn, as Christ first loved them. They share equally in the blessings of this new day and time made possible by love.

Rather than naming the things that make them different, 1 John names the things that hold this diverse people together as the family of God—the common experiences of forgiveness, of knowing God intimately, of having overcome the draw of darkness, of being strong with Christ abiding in them. Here, 1 John paints its initial picture of the new family of beloved ones being drawn together as they walk in the light, seeking to walk in the ways of Jesus, the one who loved them with radical love. This sort of family is an amazing possibility emerging for those who live the old commandment of love in new, Christ-shaped ways.

So here we are, friends—2,000 years further into this old, old story that still calls for new expression in our time. We live in the midst of this frenzied culture where we are always looking for the new and trendy thing, for the quick and innovative fix, for whatever is hot and unique. In such a time, how can this simple commandment to "love one another as I have loved you" capture attention that is so constantly divided? Though we feel like there always has to be something new to talk about, perhaps what we really need is something old. In this day and age where hating those closest to us, where lashing out against those different from us, where separating ourselves from those we wish to have power over, where judging people in loud and hateful ways is so rampant, what we need is to return to that old, old teaching—to love rooted in Christ's love. It's a love so deep that it can't help but change things. What if, as Winifred Gallagher suggested, we learned how to latch on to this new vision, loving in such a way that we are able to "create the new things that matter, while dismissing the rest as distractions"? I wonder what we'd find to be those new things that matter. I wonder what things we once thought were important that we might be forced to dismiss as distractions.

At a recent Alliance of Baptists meeting, Mahan Siler reflected on the core of who we are as progressive Christians, on what we must hold on to above and amid all other things that clamor for our attention. He began his sermon with a poem by William Stafford titled "The Way It Is." I think this poem may hold a key to how becoming those who, as Jesus and the writer of 1 John hoped, hold on to what is old even as we live into what is new. Stafford wrote,

> There's a thread you follow. It goes among things that change.
> But it doesn't change.
> People wonder about what you are pursuing.
> You have to explain about the thread.
> But it is hard for others to see.
> While you hold it you can't get lost.
> Tragedies happen; people get hurt or die; and you suffer and get old.
> Nothing you do can stop time's unfolding.
> You don't ever let go of the thread.[6]

Amid all that is old and needs to be renewed, amid all that is new and clamoring for our attention, may we be those who hold on to the thread. May we hold on to the thread of radical love that lets us know God, be family to one another, and live in a world that, despite all appearances to the contrary, is being transformed by this thread of divine love running through it. As we abide by this old, old commandment, may we live in ways that help us see the world truly being made new.

Notes

1. Winifred Gallagher, *New: Understanding Our Need for Novelty and Change* (New York: Penguin, 2011), Kindle Edition, locations 80–86.

2. Nijay Gupta, "Commentary on 1 John 1:1–2:2," *workingpreacher.org*, 12 April 2015, www.workingpreacher.org/preaching.aspx?commentary_id=2429.

3. C. Clifton Black, *The First, Second and Third Letters of John*, The New Interpreter's Bible, vol. 12 (Nashville: Abingdon Press, 1998) 389.

4. Dan Clendenin, "To Carry the Candle Against the Wind," *Journey with Jesus*, 28 April 2013, www.journeywithjesus.net/Essays/20130422JJ.shtml.

5. Black, *The First, Second and Third Letters of John*, 398.

6. William Stafford, *The Way It Is: New and Selected Poems* (Minneapolis: Greywolf, 1999).

3

Buying into the Lie[1]

1 John 2:15-29 (with John 14:15-29)

My college roommate Emily is one of the loveliest people you'll ever meet. She has, however, one delightfully exploitable flaw: she is one of the most gullible individuals I have ever known. During our second year, my earnest friend gave up dessert for the season of Lent. Around week 4, I began a campaign to convince her that banana pudding was not actually a dessert—it was a fruit salad. Logical, right? Banana *pudding*. At first she was a bit skeptical, but the detailed arguments of her future pastor roommate eventually proved so persuasive that she became convinced of the error of her ways and confessed that banana pudding was, in fact, a delicious, nutritious fruit salad. I still feel a *tiny* bit guilty about that one, but at least I have another great example of her gullibility that I had nothing to do with. I was sitting in my room one night when Emily came bursting in, a copy of our student newspaper clutched in her hand. "Have you seen this?" she screeched. She slammed the paper down on my bed and jabbed her finger at a sidebar with this headline: "Krispy Kreme Putting Crack in their Powdered Doughnuts." "Can you believe that?" she said, devastated. "I have been eating those donuts all semester! I am a drug user!" "Um, Em?" I said in response. "Do me a favor. Take a look at the date on the top of this newspaper." There it was—April 1. Always know the context, my friend.

My roommate may be an extreme example, but it doesn't take much for most of us to be swayed—for us to abandon things we thought to be true, for it to become difficult to see the difference between truth and falsehood, between what can be trusted and what is a lie. Like many human struggles, this is nothing new. Figuring out and holding on to truth was also a big issue in the early church. We have seen this as we've begun working our way through 1 John. The people addressed by this letter were seeking to be faithful editors of the gospel that had been handed down to them. They wanted to handle rightly the story of Jesus, which had been entrusted to them and which was changing their lives, and which they knew had power to change their world. Yet they were full of questions: What was most essential about their newfound faith? Whose leadership could they trust? How could they know that their relationship with Christ would be enough, sufficient in the face of all the ideas others were tossing their way?

In today's section of the letter, the writer of 1 John seeks to speak truth to some people who, like my sweet roommate, have been buying into or are tempted to buy into some lies. This passage deals a lot with the words "truth" and "lie," and that compels me to do a bit of truth-telling myself: I have a hard time with much of this section of 1 John. In fact, in this project of preaching through the whole letter, this might be the section I have least looked forward to dealing with—though I reserve my right to change my mind on that as we move further into the book. But I can't deny that there are ideas here that trouble me. How can we find truth in these words today, when we struggle as much as ever to discern what is true about our faith and the Christ we confess?

My wrestling begins at the reading's outset with the writer's strong words, "Do not love the world or the things in the world" (v. 15). That sentence makes me want to stop reading and protest. What about the fact that, as John's Gospel says, God so loved the world? Are we not to love the world God loves? Are we just supposed to retreat into our own little bubble where nothing on this earth really matters compared to the spiritual things we have come to know? Many people have read this passage and taken it to mean just that—"Withdraw, people of God! Get as far away from this evil world as you can! Have nothing to do with it! All that matters is the life to come." Such an attitude has led a lot of Christians to see little point in addressing needs connected to this earth—things like hunger, injustice, and caring for creation, just to name a few. Such people say that only the soul matters, not the flesh or the earth. But to me, such indifference doesn't sound a lick like Jesus.

Fortunately, we find that this interpretation actually doesn't make sense in the larger context of the letter. After all, if we withdraw from everyday life, how are we to live out that old-yet-new commandment the writer spoke of last week, loving others as Jesus has loved us? Obviously, the writer must mean something else. If we press past verse 15 and read on to verses 16 and 17, we get some insight into how the writer defines "the world": it is the realm driven by "the desire of the flesh, the desire of the eyes, the pride in riches." The world, it seems, is the universe driven by the arrogant presumption that we are god and God is not. The world is a sphere defined by things like material wants and the ambition to accumulate. Is such a perspective worth giving our hearts to? This is the first lie the writer wants to make sure Christians are not buying into. We deceive ourselves when we think these are the things that last, that these are, indeed, our whole world. Really, the only true and lasting life is found in obedience to God lived out in love. So, the writer asks, are we going to be defined as being "of the world," driven by the impulses deemed good by popular society, or as "of God," driven by the things God desires? Our answer to these questions reveals what and who we truly love.

From this discussion of the world, the writer moves on to another conversation that disturbs me. Yes, church, it's time—perhaps for the first and only time in my ministry here—to talk about the Antichrist. I think it's important to note that the actual word "Antichrist" appears only five times in the New Testament—all of them in 1 and 2 John, and three of those five instances in today's reading. Yet the concept has taken on a life of its own in some Christian circles and popular culture. In some Christian belief systems, it is thought that Jesus will return to earth to face an individual called the Antichrist, the greatest false messiah in Christianity—an opponent as soundly evil as Jesus is soundly good. But basically, these days it seems like "Antichrist" is just a term people use to reference someone they think is evil or don't like. It has become a weapon deployed in elaborate theological name-calling. A simple Internet search reveals that all of the following people, within the last century alone, have been publicly dubbed "The Antichrist": Mikhail Gorbachev, Bono, Sadaam Hussein, Bill Gates, Barney the Dinosaur, Prince Charles, all members of the boy band N*SYNC, just about every pope, and most every US president since FDR, who is believed to have been the first to earn that dubious honor. Such hateful absurdity makes me want to stop reading as soon as I come across this particular term.

But again, I need to look at what the writer is saying and not just at what our culture and some people's biblical interpretation have laid onto this word. The word "antichrist" literally means "one who is counter to Christ" or "one who is opposing Christ," and 1 John says some things that may startle those waiting for a singular Antichrist to inaugurate the end times. First, the writer declares that antichrists were already present in his community. There's not just one—the writer speaks of multiple antichrists! How does he identify these people who are opposed to Christ, who counter what Christ is about? Well, basically, they are folks in the community who uphold things about Jesus that are not true and put forth ideas contradicting the life and teachings of the flesh-and-blood Jesus who walked among us. Those being called antichrists are saying it takes more than knowing this Jesus to know God.

The impact of these antichrists has been grave. Such false teaching has caused something to occur that is the opposite of what Jesus would want—a schism in the community. "They went out from us," verse 19 says, showing the startling fact that these people acting in ways counter to Christ's ways are not detractors from some other faith or faraway place, but rather members of the very community addressed by this letter. It's clear by the strength of the language here that their departure has been a painful occurrence in the life of the community. To the best of our knowledge, this is the first schism in the history of the church, and for people who understand themselves as family in Christ, such a break is devastating. It has caused great trauma among the community and especially for the elder, the community leader, who is writing to them. The agony drips from each word of the rest of the chapter as the writer speaks in increasingly harsh terms, sharply delineating between truth-tellers and liars, making sweeping generalizations about "everyone" and "no one."

It can be hard to listen to rhetoric like this—yet another difficulty that made me unexcited about preaching on this text. Clifton Black describes my feelings exactly when he writes, "The elder's branding of his opponents as liars and antichrists may strike some readers as exemplifying the tendency of a lamentable kind of religious behavior: the demonization of those with whom we disagree."[2] Goodness knows we have enough of that in our own time; we don't need to hear it in Scripture, too. But Black also offers us an important reminder: "behind the pained rhetoric of 1 John 2:18-25 is a harrowing reality: For the first time in the [New Testament] record, a church has fallen apart over a matter of critical importance, a division that must surely have been experienced with shock by those whose tradition accentuated the church's unity in Christ. . . . At the time of this letter's composition, that wound was fresh, gaping, and raw."[3] And that wound spills out all over the place.

This sort of fresh pain is something we certainly can relate to as we have watched anger and wounds from injustice, divisions in communities, desires for truth, frustration with circumstances, and too many years of loss burst out in our wider community over the course of the past two weeks. We see and hear the wound in protests both peaceful and riotous, in words both vilifying others and seeking a common solution for dealing with all that is broken in our local community of Baltimore. We recognize that pain can lead to extreme statements that are hard to hear, but to which we still need to listen carefully. We need to listen beneath them to hear the bigger story being revealed. It is important to honor and not try to soften a suffering community's pain, whether we are reading an ancient letter or modern headlines.

And this is where the ancient and modern meet: in light of such pain and chaos, such confusion about what is truth and what is lie, a community trying to figure out what to do with its broken state, and counter-voices crying out all around, what shall Christians do? For all the things in this text that I had a hard time connecting with, this is the question that felt closest to home for me. And the writer's response to the community is one we need to hear: when everything seems up for grabs and we don't quite know what to do, we actually already know the things that matter. "Let what you heard from the beginning abide in you," the writer says—what you saw and heard in the life of Christ (v. 24). "If what you heard from the beginning abides in you, then you will abide in the Son and in the Father. And this is what he has promised us, eternal life" (vv. 24-25). Remember, when talking about eternal life, the writer is not speaking of some life beyond this one. It is a life lived in this world that takes on the qualities of God's life, of Jesus's life—justice, healing, peace, and love that go beyond the material and superficial, that cannot be destroyed.

"You already have what you need for this new, terrifying day!" the writer reassures them. "Remember your baptism—when you were anointed with holy oil and blessed as a child of God? Remember that Spirit Jesus promised—the One that he said would come rest on us, and teach us everything, and remind us of all that Jesus said to us, making a way for peace beyond anything possible by the self-centered ways of the world? Remember all of that? Friends, you have what you need. You have what you need to remain in Christ even when everything around you is shaking. I'm not writing to you because you need some new wisdom—you already know the truth! So stop buying into the lie that you need something more. You've got all that you need in Jesus's example! So live it. Live in a way that shows you know this Jesus and his way that is so different from the ways of our current world. Live in a way that shows the hour is here—a new day has come, and it has to keep coming. Live in a way that shows that, through Jesus, you have been and are being taught all you need to know. Then you'll have nothing to fear because, come what may, you will be living as children of God."

Sometimes, in the midst of chaos, when wounds are spilling over and things seem to be breaking up all around, truth can be hard to see. We can get quickly tossed up in the air, as shaken as my roommate on April Fools' Day. But God's truth, my friends, runs deep—it runs through the veins that flowed through the body of Jesus, and it runs through the Spirit of anointing that flows through the body of Christ even today. In times of turmoil, how might we root ourselves deep in this truth—that in the life of Christ we have seen and known all we need, and that now it's our turn to go and live likewise?

Notes

1. This sermon was preached in a community outside of Baltimore on the Sunday after protests and riots consumed the city over the death of a twenty-five-year-old African-American man named Freddy Gray, who died of a spinal injury while in police custody. At the time of this sermon, Baltimore was under a curfew, the National Guard had been called in, and people of all races and economic classes were debating the best response to the cries to correct injustices experienced in the city.

2. C. Clifton Black, *The First, Second and Third Letters of John*, The New Interpreter's Bible, vol. 12 (Nashville: Abingdon Press, 1998) 404.

3. Ibid., 405.

4

Remember Who You Are

1 John 3:1-10

It was without a doubt one of the oddest experiences of my life. I was traveling through southeastern Virginia on a rare Sunday when I had no church I was obligated to attend. On a whim, I decided to visit the congregation where my grandfather had been pastor for thirty-two years. Since he retired a month before my birth, I had never had the chance to worship in this church where my family had so much history. My dad and his brothers grew up in the parsonage next door, my parents met as babies in the nursery, and my mother's parents were buried in the cemetery out back—the same cemetery where my preteen dad stepped in a hole and broke his leg while chasing a classmate who had teased him about liking my mom.

Arriving just as worship started, I slipped in the back door and joined in the first hymn. After the service concluded, I was trying to make a quiet escape to my car when a woman made a beeline for me. She grabbed my arm and pointed at me confidently. "You," she said, "are a Thornton." My jaw hit the floor. I had never been in this church before. No member of either side of my family had been active there in over twenty years. But somehow, I was recognized. After all that time, something about my appearance or the way I carried myself made my identity immediately apparent to someone who had been around Thorntons before.

Family resemblance is a powerful identifier. Some of us physically look like our nearest and dearest. Astonishingly, this can even be true for people not biologically related! I read this week that non-blood relatives who spend a lot of time looking at one another can start to look alike. We have an unconscious tendency to copy facial expressions that we spend lots of time observing, and we can start mirroring what's in front of us such that our own muscles begin to be reshaped.[1] Who knows if this is true; but certainly family resemblance goes beyond the physical. I will never forget the first time I met a dear friend's mother. My initial reaction looking at them was, "Wow, are they really related?" But then we got in the car and, before I knew it, the mom exhibited one of my friend's most noteworthy traits: singing along loudly and confidently with every song on the radio even when she didn't know the lyrics. Fascinating the things that show us from what cloth we are cut, to whom we belong. Some of it's nature, some of it's nurture, and some of it may indeed be random, but all of it helps us figure out who we are and where we've come from—key factors in recognizing and shaping who we are becoming.

Today's section of 1 John focuses on matters of identity. The letter is addressed to a fledgling church community that needs help gaining clarity around the nature of faith and its implications for the life they are living. Throughout the letter, the writer has referred to them as "children"—both as a term of endearment and as a reminder of how green they are in this new journey with Jesus. Today, they learn for the first time not just that they are children but that they are children *of* someone. It's one of my favorite verses in Scripture, one that was our theme verse for Music and Arts Camp a few years ago. I loved reciting it with the kids every morning: "How great is the love the Father has lavished upon us, that we should be called the children of God! And that is what we are!" (v. 1). I am particularly fond of the word *lavished*—the term is translated "given" in the version we read this morning, but that doesn't hold quite the same power. "Given" makes you think of someone handing you something casually: "Okay, here you go . . . I'm giving this to you." But lavished? It's an image of someone pouring something wonderful over you, almost like a flood. It's overwhelming, someone going above and beyond to give you something so amazing, so valuable, so exquisite that it's hard to get your mind around it. And that's what the elder is speaking of here when he declares the new identity of the community: because God has lavished mysterious, extravagant love upon them, they have been made children of God. That is what they are! Unlike me walking into my family's old church, they may not immediately be recognized by others for who they are. But this does not change their identity: they are God's children, now and forever.

Becoming children of God is often described in the New Testament in terms of adoption, and I think that sense is present in today's reading. When we think of adoption, we usually think of a small, helpless one being taken in by a family that longs to lavish love on a child they can call their own. There are certainly threads of this here—becoming children of God is prompted, clearly, by lavish love, a gift that no child could earn but that God longs to freely give. But there's another dimension of adoption to consider when we look at this practice in ancient times. As New Testament scholar Nijay Gupta points out,

> In the Roman world adoptions took place, but it was not about compassion for orphans. In fact, many people were adopted as young adults or adults. Adoption was about inheritance and name. Often a man was adopted to carry on the name of a childless family. The adopted son would sever ties to the old family and this would include relief of any debt owed under the name of the old family. He would become a whole new person, in a new context, with a new inheritance and name.[2]

The adopted one would have a new mission: to bear the new family name with honor—to make the new family resemblance known, honoring his or her new ties and identity in the way he or she lived.

If we think of it in light of this idea of adoption, 1 John 3 makes it clear that becoming a child of God does not mean one can just rest on one's laurels. It is not an end point with the recipient remaining totally passive. Though nothing the recipient does will merit or earn such freely lavished status, this is just a beginning. "Beloved," verse 2 says, "we are God's children now; what we will be has not yet been revealed. What we do know is this: when [Jesus] is revealed, we will be like him." God's children have begun a lifelong journey of seeing their family resemblance intensify: in this case, resemblance to God's only begotten Son. What are the markers of such resemblance? Clifton Black identifies two "family traits" of God's children named in this passage, things that let others pick them out of the crowd. The first is that they are those who "do righteousness"—an idea that appeared at the end of chapter 2 and shows up again here in verse 7. "Doing righteousness" means participating in setting the world right, in God's justice. It means helping to bring about God's new order of things—that kingdom of God Jesus spoke of so often. The second trait, Black says, is purity, a word that may feel off-putting at first or seem narrow since we've translated purity to mostly be about sexual matters, as in "impure thoughts." Purity's meaning, however, is much broader. Black describes it as "unimpeachable sincerity"[3]—an authentic, single-mindedly transparent commitment, in this case, to living in the ways of Jesus without compromise. "Unimpeachable sincerity"—how easy it would be to identify us as belonging to a particular family if we had such a rare trait!

Living into this new identity, taking on these new traits and habits, is not going to be easy. Because of our new family ties, we are going to be living in different, distinctly identifiable ways. Verses 4-10 highlight the challenge of life as children of God. Verses 4-10 are tough in and of themselves, because at first glance they seem to claim some pretty extreme things. No one who abides in Jesus sins? No one who sins has seen or known Jesus? Those who have been born of God do not sin, indeed, *cannot* sin? All who do not do right are not from God? As I read these verses, my heart sank. How can this be right when none of us—as of yet—have reached the place of being fully like Jesus, in whom there is no sin? How can this be right when earlier sections of this very letter have seemed to admit that sin is still present in the Christian community? Remember the first verse of chapter 2, where this same author presumably wrote, "My dear children, I write this to you so that you will not sin. But if anybody does sin, we have an advocate with the Father—Jesus Christ, the Righteous One"? How does all of this hang together?

There have been many attempts to harmonize the views expressed in chapter 3 with those expressed elsewhere in the letter and throughout the New Testament. No solution is entirely satisfying, but there are a couple of ideas that help this make a little more sense to me. The first is the influence of urgency. The writer wants to make it clear that, even though Jesus provided a way to address sin, it is not okay for us to continue doing whatever we want. This is not how a child of God, bearing the new family name, would ever consistently live. Sin is not something, in this writer's view, that can be shrugged off as "no big deal"; the idea of "Hey, we're going to be forgiven so it doesn't matter how we act" is one that appalls him. As those with God's very seed living in us, as verse 9 describes it, we can't hold on to this perspective and simultaneously claim to be children of God.

Second, we need to consider 1 John's worldview, which takes a page from Jewish apocalyptic literature. When the letter speaks of "lawlessness," Jewish audiences would have known what the elder meant: the realm of chaos, disorder, and distance from God. This stands in contrast to the order of justice or righteousness, where God is revealed to be in charge. Christians, now, live in the realm of righteousness—God's reign has begun! In this realm, though sin is still present, it no longer has the last word. And in this worldview, sin is not just an individual, distinct act of wrong we commit but also, and more important, a state of being. Jesus came to destroy that realm and free God's children from an enslaved way of life, and they must not return to living under that disorder again. Even if the world around them seems to be going on the same as usual, they know everything has changed and cannot pretend to live under the old ways. After birth, there's no going back into the womb; there's no undoing the forward movement that has taken place from one realm into another.

If you need another metaphor, here's a beautiful example offered by N. T. Wright:

> John knows, of course, that Christians do still sin from time to time. . . . What he is talking about here is the whole habit of life, "going on sinning," sinning as the regular mode in which we live. We should be doing our best to avoid all kinds of sin, all the time, though we shall surely fail; but the failures must take place within a settled habit of life in which sin is no longer setting the tone. We are playing a different piece of music now, and even if our fingers slip sometimes and play some wrong notes, notes that belong to the music we used to play, that doesn't mean we are going back to play that old music for real once more.[4]

Children of God both reveal and live into their new identity as they play and sing a different score. Every day, they set out to play this music, and every day—through practice, through persistence, through God's unflagging love—they get a little closer to bearing full resemblance to Jesus.

The first time I visited the church office of my now-husband, I was captured by a set of words he had printed and then taped to the top of his computer monitor and over his office doorway: "Remember who you are and where you've come from." He says they are the words that ground him in his faith, and I don't think any phrase could better sum up what the writer of 1 John hoped his people—and what I hope we today—will remember. Remember who you are—children of God! Chosen by God's lavish love to bear God's name and God's imprint into the world, destined to grow to bear such strong family resemblance to Jesus in our appearance and behaviors that people can't help but identify us with him. And remember where you've come from. Once, you lived in a realm of lawlessness, where sin has control and final say, but not anymore! Now you live in the realm of God's righteousness and justice. These are the forces that hold sway over you now, in which you are rooted and out of which you will continue to grow.

We all bring different identities and backgrounds into the family of God—some we want to cherish and remember, and some we wish we could disown and forget. But here, for each of us, a new identity prevails: "How great is the love that God has lavished upon us, that we should be called children of God! And that is what we are!" What might it mean for you to live fully into your identity as a child of God this day and in the days to come? How might people come to see the family resemblance in you? And as we prepare to come to the table of remembrance, how might the Communion we share be an opportunity for you to remember who you are and who you'll always be, no matter where you've come from?

Notes

1. N. T. Wright, *The Early Christian Letters for Everyone*, New Testament for Everyone (Louisville: Westminster John Knox Press, 2012) Kindle Edition, 149.

2. Nijay Gupta, "Commentary on 1 John 3:1-7," *workingpreacher.org*, 19 April 2015, www.workingpreacher.org/preaching.aspx?commentary_id=2430.

3. C. Clifton Black, *The First, Second and Third Letters of John*, The New Interpreter's Bible, vol. 12 (Nashville: Abingdon Press, 1998) 283.

4. N. T. Wright, *Early Christian Letters*, 151.

5

What Is Love?

1 John 3:11–24

Listen to popular music from the last century and it becomes apparent that the nature of love is by no means clear to any of us. Based on my research, the legendary Cole Porter kicked off the lyrical question asking with his 1929 hit, "What Is this Thing Called Love?" Then came The Monotones in the 1950s, asking, "Who wrote the book of love?" and the good old BeeGees in 1977 asking each of us, "How deep is your love?" "Where is the love?" seems to be a frequently asked musical question, forming the title of songs by crooner Roberta Flack in the 1970s, boy band Hanson in 1990s, and hip-hop group the Black Eyed Peas in the early 2000s. Occasionally, singers would think they found the love but weren't quite sure: "Is this love?" asked reggae king Bob Marley in the 1970s and hair band Whitesnake a decade after that. 1984 was a particularly perplexing year, bringing us both the pleading "I Want to Know What Love Is" by rock group Foreigner and the defiant "What's Love Got to Do with It?" by Tina Turner. I'm sure you can name many other songs, but perhaps no one summed up our confusion better than Haddaway, the Trinidadian-German Eurodance artist (yes, that's a real thing) who posed both the simplest and most complex question in his 1993 hit song: "What Is love?"

What *is* love? As we've noted throughout our series on 1 John, this letter to a fledgling congregation mentions love a *lot*—more than fifty times in five chapters. Already we've learned that those who love their brothers and sisters live in the light (2:10), and that we are not to love and attach ourselves to the broken ways of the world (2:15). Last week we discovered that God has lavished such great love on us that we have been adopted as children of God, bearing God's family name and resemblance into the world (3:1, 10). But this week we really get into the details of love: what love is and what love is not. Both Jesus and this letter, again and again, state that love of God and neighbor is the most important commandment—the one on which everything hangs, on which everything depends. This makes the question of "what is love" one we must explore as fully as possible so we can be clear about the life to which we have been called.

The writer begins today's section of 1 John by reiterating the message heard from the beginning, the message heard in our gospel reading from John 15 this morning: Jesus's call to love one another. Yet the author starts by offering a *negative* example of love. He does something done explicitly nowhere else in this letter: he draws on an Old Testament text, the story of the first humans to live as brothers—Cain and Abel. Cain provides an intense example of failure to love a brother or sister. His anger and resentment boiled into hate that drove him to act in violence toward his brother, taking Abel's life. It is a story of extreme pain and agony in both the hearts of humans and the heart of God.

But how does this inform us about what love is? None of us here, that I am aware of, have actually murdered a sibling. Yet, by the definition of 1 John—and of Jesus, for that matter—we are still often dealers in death. "Whoever does not love abides in death. All who hate a brother or sister are murderers" (3:14-15). This may seem an exaggeration until we remember Jesus's words in the Sermon on the Mount: "You have heard that it was said to those of ancient times, 'You shall not murder'; and 'whoever murders shall be liable to judgment.' But I say to you that if you are angry with a brother or sister, you will be liable to judgment; and if you insult a brother or sister, you will be liable to the council; and if you say, 'You fool,' you will be liable to the hell of fire" (Matt 5:21-22). First John is making a similar point to that made by Jesus. In essence, Jesus was saying, "The surface command is do not murder, and I'm not discounting it. But remember this: carrying around your anger, insulting others, devaluing them by calling them names—these things will land you in a place that's just as bad as where murder gets you. The outcome is the same: destruction. Death, not life. Hate, not love. A continued cycle of brokenness."

So what is love? Love is not murderous and death dealing. Rather, it places a high value on the lives of brothers and sisters. And if this is love, then perhaps all those musicians were right when they asked, "Where is the love?" We live in a world where life is prematurely extinguished so often that we sometimes overlook it. The United States' murder rate remains among the highest of developed countries, and one of the cities with the highest murder rates is Baltimore, right in our backyard. Lost in the midst of the riots and protests unfurling after Freddy Graty's recent death in police custody is the horrible fact that as of last week, eighty-seven people have been murdered in Baltimore this year (2015), twenty-two more than at this time last year. Horribly, these killings are most often committed by people related to the victims in some way: brothers, sisters, spouses, parents, children. Those with whom we share the closest connections are those against whom we most often turn in violence.

These realities are more than enough to make us ask, "Where is the love?"—especially when we look beyond physical murder to matters closer to most of our hearts. Moody Smith calls it our "murderousness as a society," our tendency to put far less value on individual human life than on things like profit, power, security, and status.[1] We ignore how securing our means of life often takes life from others, and such subtle murderousness is just as deadly as actual killing in many ways. Love means the transformation of all of this—that we pass from ways of death to ways of eternal life, life of the lasting quality God desires and gives. Love is life giving rather than death dealing, and it places a premium on the lives of those around us.

Rather than just describing such life-giving love, the writer of 1 John decides to illustrate it. You want to know what love is? "We know love by this, that he laid down his life for us" (v. 16). With this statement, John gives us a story to stand in contrast to Cain's: "John doesn't offer up little vignettes from daily life to help us define love for fellow Christians; he hangs a masterpiece portrait of love in our mind's gallery. Love is nothing less than this picture of Jesus hanging on the cross, the long promised Christ crucified with common criminals, the very Son of God emptying himself of not only his dignity, but even his very life. That's what it means to love."[2] Or, as another commentator put it, "[Jesus'] self-giving death is love's story and love's shape. The church proclaims and lives love not as a vague ideal rooted in the human potential for good. Love is identified and known by what Jesus has done, and that act is the ground of all Christian thought and hope."[3]

But then comes the kicker: if this is love, then as those called to love, we, too, ought to lay down our lives for one another. Yet how many of us get a chance to love in this way, physically dying for the sake of another? Not many—but the writer makes it clear that this does not mean we don't have the chance to lay down our lives. A couple of amazing word plays happen in verse 17 that get lost in the English translation. "How does God's love abide in anyone who has the world's goods and sees a brother or sister in need and yet refuses help?" The word "goods" here is actually another Greek word for "life"—the word *bios*, which means "that by which life is sustained." The verse is saying that if we have even the bare minimum of what we need to sustain life but don't share that with a brother or sister who lacks those resources, then God's life-giving love is nowhere to be seen. Withholding basic needs from others when we have power to meet them is withholding life, and such stinginess not only hurts others but also cuts us off from being fully alive and human. The word translated "refuses help" in this verse means literally "to close or shut our bowels." It's a reminder that concrete failure to love cuts off a part of ourselves: the deeply human part that expresses and acts on compassion.

Here, we learn another answer to the question, "What is love?" Love is being moved to act on behalf of another. Love that stops at words or is only an intellectual belief or a feeling that washes over us and then passes *is not love*. "Love is more than merely understanding the problem of poverty. It is more than being moved by compassion for the poor. It is more than being able to talk a good line about what love requires. Love means actually doing something about the needs of your brother or sister. Love takes what you have in your own life and goes to work with it to alleviate the needs of a fellow believer."[4] The writer of 1 John has little time or patience for love that is talked about and not enacted. Jesus's love, after all, manifested itself in sacrificial, life-giving action. Though the expression of our love will look different, the outcome will be the same: something sacrificial and life giving.

This section of 1 John—the exhortation to love not just in word and speech but also in truth and action—was actually the text I drew upon for the first sermon I ever preached, when I was a high school senior preaching for Youth Sunday at my church. I am glad I don't have the manuscript of that sermon, but part of me would love to see what I actually said. I do remember, in spirit if not in substance, that I, in my teenaged confidence, laid a pretty heavy guilt trip on my poor congregation. I saw these words and thought—"Yes! This is it! We are hypocrites—we don't do this at all—we are all words and no action!" and then spent twenty minutes . . . um . . . *educating* people about how much we had missed the point.

But as we continue further in 1 John, we discover that my efforts as a teenager trying to interpret this passage were not very loving. Verses 19-24 teach us that "love is not guilt," even in the face of times when we have fallen ridiculously short. Many preachers use guilt as a way to spur us to action—and I fear that, in my eighteen-year-old self-righteousness, I did just that. But the writer of 1 John offers reassurance to those reeling after hearing about what love truly is, those wondering if they've done enough and knowing they haven't. If your heart seems to condemn you, sinking to the pit of your stomach in despair and grief, verses 19 and 20 say don't be afraid: God is greater than your heart and sees to the depth of it. Even as 1 John urges action, this section's final verses, in the words of Clifton Black, repudiate "any attempt by any Christian to lay a cheap guilt trip on anyone."[5] Love is not anxiety and fear and self-loathing and self-condemnation. These things are not compatible with love, which constantly draws us to abide in God so deeply that our wills become aligned with God's. These things are not compatible with the love of a God who has poured out God's own Spirit to live in us and help us in the places where we are weak.

And so, in the end, love is about action, but it is about something else, too. Only one thing can enable us to love in truly life-giving, self-sacrificing ways, and it's not our human will or ability. It is our belief in the name of Jesus. It is our trust in who Jesus is and has shown God to be. As the brilliant eighth-century monk St. Bede wrote, "In truth it is impossible to love one another in the right way if we do not have faith in Christ, just as it is impossible to believe in the name of Christ if we do not love one another."[6] Love, then, is an act of faith. It is trust in something bigger than ourselves, something beyond logic, something made possible only as we root ourselves and abide in who we claim Jesus to be. When I was growing up, one of my pastors always talked about grace being both gift and task—and this is true of love as well. Love is a task, something we must actively live; but it is also a gift—a way of being made possible only by trust in One greater than we are, who knows us and chooses to call us children of God anyway.

First John was written some 1,900 years ago, yet the things that this letter shares with us address questions we still carry today. What is love? It is that which is not death dealing but life giving. It is Jesus laying down his life and those of us who follow Jesus, actively giving of our lives for others in concrete ways. It is not guilt inducing but an expression of sheer faith—a way of being in the world made possible only by Christ's way of being among us and the Spirit's continued presence within us. In a world so often murderous and violent, so often guilt and anxiety ridden, so often all talk and little walk, so often self-reliant rather than grace accepting—what might claiming this vision of love do for us? How might the way we live out love in Christian community start answering the questions about love that the world around us, seeking that which is true, keeps on asking?

Notes

1. D. Moody Smith, *First, Second, and Third John*, Interpretation: A Bible Commentary for Teaching and Preaching (Louisville: Westminster John Knox Press, 2012) Kindle Edition, 90.

2. Scott Hoezee, "1 John 3:16-24," Lectionary Epistle, Calvin Theological Seminary, cep.calvinseminary.edu/sermon-starters/easter-4b-2/?type=lectionary_epistle.

3. Brian Peterson, "Commentary on 1 John 3:16-24," *workingpreacher.org*, 29 April 2012 www.workingpreacher.org/preaching.aspx?commentary_id=1287.

4. Hoezee, "1 John 3:16-24."

5. C. Clifton Black, *The First, Second and Third Letters of John*, The New Interpreter's Bible, vol. 12 (Nashville: Abingdon Press, 1998) 424.

6. Bede quoted in Nijay Gupta, "Commentary on 1 John 3:16-24," *workingpreacher.org*, 26 April 2015, www.workingpreacher.org/preaching.aspx?commentary_id=2431.

6

Discerning the Spirit[1]

1 John 4:1-6 (with Acts 2:1-21)

"Spirit," theologian Frederick Buechner writes, "has come to mean something pale and shapeless, like an unmade bed. School spirit, the American spirit, the Christmas spirit, the spirit of '76 . . . each of these points to something that you know is supposed to get you to your feet cheering,"[2] even if you can't always figure out why. "Spirit" is definitely an ambiguous term in our culture, one that's been overused to the point that we aren't even sure how to identify or define it anymore. Do a Google search for "spirit," and the first things that come up are Spirit Airlines, the rock band Spirit, the movie *Spirit: Stallion of the Cimarron*, Spirit Halloween costume store, and one of the Mars Rovers—which is named "Spirit."

Amid these many spirits, Scripture introduces us to the Spirit, Spirit with a capital *S*—otherwise known as the Spirit of God or the Holy Spirit, whose gift to the church we celebrate today on Pentecost. What is this Spirit? Rather than introducing the Spirit to us with a compact definition, the book of Acts gives us a story. I think that story is where we need to start if we want to understand what the Holy Spirit is, what it looks like, and what it does—a task as difficult for the early church as it can be for us today.

The day of the Spirit's coming begins with Jesus's followers huddled together in a room in Jerusalem. In the streets below, devout people from across the known world mill about, celebrating the feast of Pentecost—Judaism's harvest festival that commemorated the gift of the Law on Mount Sinai. Just as millions hit the road this Memorial Day weekend, Jews and curious seekers from all regions converged on Jerusalem, turning it into a multicultural melting pot. Surely it was a hectic scene to begin with, but the usual chaos was about to be amplified. Suddenly, like a rush of wind or a blaze of fire, Jesus's community of uneducated Galilean fishermen and housewives bursts into the street. They start speaking languages that they've likely never heard before, let alone studied enough to utter with any degree of fluency. Most of these first followers of Jesus had never been more than a few dozen miles from home; yet suddenly they are communicating in ways that can be understood by people from all over the world, comprehended even over the roaring din of the city.

It's no wonder that the crowds, upon hearing these backwoods believers speaking fluently in their native tongues, are bewildered, amazed, astonished, and perplexed, to borrow a few superlatives from Acts 2. Each can hear clearly what Jesus's followers are talking about—"God's deeds of power"—but their responses and interpretations are mixed. The cynics among them try to brush this remarkable display aside, dismissing it by assuming the Jesus followers have hit the bottle a little too early in the morning. The accusation of their being drunk makes me chuckle—it's just such a fabulous detail. Yet I have to wonder if in that moment some of the disciples remembered what Jesus, who was often accused of being a drunkard himself, said about wine: "Nobody pours new wine into old wineskins. If they did, the new wine would burst the wineskins, the wine would spill, and the wineskins would be ruined" (Mark 2:22, author's paraphrase). Now these Spirit-filled disciples have become that new wine, bursting the seams of convention as they spill into the streets. And though there is much cynicism and disorientation, some witnessing the scene are absolutely captivated, realizing something important is happening here even if they struggle to explain it. And so they begin asking the loaded question: "What does this mean?"

Peter does his best to name what this Spirit is, who it is for, and—perhaps most important—who it is from. This Spirit is not random, and it is not out of the blue. It is a continuation of the story of Jesus, who during his life did countless things that showed God bursting into this day and time, crafting a new creation where old divides no longer exist, and forming a new community of inclusion and equality and healing for all people—God's kingdom in the here and now. The same Jesus who did these things while on earth is now sending the Holy Spirit not just to dwell in a few prophetic individuals, as it had in the past, but to dwell in *everyone*—that all of our voices and lives, driven by the Spirit, may continue the work Jesus began.

By the time the Christian community addressed by the letter of 1 John came along, this Spirit had been flowing freely, as promised, for decades. The Holy Spirit's presence had made some amazing things possible, bringing together diverse people in communities committed to the way of Jesus. These communities demonstrated love for one another in ways that would have seemed impossible previously—Jews, Gentiles, men, women, rich, poor, slave, free, all together seeking to live the Gospel faithfully, embodying Jesus as best as they could for the world. Yet, as with all gifts, the beauty of the Spirit had fallen subject to abuse by the time 1 John was written. We've talked over the past weeks about the schisms and breaks the community of 1 John was facing as people held opposing ideas about what was true and what mattered most. Some individuals were trying to use their positions of power and influence to draw others to their ways of thinking rather than leading them in ways consistent with Jesus's life and teaching. One of the things some leaders were doing, it seems, was claiming to speak by the Spirit of God when, if one looked closely, it was clear they were speaking by and about a different sort of spirit altogether.

And so, 1 John offers a warning to the community: "Beloved, do not believe every spirit, but test the spirits to see whether they are from God" (v. 1). I like how Eugene Peterson translates this first verse in his modern paraphrase, *The Message*: "My dear friends, don't believe everything you hear. Carefully weigh and examine what people tell you. Not everyone who talks about God comes from God." How true that is, even today. Many people claim to speak for God, to speak about God, naming divine inspiration as their authority and Christian faith as their foundation—but not all of these really do. I was astonished this week to read through a list of organizations designated "hate groups" by the Southern Poverty Law Center and learn that eighteen of the identified organizations had the word "church" in their title, twenty-five the word "Christian," seven the word "Baptist," and eighteen the word "ministry" or "ministries." This doesn't even include the 186 Ku Klux Klan groups that, horrifically, have a cross as their central symbol. Christ, have mercy.

Just because someone says they speak for God, and are speaking by God's Spirit, clearly doesn't make it so. We have to test the spirits—to carefully weigh and examine what we hear. This is part of our responsibility and mission as those carrying the gospel into a new day, serving as its editors and ambassadors for a new time and context. How do we test the spirits, then? The writer of 1 John challenges his readers to ask a central question: does what we are hearing and seeing line up with the life of Jesus? Do the words and actions being tested confess Jesus or (as some scholars have argued that verse 3 should be translated) annul and dissolve Jesus? Do they make it seem like his life didn't matter? The Holy Spirit is not some ambiguous, amorphous thing that can take any shape it wants. Just as last week we discovered that love looks like Jesus, this week we learn that the Holy Spirit is proven by words and actions that take the shape of Christ.

It is the church's responsibility, then, to discern what spirit is true. The church's very life, 1 John seems to say, relies on us doing this. The elder reminds the church that, though it may feel overwhelming with the many spirits, voices, and messages that surround them, such discernment is something they are more than equipped to do. "Little children," verse 4 reassures, "the one who is in you is greater than the one who is in the world." It is almost as if he is saying, "Remember the story of Pentecost? The true Spirit of God, on that day, was poured out on all people. It was that outpouring predicted by the prophecy of Joel long ago: on young and old, on slaves, on men and women alike. All of you, now, are gifted with vision, able to dream the Spirit's dreams—and able to know when something is not of the Spirit. You don't have to take everything at face value, or jump after the next shiny thing that comes along—in fact, you *can't* do that. People speaking by other spirits will be the ones grabbing the headlines, getting the world's attention, making a name for themselves and garnering a following—but that cannot deter you. You know what is true, deep in your bones, because you have seen Jesus. So be discerning, church. Look for and listen to the Spirit that is true, and then live by it."

First John 4 gives the church born on Pentecost, the church born by wind and by flame into the world, its marching orders. C. Clifton Black describes who we are and what those orders consist of beautifully:

> 1 John shows little patience and even less support for an understanding of the church as a club, a special interest group, a religious recreational facility, or a YMCA. The elder's view of what should happen when the church gathers is very different: "Test the spirits to see whether they come from God!" In 1 John, the church is where one ought to find hard questioning and reasoned deliberation about crucial matters of Christian faith and practice. In this endeavor no distinction is made or hinted at between the prerogatives of clergy and laity. All within God's family are equal participants in an ongoing, evaluative enterprise; no one occupying an official or demographic niche claims special purchase on theological insight. The church that takes its bearings from 1 John resembles a household with a flawed but venerable heritage, where the children of God are pondering what it means to be faithful.[3]

Such a household of thoughtful, collaborative people certainly resonates with the story of that first Pentecost. That story, though we often focus on the pyrotechnics, is really about diverse people learning to understand one another, to seek wisdom together, to gather united around the story of Jesus and then spill out into the world to live the boundary-breaking truth. It is a continuation of Jesus's tendency to call unlikely people to follow him and speak for him, to reach people from the margins and bring them into the family of God as equally beloved participants. That such an unruly Spirit gathers so many people together makes it crucial for us to listen, to discern the Spirit—not just the spirits we need to identify as outside of the bounds of what Jesus was about, but the true Spirit that may come to us through the unexpected neighbor. We may have to realize that the one we've never been able to understand before also has that One in them who is greater than the one that is in the world. It is up to all of us, 1 John says, when we experience something that seems to be or claims to be of the Spirit of God, to pause as the people did on the first Pentecost and ask, "What does this mean?"

As the community at that first Pentecost and 1 John's community had to ask their own questions of the Spirit of God in their day, so do we in ours. It's up to us to listen carefully to whatever answers we may hear, even if they shock or surprise us. The Spirit of God shows up in a lot of places, stunningly at times, and it means we have to take time to be attentive and discern the truth. Jesus is out there still, working for community, breaking down barriers, proving that love and life are stronger than hate and death. We have to prepare to see Jesus being made known, standing in the place we least expected.

So, this Pentecost Sunday, what might happen if we took time to listen seriously and discern the Spirit? What might happen if we tuned in to unlikely messengers speaking about what they have seen and heard—the life and being of Jesus? What might happen if we realized that we all have access to God's Spirit, and that this Spirit has power to prevail over the many more ambiguous spirits floating around and seeking to grab our attention? What might happen if we let the true Spirit live in us and drive us where it may, along the risky paths of love walked by Jesus? As we bear this Spirit from this place and into the world, may we be willing to ask these questions, and then to listen to the surprising and challenging answers that are bound to come.

Notes

1. This sermon was originally preached on Pentecost Sunday.
2. Frederick Buechner, *Wishful Thinking: A Seeker's ABC* (New York: Harper One, 1993) 102.
3. C. Clifton Black, *The First, Second and Third Letters of John*, The New Interpreter's Bible, vol. 12 (Nashville: Abingdon Press, 1998) 427.

Who God Is ... and Why It Matters[1]

1 John 4:7-21

As the early church sought to make sense of the gospel, one of the biggest and most pressing questions was this: Who is God? Who is this God we have come to know in Jesus Christ? Who is this God who now lives in us by the Holy Spirit sent down on Pentecost? Emerging from the Jewish tradition, early Christians understood that there was only one God, yet now they knew this God not just as Creator or Father but also as the Son—Jesus—and as the Holy Spirit. All of these seemed equally to be God, yet they couldn't be different *gods* if there was only one *God*. So what gives?

Theologians spent Christianity's first five centuries or so arguing for hours about how one God could be three persons and not be three separate gods, about whether any person of what came to be known the Trinity—Father, Son, or Holy Spirit—was supreme over the others or had created the others. Eventually, as a way to help us remember and embrace the mysterious relational unity that is God, those early Christians put into place the holy day that we celebrate today: Trinity Sunday. It is a unique Sunday in that it doesn't commemorate an event in the life of Christ or the church but a belief held by the church based on its own experience of God.

Still, when we think about God as Trinity, it can feel a bit murky and overwhelming. I vividly remember preparing for my ordination council by spending hours on my parents' back porch reviewing my notebooks from seminary theology class. I woke in the middle of the previous night terrified I would be asked to explain the Trinity before I could be ordained. Though I tried to come up with some clever analogy or explanation to keep in my back pocket, I knew that no matter how long I studied, any attempt to make God rationally comprehensible would fall short.

This realization is reaffirmed by one of my favorite YouTube videos of all time, a cartoon titled "St. Patrick's Bad Analogies" produced by a group called Lutheran Satire.[2] In it, two snarky Irish peasants named Connal and Donnal approach their island's patron saint, St. Patrick, in hopes of getting answers about the Trinity.

"Okay, Patrick," Connal begins in his slow Irish drawl, "tell us a bit more about this Trinity thing . . . but remember we are simple people without all your fancy books and learnin', and we're hearing about all this for the first time, so try to keep it simple, okay Patrick?"

"Sure," says Patrick. "Okay, there are three persons of the trinity: the Father, the Son, and the Holy Spirit, but there is only one God."

There's an awkward pause, then Connal says, "Don't get what you're saying here, Patrick."

"Not picking up what you're laying down here, Patrick. Could you use an analogy?" asks Donnal.

"Sure," Patrick replies accommodatingly. "The Trinity is like water and how you can find water in three different forms: ice, water, and vapor."

Connal is outraged: "That's modalism, Patrick!"

"What?" Patrick asks, perplexed.

"Modalism—an ancient heresy which espouses that God is not three distinct persons but merely reveals God's self in three different forms. This heresy was clearly condemned in Canon One at the first council of Constantinople and those who confess it cannot be considered part of the church Catholic. C'mon, Patrick!"

"Yeah," says Donnal, "get it together, Patrick!"

"Okay. . . . " Patrick tries again. "Then the Trinity is like the sun in the sky, where you have the star and the light and the heat."

A look of disappointment washes over Connal. "Oh, Patrick. That's Aryanism, Patrick!"

"Aryanism?" asks the saint.

"Yes, Aryanism—a heresy which states that Christ and the Holy Spirit are creations of the Father and not actually one in nature with him, just like light and heat are creations of the star and not actually the star. That's a bad analogy, Patrick."

"Yeah, you're the worst, Patrick," Donnal echoes.

Wearying, Patrick tries again. "Okay—the Trinity is like this three-leaf clover here."

But Connal interrupts: "I'm gonna stop you right there. You're about to confess partialism, Patrick."

"*Partialism?*"

"Yes, Partialism—a heresy which asserts that the Father, Son, and Holy Spirit are not distinct persons of the Godhead but are different parts of God, each composing one third of the divine."

The exchange goes on and on, with Patrick making valiant attempts and the brothers shooting down every suggestion. Finally, Patrick loses it and just spouts off: "Fine! The Trinity is a mystery which cannot be comprehended by human reason but is understood only through faith and is best confessed in the words of the Athanasian creed, which states that we worship one God in Trinity, and Trinity in Unity, neither confusing the Persons nor dividing the substance; that we are compelled by the Christian truth to confess that each distinct person is God and Lord and that the deity of the Father and the Son and the Holy Spirit is one, equal in glory, coequal in majesty."

There's a lengthy pause, after which Connal says, "Well why didn't you just say that in the first place, Patrick?"

"Yeah," Donnal agrees, "quit beating around the bush, Patrick."

As Patrick stands looking befuddled, happy music plays in the background and the Irishmen go off to celebrate their conversion.

Though the word "Trinity" never appears in Scripture, we see the three persons of God relating to one another and to us throughout the New Testament, including in today's reading from 1 John. First John paints a picture of a God who is relationship in God's very being—and who has now made us part of that relationship. If I try to dissect the ways the Father, Son, and Spirit show up in today's reading, I'll probably quickly end up in the same boat as poor Patrick, reducing or simplifying God in ways that don't work. But what 1 John gives us is a glimpse of who this God is: Father, Son, and Spirit.

Based on our reading of this letter so far, 1 John's conclusion about God's nature should not come as a surprise. God, the writer says, is love. But I think we have to be careful—as 1 John is—not to reduce the fact that God is love to some sort of amorphous, mushy thing. God is not just love in any manifestation, but a very specific type of love. In Greek, there are several different words for love, and not all love is created equal! First John doesn't use the Greek word *eros* to talk about God's love; *eros* is love earned or merited by the beloved, love that can flame up or flame out. Nor does it use the word *philos*, which is love for a member of the family—one we are obligated to by blood. Rather, 1 John uses an altogether different word, *agape*, which is described as "love for the unworthy stranger, even the sinful rebel"³—love that serves the other regardless of merit or changing circumstances, not out of obligation or for personal gain but in a spirit of self-sacrifice and utter self-giving.

This is the love that God is, that forms God's very core and dictates God's very life. It is all that God has been, is, and will be—a love that is not abstract but "passion expressed in action."⁴ First John holds in mind one action in particular as evidence of the love that God is: the gift of God's own Son, Jesus, to a world that did nothing to earn or invite such a gift. Some scholars have thought verses 9 and 10 in today's reading offer further reflection on their more famous older cousin, John 3:16: "God's love was revealed among us in this way: God sent his only Son into the world so that we might live through him. In this is love, not that we loved God but that he loved us and sent his Son to be the atoning sacrifice for our sins." I love how Brian Peterson describes the importance of defining the love that God is in this specific way:

> This insistent rooting in the sending of the Son . . . gives this love a particular character quite different from the sentimental or self-serving content that we otherwise might use to define what "love" means. This is the sense in which we must say that "God is love." We cannot reverse the elements of that claim and say "love is God." We would then remake God in the image of an attitude, or ideal, or emotion. God is love because God has been made known in the act of sending and giving the Son for us, the action that is perfect and eternal love.⁵

Everything, the writer of 1 John says, hinges on the fact that God has first loved us in this way. Absolutely everything. This is the baseline out of which we live and which transforms our reality when we really grasp it. We have to consider what kind of love God is, because this knowledge determines who we are and how we live in response. Though I fear bad analogies after the Patrick video, I really appreciate the analogy that David Lose offered in his own reflections about the reality that God is love:

> Imagine with me for a moment the delight you would experience in discovering that you had a long-lost uncle or aunt who had made you the heir to their estate. Can you see it? You'd wake up one morning and discover that they had left you riches beyond count, that your major financial worries were over, and that you really didn't have to worry all that much about the future. If that scenario happened, how would you feel? What would you do? Or, more to the point, what would you

do differently? And here I don't mean what would you run out and buy—though I suspect that most of us would treat ourselves to something. Rather, what would be different about your day-to-day attitudes, practices, habits, and outlook? How would knowing that your future is absolutely secure change your present?[6]

This is exactly the sort of transformation 1 John imagines as we root ourselves in the fact that God is love—love of the unmerited, nonrepayable, self-giving sort that will never change. Because God has shown and invited us into this sort of love, the writer says, we are now free to do two related things. First, we are free to embody God's love as we love others. Included forever in the love of God, we now become physical signs of God's love to the world. We become those who love the unworthy stranger with an outpouring of *agape* that helps the world see who God is just as clearly as God's love of us through Christ taught us who God is. The church does not *become* God—we shouldn't get confused and start thinking about ourselves as the fourth person of the Trinity. Yet if we are in communion with the God who is love, God's love will pour itself out on others through us. Loving can be the hardest and scariest and riskiest thing in the world, if we truly love not just those who will reciprocate but also those who may rebel against us. If we truly believe in and abide in the love God has for us, however, we will gain the ability to extend this kind of love toward the least likely candidates—candidates as undeserving as we were when God first chose to love us.

And this brings us to the second thing that happens when we come to know, deeply and truly in our bones, that God is love: we are liberated from fear. Much of 1 John's fourth chapter repeats things we've seen and talked about earlier in this letter, but the fear piece is new. First John 4 says that when love is perfected—literally, made complete—it drives out fear. So much of what we do in life is motivated by fear. We talked about this reality at length in our congregational discussion of the movie *Selma* last Sunday night. So much of the racial tension and divide witnessed throughout the civil rights movement—and today—was and is driven by fear of those who are different from us, fear that if others are accorded the same rights and power as we are, then we may no longer be enough or have enough. But God's love, when it abides deeply in us, makes such fear impossible. Imagine a life where fear is impossible! Judith Jones describes the potential for this as she reminds us of the impact of knowing that God is love can have on our lives. "When we open ourselves to the warmth and light of God's presence," she says, "we find that even our deepest, darkest secrets and the ugliest parts of ourselves are not beyond God's reach. Nothing in us is so broken or so filthy that God is unwilling or unable to touch it. God embraces us as we are, loves us as we are, and works in us to make us clean and whole and new. Upheld, surrounded, enfolded by such love, who could be afraid?"[7] Suddenly our fellow humans aren't those to be feared, but those to be loved. The love God has lavished upon us becomes big enough for us all.

We may not be able to explain God perfectly. We may not be able to explain who God is systematically or have a perfect analogy that makes all the light bulbs go on in our heads. We have barely scratched a surface that goes on to unimaginable heights and depths. But maybe all we need to know is this: the truth that God is love. God's love is made complete as we love each other, driving fear away. God who is relationship—Father, Son, and Holy Spirit—is drawing us ever more into God's self-giving love. Maybe, if we rooted ourselves in this, we might be transformed in such a way that God would be known to abide in us and be made visible to a watching world. The more I think about it, the more I think knowing that God is love constitutes a more-than-sufficient God for me, for you, for all of us. Thanks be to God for such a gift—thanks be to God for being the one who, in first loving us, made the love that binds us together possible.

Notes

1. The sermon was originally preached on Trinity Sunday.

2. Published 14 March 2013, www.youtube.com/watch?v=KQLfgaUoQCw.

3. Scott Hoezee, "1 John 4:7-21," Lectionary Epistle, Calvin Theological Seminary, cep.calvinseminary.edu/sermon-starters/easter-5b-2/?type=lectionary_epistle.

4. Judith Jones, "Commentary on 1 John 4:7-21," *workingpreacher.org*, 3 May 2015, www.workingpreacher.org/preaching.aspx?commentary_id=2448.

5. Brian Peterson, "Commentary on 1 John 4:7-21," *workingpreacher.org*, 6 May 2012, www.workingpreacher.org/preaching.aspx?commentary_id=1288.

6. David Lose, "Trinity B: Three-in-One Plus One!" 25 May 2015, www.davidlose.net/2015/05/trinity-b-three-in-one-plus-one/.

7. Jones, "Commentary on 1 John 4:7-21."

8

Bearing Witness

1 John 5:1-12

In some Christian traditions, often in preparation for confirmation, Christian formation includes memorizing a catechism or studying a series of questions and answers that help one understand the meaning of things like the Creed and the Lord's Prayer. Martin Luther first made a question-and-answer format of catechism popular in the 1500s, thinking that asking questions was the best way to help those new to faith learn the essential truths of what they professed to believe. One of the most famous catechisms, the Westminster Shorter Confession, begins by asking, "What is the chief end of man?" Then comes the reply: "Man's chief end is to glorify God, and to enjoy [God] forever." Then another question: "What rule has God given to direct us how we may glorify and enjoy God?" And another answer: "The word of God, which is contained in the scriptures of the Old and New Testaments." It goes on like this for a whopping 107 questions and answers—which makes me think, if this is the Westminster *Shorter* Confession, I probably don't even want to *look* at the Larger Confession.

As we reach the end of the letter of 1 John, we find that this question-and-answer format for affirming and learning the essentials of faith was not something new to Martin Luther. Through four chapters of this book, we have been listening to the writer instruct, correct, and encourage a community of young Christians seeking to make sense of the gospel and apply it to their own time and context. The beginning of chapter 5—the letter's conclusion—doesn't bring us any new revelations, really, but rather draws all the ideas of the letter together, providing a sort of review. At times throughout this letter, the writer has sounded so convoluted that his line of thought is hard to follow. At first glance, the letter's final chapter seems equally chaotic. Scholar C. Clifton Black, however, helped me see something: that in this section, though the reasoning swirls so much that the reader may experience "verbal vertigo," a sort of pattern does emerge: the writer is answering questions about faith.[1] The letter's conclusion becomes a sort of question-and-answer session. Even though the questions being asked remain unwritten, one can hear them between the lines, connecting the ideas to each other and taking us deeper into the meaning. The result is a conversation not unlike the question-and-answer of catechism.

Try hearing the first five verses of our passage this way, imagining the questions interspersed. The writer starts by reiterating a key point of the letter: if we trust that Jesus is the Messiah, we become a child of God.

Q: Well, if that's true, how should we respond?

A: You should love the parent—God—and the offspring—both Jesus, God's Son, and the children of God now around you (v. 1).

Q: But how can we be certain that we are showing love to God's children?

A: If you love God and obey God by loving others (v. 2).

Q: Well, how do we love God?

A: By keeping God's commandments—especially that big one of loving your brothers and sisters (v. 3).

Q: That's going to be hard, isn't it?

A: Not really. God's commands aren't burdensome (v. 3; see Matt 11:30).

Q: If we do all of this, love God and love our brothers and sisters, what will happen?

A: We will show that we are begotten of God just as Jesus was, and we will conquer the world.

Q: What does this conquest look like?

A: The world will be overcome by our faith (v. 4).

Q: But who can actually overcome the world, with all its brokenness?

A: The one who trusts in Jesus, God's Son (v. 5, an answer that brings us full circle, back to the initial statement in v. 1).

I feel like I need to stop here and talk about this language of conquering or overcoming the world because, honestly, it troubles me. Is that really the goal of our faith? Hearing the word "conquer" brings to mind a lot of militaristic images. It brings up things like the Crusades, missions to subdue everyone who does not believe in Jesus, imposing our faith by force. It makes me think of fighting zealously, beating others down, bulldozing a path to glory—things that the Christian faith has taken up at times but, I think, when you look at the life of Jesus, taken up in grave error. Jesus didn't do any of these things—in fact, he intentionally rejected them. So there's another question:

Q: What does it mean to conquer—or, to use a better synonym, overcome—the world?

A light bulb went on for me when I read a reflection by Jodi-Renee Adams. She, too, was struggling with the military language of conquering or overcoming found in this passage until she had a new experience that shed light on what 1 John might have intended. She tells the story of attending the premiere of a symphony dedicated to a friend's brilliant and mentally-ill brother. She went along to the concert hall but admits that she didn't go into the concert expecting anything profound. She'd heard a lot of classical music in her life, and didn't anticipate this being anything different than countless concerts she'd attended before. But as she listened, she was drawn in, overwhelmed by an unexpectedly profound performance. It overcame her, she said—"overcame my cynicism, my musical elitism, my grumpy and tired state."[2] She couldn't resist the beauty of what she was hearing and seeing and experiencing; she was overcome by the power of it all. This, perhaps, is the way 1 John is talking about the power to overcome—overcoming the hardened skeptics and cynical ways of the world with the love talked about throughout this letter and reiterated through the questions and answers of the previous verses. When we demonstrate extravagant love of God and neighbor that reflects back God's extravagant love of us, the world can't help being overcome by it. The world can't help being won over by what they hear and see and experience. That's a powerful visual of what our faith can bring about.

Yet, for the world to be won over by our lives, we first have to be won over ourselves. And that brings us to the second half of today's reading, which raises for the first time in this letter the idea of *witness* or *testimony*. As he uses these words nine times in a span of six verses, the author is intentionally emphasizing a key theme from the Gospel of John. Throughout that book, the importance of testimony about Jesus is reiterated again and again. John is a veritable litany of witnesses testifying that Jesus is who he seems to be—the one sent by God, God's own Son. John the Baptist bears the first testimony, and, at the Gospel's end, the Beloved Disciple bears witness. In between, Jesus is testified to by God, by the Spirit, and—in our Gospel reading this morning—by Jesus himself. That Gospel is full of voices from every corner seeking to see the world overcome by the good news of who Jesus is.

But in today's reading, the writer highlights some different sources of testimony. First, he talks about "the water and the blood"—a reference that has caused a lot of debate in scholarship (cf. vv. 6, 8). Most people believe that the reference to water is meant to bring to mind Jesus's baptism, and the blood is a reference to his death. In other words, the phrase encapsulates the whole of Jesus's life and ministry—including his humiliating, suffering death—and says that all of these things offer witness to who Jesus is, to the power of God's love demonstrated through him. The testimony was heard in fullness from the cross, where Jesus was pierced with a spear and "at once blood and water came out" (John 19:34). The water and blood references may also refer to the way Christians, both in 1 John's community and today, add their own testimony to the testimony of Jesus's life, making their own affirmation of what they hold to be true by participating in the two sacraments or ordinances Jesus commanded of his followers: passing through the waters of baptism, and sharing his body and blood at the table of Communion. All of these things—Jesus's life, Jesus's death, and our sacred participation in these things through baptism and Communion and being filled with God's Spirit—come together to bear witness in a powerful way to the world, to testify to this love that has overcome us, love that can overcome anything.

As we are overcome by this testimony, and begin to overcome the world by bearing witness to it with our lives, the writer says that something amazing will happen. A new form of testimony will take place: it will become evident that God, through God's Son Jesus, has given us eternal life. I know I've said this before, but I feel like the idea of eternal life has been so misconstrued that I need to reiterate it again: eternal life is not just life that goes on beyond death. It is "life of a different quality visible even now."[3] As New Testament professor Audrey West explains, "Both the Gospel of John and 1 John understand eternal life to be a present reality as well as future promise for those who believe in Jesus Christ. 'Life' in this sense . . . has to do with a quality of existence that death cannot destroy. That is, it is 'eternal,' not in the sense of lasting forever, but in its quality, in its manifestation in the here and now."[4]

How does life of such quality become a present reality? First John has made it clear throughout the letter: this new kind of life is made manifest in the sacrifices we make for one another, in the ways we share freely with those in need, in trusting Christ for our life rather than the securities the world offers, in how we love others freely and without fear—in short, as we walk like Jesus walked in the way of love. As we do these things, a whole new testimony is proclaimed, showing that everything Jesus was and is, all that he said and did, and the God he made known, is all true.

So the beginning of this convoluted final section of the letter leaves us, appropriately, with a question to answer: How have we been overcome by the love of God? And how shall we let our overcome-ness be seen? How will it flow forth in life of a different quality—one that, by the resonance of its beautiful witness, overcomes the world with the truth of who God is and of all God hopes and desires for each of us?

These are good questions to hold in mind as we come together at the table this morning, gathering around to bear witness and offer testimony to the reality of who Jesus is and to the power of his love. Here, as we remember Christ's body broken and blood spilt, we have a chance to be overcome as we experience this powerful picture of love that is life laid down. As we eat and drink together today, how will our lives grow to bear deeper witness to who Jesus is? Let us reflect on these things as we prepare to come to Christ's table together.

Notes

1. C. Clifton Black, *The First, Second and Third Letters of John*, The New Interpreter's Bible, vol. 12 (Nashville: Abingdon Press, 1998) 434. This section draws heavily on and is indebted to Black's ideas presented on pages 434 and 435.

2. Jodi-Renee Adams, *The Burden of a Not-So-Burdensome Commandment*, published on *The Hardest Question*, 6 May 2012, thq.wearesparkhouse.org/featured/easter6epistle/.

3. Audrey West, "Commentary on 1 John 5:9-13," *workingpreacher.org*, 20 May 2012, www.workingpreacher.org/preaching.aspx?commentary_id=1305.

4. Ibid.

What We Know

1 John 5:13-21 (with John 14:1-14)

In fall 2014, Internet listeners across our nation became enthralled with a podcast produced in collaboration with WBEZ Chicago public radio. *Serial*—a spinoff of the well-known *This American Life* radio program—sought to tell a true-life story over the course of a series of episodes, re-examining the facts and helping listeners develop their own conclusions. The first season held particular interest for me as it revisited events that happened right here in Baltimore—the 1999 murder of Hae Min Lee, a student at Woodlawn High School, and the subsequent conviction of her ex-boyfriend, Adnan Syed, who was sentenced to life in prison. Over the course of eleven episodes, *Serial*'s investigative team made it their mission to "follow up on long-dormant leads, recheck alibis, and question assumptions"[1] as they reinterviewed key parties and consulted experts in a variety of fields. They struggled to piece together what really happened in a tangled case with lots of components that didn't seem to add up. Their findings made one wonder, at times, how Adnan was convicted based on largely circumstantial evidence. When it came time for the much-anticipated final episode, I along with millions of listeners grew excited when I read the title of the podcast: "What We Know." It was advertised with a promise: "After 15 months of reporting, we take out everything we've got—interviews and documents and police reports—we shake it all out, and we see what sticks." After eleven episodes of speculation, I felt like we were going to reach a certain conclusion, to wrap this story up neatly and know the truth beyond a doubt.

The "What We Know" episode, however, didn't offer this sort of satisfaction. I don't want to spoil it for anyone who hasn't listened to the podcast, but basically the ending—while reiterating the facts and presenting a couple of new twists—left the story open-ended. At times the episode felt scattered, like the crew was trying to find a way to conclude but wasn't sure how to put a bow on this real-life case that is still ongoing. One review of the finale described it well:

> Anyone who is expecting the 12-episode podcast to wrap up like a scripted series . . . will invariably be disappointed. There's no surprise ending. The butler didn't do it. But to be fair, [they] never promised we would have hard answers by the end of [their] investigation into this 1999 murder. Part of the appeal of "Serial" all along has been that we've all gotten to be amateur sleuths, speculating on everything, asking "what if" to infinity. . . . So we'll continue with the "what ifs" until there are more answers . . . or more questions.[2]

Though on a very different topic, the conclusion of 1 John feels a bit like the conclusion of that *Serial* podcast. We haven't gone twelve episodes yet, but this is our ninth week of reading this book together. Following it through all of its twists and turns over the course of two and a half months is enough to get us asking, "How is this all going to end up?" Today, our final episode from this letter meanders around some more. Instead of tying everything up with a bow, its final words to people in an early church who are trying to figure out what it means to live the story of their faith in Christ leave us with as many questions as answers. It says some things that confuse, offers a few new ideas, and raises questions that cause us to speculate about what the writer is really saying.

If, then, we were to sum up "What We Know" out of these last verses—and this seems to be the point since the writer begins his conclusion by telling readers that he has written these things "so that you may know," and then uses the refrain "we know" six more times in this passage—what *can* we know? The first thing the writer emphasizes is the importance of prayer—an interesting thing to focus on here since prayer hasn't gotten much face time throughout the letter thus far. But in the end, the writer wants to remind readers of the responsibility and power of prayer. His words in verses 14 and 15 about asking and receiving bring to mind the words of Jesus in the Gospels—"I will do whatever you ask in my name," Jesus said at the end of today's Gospel reading, "so that the Father may be glorified in the Son. If in my name you ask me for anything, I will do it" (John 14:13-14).

In the Sermon on the Mount, Jesus said something similar: "Ask, and it will be given you; search, and you will find; knock, and the door will be opened for you" (Matt 7:7). Many faithful Christians have struggled with these words, as so often we *don't* get what we ask for in prayer—even when our intentions are earnest and, we feel, in line with God's. But I think the writer of 1 John is not trying to make the point that we will actually get each specific thing that we ask for. He is encouraging us to pray boldly, trusting that when we come to God honestly and openly, God will hear our prayers and petitions and respond faithfully to them. Prayer, the author wants us to remember, has power—real interaction between God and humanity takes place. It provides a chance for us to participate in God's redemptive work, particularly as we pray for those who are struggling, who are trying to walk in the light but stumbling along the way. Clifton Black sums it up well:

> Prayer, for the elder, is not a form of abracadabra or self-interested manipulation. Prayer, rather, is a force that promotes restorative life, bestowed on us by a mercifully responsive God (5:16). In intercession for their brothers and sisters, Christians actually participate in Christ's priestly ministry of atonement for the world (2:1-2; 5:16-17) . . . . Whether framed as intercessions for others or petitions for ourselves, prayer in 1 John, as in the Bible generally, is enacted in the faith that a genuine conversation between God and humanity occurs, out of which God gives shape to the future.[3]

Yet the writer also wants his readers to know that sometimes, prayer actually *isn't* the answer. First John addresses again the troubling issue of continued sin in the Christian community (vv. 17-19) by pointing out that sin has diverse manifestations, and that our responses have to be varied as well. I think this distinction is what is behind the troubling words in verse 16 that "there is sin that is mortal; I do not say that you should pray about that." There has been endless scholarly debate about the distinction 1 John seems to make between mortal and non-mortal sin or, to take 1 John's language more literally, between sin that leads to death and sin that does not lead to death. The church has, at times, tried to explain this through designating different types or levels of sin. As early as the late second century, Tertullian used these verses to classify some sins as unpardonable: murder, idolatry, injustice, apostasy, blasphemy, adultery, and fornication. By the twelfth century, Thomas Aquinas was talking about how different sins require different levels of action to be forgiven. And by the sixteenth century, Catholic moral theology distinguished between mortal sin—"a deliberate violation of a serious law of God, forgiveness of which normally entailed the sacrament of penance"—and venial sin—a violation of a more minor law of God, which could be forgiven through prayer and participating in the sacraments and acts of charity.[4]

I don't know about distinguishing between sins and their requirements so legalistically, but what I think can be discerned from these somewhat confusing verses and centuries of church reflection on them is that sometimes prayer is not enough. Sometimes inflicted wrongs are so great that for there to be forgiveness, for there to be the possibility of life beyond them, we have to do more than pray. In the wake of the horrific 2015 shootings at Mother Emmanuel AME Church in Charleston, the hashtag "Pray for Charleston" was trending around the country. People across racial and religious lines gathered together for vigils to pray for the victims and their families, to pray for the shooter, to pray for an end to racism. But I think this is one of those cases where it is not adequate just to pray and assume all will be well. We can pray all we want, but prayer alone won't change the scourge of racial-motivated hate that is continuing to lead to death in America. Prayer alone is not sufficient to bring us out of mortal danger. There has to be true repentance—a turning from old ways to new ones in thought and actions. The sin of racism in our nation is so pervasive that we must take concrete steps toward reparation and reconciliation; we must take action beyond prayer to actually make changes that can be life-giving rather than life-taking. Sometimes, moving from death to life means marching outside of the Capitol and Supreme Court buildings. Sometimes, it means taking hard personal steps ourselves or challenging others to take them. Who knows what sins that lead to death the writer had in mind; but certainly we can see sins in our society and in ourselves that require more than prayer, especially if we are not merely seeking to move past or feel better about them but to actually participate in God's healing redemption of the world.

So, then, at this juncture in our last episode, what do we know? We know that prayer is a powerful part of our identity in Christ, which the writer reiterates in verses 18 and 19 as something we know beyond doubt—that we are born of God, children of God. Yet he also wants us to know that this certain identity in Christ means participating in the concrete acts of reconciliation and healing that lead from death to life. At least, among my many continued questions about the problem of sin and how it is addressed in these verses, that is what I *think* we can know about this.

There is one thing, however, that I am certain the writer wants us to know above all, something he wants as the bedrock on which we plant our questions and watch them grow. It is the drum he has been beating throughout the letter—above all, we must know and hold on to the truth about who Jesus is.

In verse 20, we get one of the few straightforward, bold assertions in the New Testament that Jesus is God, the One who is eternal life, life of a different quality now and in the future—the One who is true. This bold assurance leads to the strange, dangling conclusion of the whole book: "Little children, keep yourself from idols" (v. 21). I don't believe this last warning stemmed from the writer being afraid the Christians would run off and worship pagan statues, as we usually picture when we read biblical statements about idolatry. Rather, I think this was the writer saying, "Dear beloved children of God, don't settle for anything less than the full truth of who God is. Don't worship a watered-down, lesser version. Hold on to what you know." It is what Jesus assured his disciples on their last night together when Thomas fearfully asked, "How can we know which way to go?" "If you know me," Jesus said, "you will know my Father also. From now on you do know him and have seen him." (See John 14:5-7.) This truth—who Jesus is—is the ultimate thing we need to know for all the questions that remain.

And so we have come to the end of our long, winding journey through this letter. What I both hate and love about how 1 John ends is that, like the ending of the *Serial* podcast, it's not an ending at all. It leaves us with questions to explore and answer about who we are, who God is, and what all this means for how we live together in the world. It ends as a story still to be written as we continue as editors of the gospel, embracing Jesus and learning what his life and death mean for the lives we lead today. As Clifton Black puts it, "With an unexpected warning (v. 21), 1 John ends as abruptly as it began—and just as appropriately. Sounding the depths of divine love and human responsibility, an epistle like this cannot end. By its very nature, there can be for 1 John no full stop. There can only be, as it were, a colon, a directional indicator of how the rest of the church's life will continue, along the limitless horizon of God's love."[5] As we pray and as we act, as we seek to live knowing who we are and who the God is that we serve and worship, how will we continue the story? It is my prayer that we, as those gathered in this place to be Christ's church, will keep asking questions, loving one another unreservedly, and digging deeper to learn what it truly means for us to live as children of God both this day and beyond.

Notes

1. Amy Mulvihill, "Baltimore Teen's Murder Re-Examined in New Podcast: Makers of This American Life Delve into Questions Surrounding the 1999 Murder of a Woodlawn High School Senior," *The Baltimore Sun*, 6 October 2014, www.baltimoremagazine.net/2014/10/6/1999-murder-of-baltimore-teen-re-examined-in-new-podcast.

2. Paula Bernstein, "'Serial' Podcast Finale: What We Know (and What We Don't Know)," *IndieWire*, 18 December 2014, www.indiewire.com/article/serial-podcast-finale-what-we-know-and-what-we-dont-know-20141218.

3. C. Clifton Black, *The First, Second and Third Letters of John*, The New Interpreter's Bible, vol. 12 (Nashville: Abingdon Press, 1998) 444–45.

4. Ibid., 443–44.

5. Ibid., 441.

Part 3

2 John

by Abby Thornton Hailey

Making Connections

2 John

We live in a snapshot culture, now more than ever. We love quick photos that capture the moment, or at least a glimpse of it, preserving it for all time—and we love sharing those photos with others in ways that connect us. Consider these statistics:

- As of 2014, over 1.5 billion new photos were being shared on social media platforms like Facebook, Instagram, and Snapchat every day. *Every. Day.*

- Estimates are that in 2015, the number of photos taken and shared on social media would be over one trillion. *One trillion.*

- Thanks to so many people in Western and Asian countries having a camera with them at all times courtesy of their smartphones, we have now snapped more photos in a single year than were taken on film in all previous history.

- Every two minutes, we take more pictures than all of humanity did throughout the 1800s.

- If all the photos taken in a year were printed out as a standard 4 by 6 and stretched out end to end, the pictures would cover more than 450 million miles—that's more than the distance to the sun and back 2.5 times.[1]

I don't know how exact those numbers are, but the concept is staggering. We have an unprecedented ability to document what is going on around us and share it with others. We can preserve any given moment for posterity, conveying an emotion, expression, and beauty that is hard to capture using only words.

We have no pictures from the early church. I wish we did. But the closest thing we have to snapshots of the first members of our family of faith comes near the end of the New Testament, in a cluster of books so tiny they're easily overlooked. The letters of 2 John and 3 John are one chapter apiece and are rarely read in church life. Neither of them appear in the Revised Common Lectionary that many churches draw upon for their Sunday readings. Until beginning work on these sermons, I am not sure I had ever spent time with these final New Testament epistles beyond the very earnest teenage year I read all the way through the Bible—and by the time I got to these final chapters, I was probably cruising toward the finish without a whole lot of thought, just grateful to hit books that were so short!

But these letters, in their brevity, offer precious glimpses into early communities of faith. Second and Third John are the two shortest books in Scripture; each could have been accommodated on a single 8 by 6 inch papyrus sheet, making them more like postcards than letters.[2] With so little to work with, and so much time passing since the letters' composition, it's hard to know all of what was going on with the communities these letters addressed. We are missing a *lot* of context.

My extended family is having a big reunion in a couple of weeks, and in preparation for it we have been emailing back and forth scans of old family pictures we have found from the early 1900s, trying to see if anyone knows something about them. Who is in this picture, when was it taken, and what is going on here? These short letters in the Bible are kind of like that; there's a lot of guesswork involved. But still, if a picture holds a thousand words—far more than the 245 that make up 2 John—then in this snapshot we can gain glimpses of the particular goals and struggles of an early church that resonate with ours today.

Traditional letters in the first and second centuries had three parts: a greeting, a body that included a request, and a closing. Just from the greeting, I think we can learn a lot about this moment in the life of the community. The letter is addressed to the "elect lady and her children"—immediately, the people are reminded that they are a family. The familial language continues with the references in verse 3 to "God the Father and . . . . Jesus Christ, the Father's Son." That their family includes not just their church but others too is perhaps implied by the blessing the writer bestows on the Lady and her children in verse 3. "Grace, mercy, and peace" is a greeting often seen in Paul's letters. Subtly, then, they are being connected to other churches they may never meet but with whom they are united by love and truth—the truth being Jesus Christ himself.

That the purpose of this letter is to help believers make connections becomes further solidified when we realize how much of 2 John's language we have heard before. We spent nine weeks reading the letter of 1 John together, and if you were here any of those Sundays, you likely felt a sense of déjà vu as you heard this epistle read today. Second John's words and ideas overlap overwhelmingly with its longer predecessor. It seems the purpose of this follow-up correspondence was not to present new ideas but to reconnect the people with the basics of their faith. Encountering words like "love," "truth," "abiding," and "walking" in the opening frames of this letter would have led the community to start firing on all synapses, making connections with what the Elder had written before. It's almost like a CliffsNotes version of 1 John—a reminder of the core things they needed to hold on to and reconnect with as a community.

The central request of this letter is one that will sound familiar to anyone with a basic knowledge of Christianity and, especially, of the Gospel of John and John's first letter: "Let us love one another. And this is love, that we walk according to his commandments; this is the commandment just as you have heard it from the beginning—you must walk in it" (2 John 5–6). Here we make connections with the words of Jesus: "I give you a new commandment, that you love one another. Just as I have loved you, you also should love one another" (John 13:34); and the words of 1 John, "Whoever says, 'I abide in him,' ought to walk just as he walked. Beloved, I am writing you no new commandment, but an old commandment . . . . For this is the message you have heard from the beginning, that we should love one another" (1 John 2:6-7; 3:11). This is a strong refresher course on what unites the community as family.

Yet then comes a section that feels oddly disconnected from these calls to love. Verses 7-11 do resonate on some level with 1 John's warnings about deceivers who are trying to pull the community apart, but there is also an edge here that feels new. As you may remember from when we talked about 1 John, the early church community was being threatened by a group that, best as we can tell, insisted that Jesus's life in the flesh did not matter—that neither the teaching of Jesus nor the teaching they had received about Jesus really made a difference in the end. These seeds of doubt had sown a great deal of havoc in the church or churches that received 1 John. Now, the Elder fears that same sort of damage could be done by false teachers in the community 2 John addresses.

But I have to confess, I have a hard time with the harshness of the language here. The Elder seems to be encouraging the community to sever all connection with those in their number who have gone astray and are leading others astray. This is hard to swallow on the heels of so much talk about love. What is the loving response when some in the community act in ways that could be deeply harmful? This moment in time is an important snapshot for us to see even if it is a painful one, because churches have wrestled with this question across the millennia. Initially, New Testament scholar Moody Smith's reaction to this section resonated with my own:

> Perhaps the unique feature of this letter is best left unheeded, namely, the warning not to show hospitality or even friendliness to those who espouse false doctrine and do not walk in love. Shunning may still be practiced by the Amish, but it is not in good order in modern society or modern churches. To be inhospitable and unfriendly is bad form. Incivility neither has, nor needs, defenders. In the face of it, normal human relations suffer. There is a sufficiency of bigotry and intolerance about, so that we do not need the Second Epistle to encourage it.[3]

So what, then, do we do with instructions like this in the midst of a Holy Book we are called not to brush aside but to take seriously?

In my research on our Instagram culture this week, a friend told me about a project done by women to take pictures of as many moments of one day in their lives as possible. The OneDay project pointed out that "we often share the pretty details of our days . . . the new haircut, the fabulous shoes, the fun night out with friends. But we don't often snap and share the mundane stuff: the commute, the sinkful of dirty dishes, the to-do list."[4] Even less often do we include the nightmarish moments—we are more likely to snap and share a picture of our kids all dressed up for a wedding than we are of them throwing a tantrum on the floor, or that moment when we scream at them in frustration. But life includes all of these moments. And with these words of the Elder, we are getting some real-life humanity included as Holy Scripture. It's an acknowledgment that moments like this are part of the life of faith too, moments when fear looms large, when we wrestle with the right response to people with whom we disagree and whom we may feel are living in harmful, damaging ways. Sometimes, the only route is to sever a relationship.

Yet this moment, when seen within the larger picture, does not mean the church should err on the side of fearful exclusion. Though sometimes we tragically fall to that side, it doesn't trump the bigger picture of love. This is a glimpse of a less-pretty moment in church life that reminds us of our continual struggle to live faithfully. Sometimes we are successful in that calling, and sometimes we fall woefully short. All of this is part of life together—the struggle to discern what really matters, where we are in line with who Jesus was and what he taught, and where we are not. As N. T. Wright astutely put it, "We need to be sure we are standing on the firm ground of the gospel, not on a point that just happens to embody our particular prejudices."[5]

This, my friends, is why we need each other. The letter ends affirming this truth. It's lovely to send letters or, in today's world, share photos, but nothing is a substitute for the connections we make when we are together. "Although I have much to write to you," the Elder concludes, "I would rather not use paper and ink; instead I hope to come to you and talk with you face to face, so that our joy may be complete" (v. 12). This verse holds so much truth. N. T. Wright again shares brilliant insight:

> This is, perhaps, a reminder to us today, with our multiple electronic communications making even letters, for many, a thing of the past, that full human life involves full, bodily, facial contact and meeting. We are in danger today of adopting, without reflection, styles of behaviour which devalue the deep truth of genuine humanness. John would gently urge us to take every opportunity to put this right.[6]

In the end, we need to be together. This is why, despite our busyness, we don't just meet in an online chatroom for worship. This is why, though text messages help us stay connected, they cannot substitute for eye contact and body language and a warm embrace. This is why, every year, members of our congregation make the flesh-and-blood trek to West Virginia that we will be repeating this week through our annual mission trip. We go to physically be with brothers and sisters there, to watch their kids grow, and to walk with them through the ups and downs of life in a depressed and forgotten corner of our country. We could just send them money to fix up their homes; but like the community of 2 John, who was reminded of the love of the Elder and their Elect Sister, these friends need to know that they are not alone, and we need to be transformed by the relationships they offer. We maintain these connections so we can practice loving each other over the long haul. This, in the end, is what the life of faith is all about.

So this week, where can you make and maintain connections? Who are you called to connect with not just on the level of casual conversation but also with the deep love and care of family? Where do you need to reconnect with the heart of your faith, the things that really matter? Who do you struggle to connect with because of differences or pain, and where do you need to either draw back for a time or draw closer? Who do you need to be with in the flesh, even when spending time together in this way doesn't feel as efficient? These are big questions from a little letter; but as we answer them together, we just might share with the world a bigger picture of what it means for us, in this time, to follow Jesus together.

Notes

1. Paul Worthington, "One Trillion Photos in 2015," *mylio.com*, 11 December 2014, mylio.com/true-stories/tech-today/one-trillion-photos-in-2015-2/; Benedict Evans, "The Explosion of Imaging," 3 July 2014, ben-evans.com/benedictevans/2014/6/24/imaging; Caroline Cakebread, "People Will Take 1.2 Trillion Digital Photos This Year—Thanks to Smartphones," *Business Insider*, 31 August 2017, www.businessinsider.com/12-trillion-photos-to-be-taken-in-2017-thanks-to-smartphones-chart-2017-8.

2. C. Clifton Black, *The First, Second and Third Letters of John*, The New Interpreter's Bible, vol. 12 (Nashville: Abingdon Press, 1998) 448.

3. D. Moody Smith, *First, Second, and Third John*, Interpretation: A Bible Commentary for Teaching and Preaching (Louisville: Westminster John Knox Press, 2012) Kindle Edition, 146–47.

4. Katie Gibson, "OneDayHH: Sharing the Details," 24 October 2014, katie-leigh.wordpress.com/2014/10/24/onedayhh-sharing-the-details/.

5. N. T. Wright, *The Early Christian Letters for Everyone*, New Testament for Everyone (Louisville: Westminster John Knox Press, 2012) Kindle Edition, 179.

6. Ibid., 180.

Part 4

3 John

by Abby Thornton Hailey

Welcome and Authority

3 John

When we traveled to West Virginia to begin our mission trip on Monday, most of our drive was on the interstate; but for the last hour or so, we wound through rural areas and microscopic towns. We passed a lot of fields, countless animals, and churches of all stripes. As we passed church after church, I told one of our youth who was riding with me about how my husband and I have a sort of ongoing game we play in the car. Whenever we pass a Baptist church, my husband (who is an Episcopalian priest) asks, "What about that church—would they like you there?" What he means, of course, is would they welcome me as a female pastor—something that many Baptist churches don't agree with. For most churches I have to say, "Probably not, dear"—though, to be fair, you can't always judge a congregation by its exterior.

Anyway, this got the teenagers and me talking about differences between churches. When we drove past a Methodist congregation, one asked jokingly, "Would they like you there?" I was able to say "most likely" with confidence—the Methodists, as a denomination, have been ordaining women for a while, and a female pastor isn't an unusual sight. Then she asked, "Well, how are Methodists different from us?" Though I went to a Methodist seminary, I actually struggled to come up with a definitive answer. They understand and observe baptism and Communion a bit differently, of course, but the biggest difference I came up with—and the big reason becoming a Methodist pastor never appealed to me, though many in seminary tried to get me to cross over—is the way they are organized. Methodists have bishops who help set larger policies and doctrines for the church by which all congregations must abide. The bishops decide which pastors serve where and for how long. There is a lot more hierarchy in that system. You must answer to people above you and honor their authority, and the idea of being under a bishop . . . well, let's just say that though it works for some, it has never appealed to me.

On that drive, the youth and I touched on two of the things that churches most often part ways over: who is welcome, and who is in charge? These questions have divided us again and again throughout history. The early church struggled with whether they should welcome Gentiles as well as Jews, and whether people who were previously regarded as unclean—such as eunuchs—should be welcome. Time and again, the church kept finding that the answer was yes. But the question of who is welcome keeps popping up and dividing us. In the 1840s, the first major Baptist denomination split occurred between the Southern Baptist Convention and the more northern American Baptists over the question of slavery. In the 1980s, one of the things that split the Baptists again was the question of the welcome and inclusion of women in church leadership not just as children's teachers but as preachers and pastors—as well as whether conservative Baptists would welcome and allow those with more progressive views to be in leadership. These days, many denominations are splitting over the question of welcoming our LGBTQ siblings. The question of who is in and who is out and who can be gathered with us at Christ's table seems to continually tear the church apart.

Likewise, the church has divided throughout history over questions of authority and power. Phyllis Tickle, in her fabulous book *The Great Emergence*, claims that every 500 years or so the church has experienced a new era of splitting and reinventing itself—and that most of these shifts have centered on questions of authority. In the fifth century, a church that had been a minority on the fringes of society began to gain authority in culture as a majority force. Then, in 1054, the church experienced a great schism over the question of the authority of the pope. Five hundred years later came the Reformation, with Protestants emerging and granting authority to the Scriptures alone. Today, Tickle writes, the authority of the Scriptures is being challenged, and there are questions about where authority will lie for a generation that recognizes and trusts authority less and less. In her newer writings, Tickle posits that the church is placing increased authority these days on the guidance of the Holy Spirit.[1]

So throughout history these have been big questions for us—who is welcome, and who is in charge. And these are not new questions; they dominate the early church letter of 3 John. We have read the books of 1 John and 2 John together over the last months, and N. T. Wright uses a nice metaphor to describe how these letters relate to one another. He compares the Epistles of John to something like Google Earth:

> ... the kind of software that lets you zoom in, all the way from satellites in space, on a particular country, then a particular town, then a particular street, and finally on just one house. Sometimes there are photographs of the house which enable you to recognize someone's car in the street, or a familiar object outside the building. . . . The three letters of John have this zooming-in effect. The first letter could be addressed to almost any church . . . [and] taken and applied at once to churches anywhere else in the ancient or the modern world. Then, in the second letter, it's clear that John is writing to a particular church. . . . Now, in the third letter, he is writing to one particular church leader.[2]

Here we get the most specific picture of church life so far—yet, since 3 John is the shortest book in Scripture at only 215 words, it's a picture that offers few concrete details. We don't really know who Gaius was, or his particular role in the church. He may have been a leader in whose home the congregation met. All we do know is that the Elder—the same one who wrote 2 John and probably 1 John as well—wanted Gaius to know that he was in the same family circle, the same community of love as the recipients of those previous letters. Gaius is named as a source of joy, beloved as one of the Elder's own children.

As we move from the greeting to the body of the letter, we hit our first big issue: that of hospitality or welcome. We find that Gaius is living out his belovedness in a significant way, through hospitality. The Elder seems to have written this letter largely to commend Gaius for his reception of early Christian missionaries and to encourage him to keep up this welcoming practice. In the early church, Christians were on the fringe, viewed with suspicion, and often excluded for beliefs and practices that differed from the mainstream. Because of this, "traveling missionaries, or even Christians who were simply traveling on ordinary business, would be very much dependent on local groups of believers for board and lodging."[3] Their very lives depended on being welcomed by fellow followers of Jesus.

Early Christians struggled to find the same balance we struggle with in hospitality today: wanting to offer open welcome without enabling freeloaders or letting damaging people into the community. But Gaius, apparently, excelled in the art of hospitality, and the Elder wanted him to know how important this work was. "Beloved," he writes, "you do faithfully whatever you do for the friends, even though they are strangers to you" (v. 5). This is more than a pat on the back. The Elder reminds Gaius that his hospitality and care for his fellow Christians are actually how his faith is activated. Such action is how faith becomes real; apparently, there is no true faith unless one is showing welcome.

The Elder also affirms the countercultural way that Gaius offers hospitality. He does not try to gain status over those he welcomes, or make them beholden to him, or demonstrate his own power. Instead, Gaius puts those he welcomes on an equal playing field with himself, demonstrating that they are all "co-workers with the truth" (v. 8). In a society based on patron-client relationships, such equality and partnership between settled leaders and newcomers who wander in would have been almost unheard of. But the Elder makes it clear: expressions of hospitality and welcome are meant to bring all together on equal footing as brothers and sisters.

Some, however, were not excelling as Gaius was. The Elder calls out one individual in particular: Diotrephes. The Elder has several bones to pick with Diotrephes: that he "likes to put himself first"; that he "does not acknowledge our authority"—a complaint that, in the Greek, literally reads more like he "does not receive or accept us"; that he is "spreading false charges" about some other church leaders and members; that he "refuses to welcome the friends"—likely, some associates or delegates of the Elder; and finally, that he refuses to welcome those who extend welcome to the Elder and his friends, even throwing out of the church those who practice hospitality and offer welcome.[4] Because of Diotrephes' actions, it appears that the church is endangered not only by his tendency not to extend welcome but also by a power struggle developing between different factions of the church. Here come our authority issues! Who should the people listen to? Diotrephes, with his passionate refusal to welcome the Elder, perhaps because of a theological difference or because of a fear that the Elder is encroaching upon his territory? Or the Elder, who seems to have been nurturing this community for some time as either an unofficial or an authorized leader? Whose wisdom will they trust? How can they know what is right? This is a moment that could break the church if some go Diotrephes' way and others, the Elder's way.

The Elder cannot address these problems from a distance, and so he makes clear his intention to come be with them face to face, to work through these conflicts together in community. In the meantime, though, he urges them to one more act of welcome: to embrace Demetrius, who it seems the Elder is sending as some sort of emissary. The Elder speaks highly of this friend and encourages the community to be hospitable to him. John's friends "testified to [Demetrius's] faithfulness to the truth"—and truth, you will remember, is always a synonym for Jesus in the John letters (3 John 3). Welcoming this stranger, then, is welcoming Christ, just as we heard in our Gospel reading this morning (see Matt 25:31-40)—and this is what the church must be about above all.

The letter ends on this note. Never in this letter is the name "Jesus" or "Christ" explicitly used, but as Wright again points out, 3 John and especially its conclusion, "breathes the spirit of Jesus just as strongly as its much longer cousins. It speaks, as in the closing verse, of 'peace': not the easy peace that comes from ignoring the problems, but the deeper peace that comes from confronting them in the knowledge that truth and love are the two arms with which God in Jesus now enfolds both church and world in one embrace."[5] This, my friends, is why this letter matters so much today. We are often divided by the same things that threatened Gaius and his church community—the question of who is welcome, and the question of who or what we listen to for guidance and authority.

In this postcard-size snapshot of faith from the early church, Clifton Black writes,

> reading 3 John is a bit like studying a cracked, sepia-tinted photograph in a family album. Although at first we do not recognize the faces of Gaius, Demetrius, Diotrephes, or the elder, and while their braided histories are long forgotten, slowly we perceive traces of ourselves in their affections and petulance, their grudges and gratitude. In particular, 3 John holds a mirror to the church of our own day, inviting us to consider the sometimes divisive consequences of deep religious convictions.[6]

Today, we continue to break fellowship over wanting to exclude some people when Jesus said he came that none would be lost. We continue to break fellowship over power struggles regarding who is in charge when, clearly, we know that there is one Lord and God over us all. The same things that threatened the early church threaten us still—so often our tendency to refuse welcome out of protectiveness or fear, or to want to grab control or to be faithful to a particular human leader, can leave us broken, torn apart. How might this letter—in all its rich humanity—challenge us to deepen our welcome and open our hearts to be led by the Holy Spirit, living as children of a common parent in a way that shines light and joy rather than division to the world?

Introduction to Communion after Sermon:

As we come to this table, we are reminded of Christ's welcome: the invitation he offered was for all to join in his feast, not just the good but also the broken, not just those on the right path but those who were in the very act of wandering away. As he invited his disciples to gather as family and break bread and drink the cup, so Christ invites each of us to eat and to share, declaring that all are welcome. And the way we share this meal here in this community, I think, says a lot about who we believe is in charge: Jesus invites us all to the table as equals, and we gather in a circle to offer the bread and the cup to one another as brothers and sisters called together by the same God to live under the same Lord. So today, wherever you are coming from, you are invited to come and join as an equal at this table, to be fed and nourished, to know this is a place where you are welcomed by One whose love never ends. Let us gather here in a circle at the front at the table of our Lord and celebrate this meal that helps unite us as one family in Christ.

Notes

1. See Phyllis Tickle, *The Great Emergence: How Christianity Is Changing and Why* (Grand Rapids: Baker Books, 2008); *The Age of the Spirit: How the Ghost of an Ancient Controversy Is Shaping the Church* (Grand Rapids MI: Baker Books, 2014).

2. N. T. Wright, *The Early Christian Letters for Everyone*, New Testament for Everyone (Louisville: Westminster John Knox Press, 2012) Kindle Edition, 183–84.

3. Ibid., 184.

4. C. Clifton Black, *The First, Second and Third Letters of John*, The New Interpreter's Bible, vol. 12 (Nashville: Abingdon Press, 1998) 464.

5. Wright, *Early Christian Letters*, 190.

6. Black, *First, Second and Third Letters of John*, 467.

Praise for *Preaching the Word: John, 1–3 John*

Prince Raney Rivers and Abby Thornton Hailey are gifted pastors and wise, trusted interpreters of Scripture. In this volume they offer profound insights into some of the most important yet challenging texts of Scripture: the Gospel and Letters of John. Their insights are illuminating for laity and clergy alike, and careful study of the biblical texts and this volume together will draw us all closer to the God of Jesus Christ by the power of the Holy Spirit. An impressive accomplishment!

—L. Gregory Jones
Dean of Duke Divinity School,
Williams Distinguished Professor of Theology and Christian Ministry

In this fine volume, Prince Raney Rivers and Abby Thornton Hailey explore the content of the Johannine corpus with insightful commentary and pastoral response. The book offers careful exegesis of the texts and their essential role in shaping Christian religious experience, discipleship, and ministry in the Church and the world.

—Bill J. Leonard
Professor Emeritus, Wake Forest University

The Johannine literature represents a poetic and theological alternative to the majority of the New Testament writings and therefore presents a special challenge to the preacher. Out of their evident devotion to Scripture and extensive pastoral experience, Prince Rivers and Abby Hailey have produced an incisive and timely guide for both preacher and student alike. Everyone, including attentive congregations, will benefit from this book.

—Richard Lischer
Duke Divinity School, Author of *Reading the Parables*

There might be better preachers out there than Prince Rivers, but I don't know any. To sit in on his sermons to his beloved church as he gazes at Jesus through John's prism is a delight—it makes me want to preach, shout, believe, and live.

—Jason Byassee
Vancouver School of Theology

Birthed from the heart of two pastor-preacher-teacher-scholars, Prince Raney Rivers and Abby Thornton Hailey's commentary on the Gospel of John and John I, II, & III is an exceptional volume that is fresh, provocative, and faithful. Rivers and Hailey combine insights gained from their experience as faithful pastors and skilled preachers with the best of biblical scholarship to produce an accessible guide for anyone wishing to venture with confidence into the theological world of the Gospel of John and the Johannine epistles. Preaching the Word's sermonic form makes this commentary an invaluable resource for pastors, preachers and teachers endeavoring to nurture loving, Christ-centered, boundary-less communities in which all are known as sisters and brothers in the household of faith. Whether you are a veteran preacher, a student in theological education, or a person in the pew seeking to learn more about the Johannine corpus, this commentary will light the way.

—Veronice Miles
Associate Professor of Preaching, Wesley Theological Seminary

A tremendously alive, engaging, fresh, practical, and preachable approach of the books of St. John: laced with scholarly integrity and pastoral stories which calls and causes one to desire to embrace the abundant life through Jesus Christ as Lord.

—Dr. Clifford A. Jones, Sr.
Friendship Missionary Baptist Church

www.ingramcontent.com/pod-product-compliance
Lightning Source LLC
Chambersburg PA
CBHW071236160426
43196CB00009B/1087